STUDYING HEALTH

 OPEN UNIVERSITY PRESS

 TheOpen University Health and Disease Series, Book 2

The U205 Health and Disease Course Team

The following members of the Open University teaching staff and external consultants have collaborated with the authors in writing this book, or have commented extensively on it during its production. We accept collective responsibility for its overall academic and teaching content.

Basiro Davey (Course Team Chair, Lecturer in Health Studies, Biology)

Gerald Elliott (Professor of Bio-physics)

Richard Holmes (Senior Lecturer, Biology)

Kevin McConway (Senior Lecturer in Statistics)

Perry Morley (Senior Editor, Science)

Stephen Pattison (Lecturer, School of Health, Welfare and Community Education)

Clive Seale (Lecturer in Medical Sociology, Department of Sociology, Goldsmiths' College, University of London)

The following people have contributed to the development of particular parts or aspects of this book.

Sylvia Abbey (course secretary)

Steve Best (graphic artist)

Geoff Einon (critical reader), Lecturer, Department of Biology

Lucille Eveleigh (course co-ordinator)

John Greenwood (librarian)

Marion Hall (course manager)

Tim Halliday (critical reader), Professor of Biology

Martyn Hammersley (critical reader), Reader in Educational and Social Research, School of Education

Pam Higgins (designer)

Sarah Keer-Keer (picture researcher)

Julie Laing (BBC production assistant)

Jean Macqueen (indexer)

Rissa de la Paz (BBC producer)

Caroline Pond (critical reader), Reader, Department of Biology

Roger Sapsford (critical reader), Senior Lecturer in Research Methods, Department of Psychology

Liz Sugden (BBC production assistant)

Doreen Tucker (text processing compositor)

Authors

The following people have acted as principal authors for the chapters listed below.

Chapters 1, 6 to 8, and 10

Kevin McConway, Senior Lecturer in Statistics, Department of Statistics, The Open University.

Chapters 2 and 9

Basiro Davey, Lecturer in Health Studies, Department of Biology, The Open University.

Chapters 3 and 5

Clive Seale, Lecturer in Medical Sociology, Department of Sociology, Goldsmiths' College, University of London.

Chapter 4

Mary James, Lecturer, Department of History, University of Essex.

External assessors

Course assessor

Professor James McEwen, Henry Mechan Chair of Public Health and Head of Department of Public Health, University of Glasgow.

Book 2 assessors

Professor Ludmilla Jordanova, Professor of History, Department of History, University of Essex.

Dr Mark McCarthy, Director of Public Health, Bloomsbury and Islington Health Authority, London.

Acknowledgements

The Course Team and the authors wish to thank the following people who, as contributors to the first edition of this book, made a lasting impact on the structure and philosophy of the present volume.

Nick Black, David Boswell, Sheila M. Gore, Alastair Gray, Jennie Popay, Steven Rose, Phil Strong.

The Open University Press, Celtic Court, 22 Ballmore, Buckingham, MK18 1XW.

First published 1985. This completely revised edition first published 1994.

A catalogue record of the book is available from the British Library.

Library of Congress Cataloging-in-Publication Data

Studying health and disease / edited by Kevin McConway.
    p. cm. — (Health and disease series : book 2)
  "This text forms part of an Open University second level couse" —T.p. verso.
  "Completely rev. ed. " —Acknowledgements P.
  Includes bibliographical references and index.
  ISBN 0-335-19252-1 (pb) : £12.99
    1.   Epidemiology—Research—Methodology.
2. Research—Methodology. I. McConway, Kevin, 1950- . II. Series.
  [DNLM: 1. Epidemiologic Methods. 2. Research—Methods. 3. Social Medicine—methods. WA 20.5 S9336 1994]
RA652.4.S78 1994
610' .72—dc20
                                          93-43194
                                               CIP

Edited, designed and typeset by the Open University.

Printed in the United Kingdom by Butler & Tanner Ltd, Frome and London.

ISBN 0 335 19252 1

This text forms part of an Open University Second Level Course. If you would like a copy of *Studying with the Open University*, please write to the Central Enquiry Service, PO Box 200, The Open University, Walton Hall, Milton Keynes, MK7 2YZ.

2.1

7086C/u205b2i2.1

Contents

About this book

A note for the general reader

Studying Health and Disease gives a broad introduction to the main methods of research and investigation used in the area of health and disease. Its overall aim is to provide readers with a critical understanding of the ways in which our knowledge of health and disease was arrived at. To do that, it describes the basic methods of investigation used by social scientists, historians, statisticians, demographers, epidemiologists and biomedical researchers. It uses a range of examples to illustrate how the different methods are related and how they differ.

The book contains ten chapters which can be grouped as follows. After an introductory chapter, Chapter 2 provides an outline of the nature of scientific research. Chapters 3 to 5 cover historical and social science research methods as used in the study of health and disease. These chapters cover both quantitative (i.e. numerical) and qualitative (non-numerical) methods. Chapters 6 to 8 are concerned with quantitative methods that can be applied to groups of people; they deal with statistics, with demography (the study of populations) and with epidemiology (the study of the distribution and determinants of disease). Chapter 9 provides an introduction to biomedical research methods, and the book ends in Chapter 10 with an example of a study that involved a wide range of the methods discussed in earlier chapters.

The book is fully indexed and referenced and contains an appendix of abbreviations and an annotated guide to further reading.

Studying Health and Disease is the second in a series of eight books on the subject of health and disease. The book is designed so that it can be read on its own, like any other textbook, or studied as part of U205 *Health and Disease*, a second level course for Open University students. General readers do not need to make use of the study comments, learning objectives and other material inserted for OU students, although they may find these helpful. The text also contains references to a Reader of previously published material[1] prepared in association with the OU course: it is quite possible to follow the text without reading the articles referred to, although doing so will enhance your understanding of the contents of *Studying Health and Disease*.

A guide for OU students

Studying Health and Disease introduces the main methods of investigation used in the study of health and disease, and it aims to provide you with the knowledge necessary for making a critical appraisal of the many types of evidence presented to you elsewhere in the course. The structure of the book is outlined in the 'Note for the general reader' above, and is described further in Chapter 1.

Study comments, where appropriate, are given in a box at the start of chapters. These primarily direct you to important links to other components of the course, such as the other books in the course series, the Reader, and audiovisual components. Major learning objectives are listed at the end of each chapter, along with self-assessment questions that will enable you to check that you have achieved these objectives. The index includes key words in **bold** type (also printed in bold in the text) which can be looked up easily as an aid to revision as the course proceeds. There is also a list of further reading for those who wish to pursue aspects of study beyond the scope of this book.

The time allowed for your work on *Studying Health and Disease* is three weeks, or about 30–36 hours. The following table gives a more detailed breakdown to help you to pace your study. You need not follow it slavishly, but try not to let yourself fall behind. Depending on your background and experience, you may well find some parts of this book much more familiar and straightforward than others. If you find a section of the work difficult, do what you can at this stage, and then return to the material when you reach the end of the book.

There is a tutor-marked assignment (TMA) associated with this book; about three hours have been allowed for completing it, *in addition to* the time spent studying the material it assesses.

[1] *Health and Disease: A Reader* (Open University Press, 1984; revised edition 1994).

Study Guide for Book 2 (total 30–36 hours, including time for the TMA, spread over 3 weeks). Chapters 1 and 10 are very short; Chapters 2 to 9 are approximately the same length. You should pace your study accordingly. The TV programme 'Therapies on trial' is relevant to Chapters 8 and 10.

1st week

Chapter 1 — **Introduction**

Chapter 2 — **The nature of scientific research**

Chapter 3 — **Qualitative methods in sociology and anthropology**; listen again to audiotape 'Why me? Why now?'

Chapter 4 — **Historical research methods**

Chapter 5 — **Quantitative methods in social science**

2nd week

Chapter 6 — **Analysing numerical data**

Chapter 7 — **Some basic ideas of demography and epidemiology**

Chapter 8 — **Investigating causes and evaluating treatments**; TV programme 'Therapies on trial'; read part of the *Reader* collection of articles on 'Ethical dilemmas in evaluation'

3rd week

Chapter 9 — **Biomedical research methods**

Chapter 10 — **The web of explanations**; audiotape 'Data interpretation: the programming hypothesis'; TV programme 'Therapies on trial' is also relevant to this chapter

TMA completion

Cover photographs

Background: Mammalian fat-storage cells, viewed through a light microscope, magnified 2 000 times (Photo: Mike Stewart). *Middleground*: Plotting the distribution of disease on a map, such as this one of part of Greater Manchester, is an important technique in epidemiological research (Map drawn by Steve Best). *Foreground*: Interviews with users of health services play a key role in social science research (Photo: Mike Levers).

One approach to the study of health and disease: an anatomy lesson in 1581 at the Barber-Surgeons' Hall, London. (Source: Glasgow University Library)

1 Introduction

What are health and disease?

This book is about discovering how to describe and explain health and disease and about understanding the relationships between different types of description and explanation. The previous book in the series[1] demonstrated that there is more than one justifiable set of beliefs about the nature of health and disease. Beliefs about what illness is and what makes us ill have changed radically over time, and even now differ between different societies, and between different groups within a single society. Lay conceptions of health differ from those of professional healers. Members of the orthodox medical profession differ radically from alternative practitioners in their views, not only on the nature of disease, but on the question of when and how therapies should be evaluated.

□ Orthodox medical practice differs considerably from one place to another. Can you give examples of this variability?

■ You might have thought of the studies carried out in the early 1980s on rates of use of common surgical procedures in different countries; for instance, in one study doctors in New England removed tonsils at four times the rate of doctors in Norway. Or you might have mentioned variation in disease categories between different countries—German doctors treat low blood pressure as a disease more commonly than doctors elsewhere, for example.[2]

How can we make sense of this diversity of belief and practice? Social anthropologists would take it as a major starting place for their discipline; they aim to describe and explain the patterns of belief and practice in the context of the society in which they exist and that gives rise to them. Doctors might take a different view; they might seek to establish a consensus view of which among a diverse set of practices is the best way of treating a particular disease.

[1] *Medical Knowledge: Doubt and Certainty* (Open University Press, revised edition 1994).

[2] These examples were introduced in *Medical Knowledge: Doubt and Certainty*, Chapter 6.

□ Do you think a social anthropologist and a doctor would give the same answer to questions like 'What is health?', 'What is disease?' or 'What is disability?'

■ One cannot generalise about what *any* individual doctor or anthropologist would say; but it seems fairly unlikely that the members of these disciplines as a whole would agree on things like this. An anthropologist may well feel that questions like this have no single meaningful answer when taken out of a cultural context. A doctor may well have views on these questions that arise from training and experience; these views are likely to be similar to those of other doctors working in the same general area.

Whatever disagreements there might be on broad questions like 'What is disease?', most people in Western culture would agree that a person whose body had a major infection of the tuberculosis (TB) bacterium was suffering from a disease. Yet that does not deal with the question of what *caused* the person to become ill. The difficulty here is that there are several different kinds of explanation.

□ Write down as many different ways as you can think of to complete the sentence 'This man has tuberculosis because…'

■ Here are just a few examples of the sort of answers people might give:

'This man has tuberculosis because certain bacteria entered his body.'

'… because he wasn't immunised against TB.'

'… because his mother had it and he caught it from her.'

'… because he was too poor to heat his flat properly.'

'… because his country is overburdened with debt to banks from industrialised countries.'

'… because characteristic lesions have formed in his lungs.'

'… because he was run down after being unemployed for years.'

Of course, there are many more possible answers.

These explanations differ radically in their nature. The causes of illness range from micro-organisms to the global economic system. Yet it is possible to imagine a scenario in which they are all valid at the same time. This book looks at some of the approaches and methods that might be used to investigate the validity of explanations like these.

Diverse methods

In order to give the book a usable structure, we need a way of categorising explanations of health and disease, and of classifying the methods by which the explanations are produced. How might this be done with the explanations for TB? Some view the disease as a consequence of something that happened in the past—'unemployed for years'—while others relate it to the state of affairs at present—'lesions in his lungs'. In some of the explanations, the man's TB is seen in terms of what is happening to parts of his body—'lesions in his lungs'—or to him as an individual—'he was run down'—or to him as a member of a particular group or society—'his country is overburdened with debt'.

This distinction between *different levels of explanation*—the level of parts of a person, the level of the individual person, or the level of groups of persons—is a pervasive one in the way that knowledge is divided up in our society. Very broadly speaking, *biological* explanations operate at the level of what is going on in parts of an individual's body, while *social scientific* explanations operate at the level of the whole person, and of groups and societies.

◻ Where would you say that *medical* explanations fit into this system of levels?

■ You will probably have met medical explanations that fit in at all three of the levels. Doctors are perhaps most clearly concerned with what goes on within an individual's body; yet many of them stress the influence of behaviour and lifestyle on the state of the body, and the importance of their own interactions with individual patients. Some doctors are concerned with patterns of disease in societies and with explanations of disease that relate to unemployment and other manifestations of how societies operate. Generally speaking, though (and certainly in the eyes of many critics of medicine), medical explanations are very often concerned with parts of the body. (These are often termed 'biomedical' explanations.)

The previous book in this series spent some time describing the nature of medical knowledge and explanation, as well as outlining some of the methods by which this knowledge is produced and validated. This book will consider the explanations of health, disease and disability, and the tools involved in developing and investigating such explanations, in four areas of study: history, the social sciences, epidemiology and biology. To a considerable extent, each of these areas of study has its own distinctive collection of methodologies, but the boundaries between these areas (and that of medicine) are not always clear-cut; for instance, there are strong historical aspects in some social science research, and epidemiology arose essentially as a branch of medicine and is still sometimes seen that way. Yet we have to start somewhere, and these divisions seem a reasonable place.

We should make it clear that these four areas do not by any means cover the entire range of knowledge relevant to health, disease and disability. They do not cover even the fields of knowledge touched on in this series of books. For instance, the next book in the series,[3] as well as later books, include material arising from economics (the study of the production, distribution and consumption of wealth). Economics has its own distinctive research methods; but it also shares research methods with other social sciences. We therefore feel that you will have learned enough about the methodology of areas of study like economics from the four areas we do describe in this book to prepare you for your study of the rest of the series.

The first area of study, and collection of methodologies, we shall cover is that of the social sciences.

◻ The previous book in this series contained a great deal of social scientific description and explanation; for instance, the work of social anthropologists on meanings of health and health beliefs, the work of Illich and others on the concept of medicalisation, and much of the work on doctor–patient interactions. On the basis of your experience of that book and of the social sciences more generally, how would you characterise the position of social scientists in explaining health and disease?

■ Social scientists give a central importance to the *meaning* of health and disease, and study how this is determined within societies. Social scientists are concerned with *interactions* of all kinds between individuals and between groups of individuals, and

---

[3]*World Health and Disease* (Open University Press, 1993).

seek explanations of health and disease that relate to these interactions. Social scientists are *not* primarily concerned with what goes on inside an individual's body.

A traditional distinction in the social sciences is that between *qualitative* and *quantitative* methods and approaches. In very crude terms, qualitative social science concentrates on *describing* meanings and their diversity, while quantitative social science concentrates on *counting* or *measuring* things (which might be meanings). This distinction is reflected in this book; qualitative social science is covered in Chapter 3, and quantitative social science in Chapter 5.

History has qualitative and quantitative aspects as well. The role of history in studying and explaining health and disease was made clear by its prominence in the previous book in this series, and from that book you may be familiar with some of the products of historical research in relation to health, disease and disability. Chapter 4 in this book describes how historical research is done. It is placed between the qualitative and quantitative social science chapters because aspects of historical research are connected with both these methodologies.

The third of our four areas is perhaps the least well-known and the hardest to characterise. Epidemiology seeks to investigate which groups of people suffer from which diseases, and why they have those diseases. Epidemiological methods can give guidance on how people should be treated. Epidemiologists are less concerned than are social scientists about the diverse *meanings* of disease; typically, they accept a medical definition. Epidemiologists do not restrict themselves to considering either biological or social explanations of the causes of illness; they study both. For example, epidemiological studies of the causes of tuberculosis would involve its relationship to poverty as well as the question of how the bacteria are transmitted from one person to another. What is distinctive about epidemiology is that it uses methods that involve groups of people, often as large as whole populations or societies. Chapters 7 and 8

describe epidemiology and its methods; and, because these methods involve a certain amount of numerical data, Chapter 6 outlines some methods for dealing with such data.

Finally we turn to biology, which we might describe as the study of living organisms. Human biology often describes phenomena at the level of parts of the individual. Biological explanations in health and disease would typically refer to the structure and function of parts of the body—that is, to how they are put together and what they do in the body—and to their interaction with other organisms such as bacteria, and with the chemical and physical environment. Different biological sciences are concerned with different aspects of the body and its workings, from molecules within the body's cells to groups of organs, such as the digestive system, taken as a whole. Often a biological explanation in health and disease will contrast the 'normal' structure or function of part of the body with some *pathological* structure or function, which is seen as leading to (or *being*) the disease. Yet not all biological explanation is concerned with parts of the individual. A rather different class of biological explanations involves putting humans and other species in an *evolutionary* context—that is, in the context of how the species arose. Evolutionary explanations are becoming increasingly important in health and disease. Chapter 9 covers the research methods used by biologists.

To round off the book, Chapter 10 provides a brief case study of how methodologies from all the previous chapters can come together in a single major investigation.

One thing that these varied areas of study have in common is that they have all been described as *sciences*. (History is usually described as a humanity, or as one of the arts, in *contrast* to sciences; but as Chapters 2 and 4 will make clear, historical methods have much in common with those of the social sciences.) The notions of science and of scientific research are very important throughout our culture; and they are central to the concerns of this book. Therefore we turn in the next chapter to the question of what constitutes scientific research.

OBJECTIVES FOR CHAPTER 1

When you have studied this chapter, you should be able to:

1.1   Outline some of the problems that arise in defining and explaining health and disease.

1.2   Explain in very broad and general terms how social scientists, historians, epidemiologists and biologists view health and disease, and give examples of the sorts of question each of these areas of study is most suited to answer.

QUESTIONS FOR CHAPTER 1

Question 1 (*Objective 1.1*)

Is it possible to say that any disease has only one valid explanation of what caused it? Explain your answer.

Question 2 (*Objective 1.2*)

Drawing on what you know of hysteria from the previous book in the series, describe which of the following questions about hysteria could best be answered by a social scientist, an historian, an epidemiologist or a biologist.

(a)   How did the medical definition of hysteria develop and change during the nineteenth century?

(b)   Is there any evidence that the physical structure of the brain changes in persons diagnosed as hysterical?

(c)   How common was hysteria in parts of London of different social status in the 1960s?

(d)   How do lay ideas of hysterical behaviour compare with medical ideas?

2 The nature of scientific research

This chapter builds on the discussion in Chapter 2 of *Medical Knowledge: Doubt and Certainty*[1] *of sociological and anthropological approaches to studying lay beliefs, which revealed health and illness as 'contested states' and discussed the philosophical view known as relativism. It also noted the appeal to science in claims about the efficacy of health products or remedies for common ailments. You may find it useful to skim very quickly through that chapter now. Chapter 7 of the same book also refers to relativism and the idea that disease categories may be socially constructed.*

Introduction

The study of human health, disease and disability is a challenging task, as Chapter 1 made clear. It requires great care if the results of research are to be directly or indirectly useful in increasing our understanding of these states and alleviating or preventing suffering. Despite the existence of a rich culture of lay beliefs about health and illness, drawn in part from pre-scientific traditions, the majority of people in industrialised societies in the twentieth century give greater weight to the explanations and remedies derived from scientific medicine. 'Research' in many fields of investigation has become synonymous with 'science', and scientific methods of research have become the most pervasive tool for investigating health and disease (and much else besides).

In this chapter, we will explore popular images of science and scientists to derive a 'shared meaning' of what science *is* and what is generally considered to fall outside science. This leads into a discussion of what are known as *scientific methods of investigation* and

[1]*Medical Knowledge: Doubt and Certainty* (revised edition 1994).

scientific reasoning. Finally we consider science from an idealised viewpoint derived from the reports and research articles published by scientists, and then from a 'behind the scenes' look at what scientists actually do when they go to work. We ask whether the idealised version of science conceals the extent to which it is also a social activity.

What is science?

☐ What images are conjured up for you by the words 'scientist' and 'scientific research'?

■ Perhaps you thought of earnest people in white lab coats, with test tubes and a microscope, electrodes, a nuclear reactor, astronomical telescopes or a hypodermic syringe; or perhaps they were dressed in fireproof suits taking measurements on a volcanic crater, or crouched in a 'hide' observing animals. Depending on your viewpoint, they may have been engaged in research dedicated to improving the quality of life on earth, or 'tinkering with nature' in a manner that might unleash destructive forces.

What these images have in common are the idealised features of modern science, which in popular culture generally refers solely to the **natural and physical sciences**, that is the study of all aspects of the natural and physical world by scientific methods. Traditionally, the natural sciences are *biology*, the study of the structure and activity of living organisms; and *Earth sciences*, the study of the structure of the Earth itself and the activity of its crust and its magnetic fields. The physical sciences are *chemistry*, the study of the properties and interactions of the chemical atoms and molecules from which the world is made; and *physics*, the study of subatomic particles and the forces that govern the properties of matter in the universe.

These scientific disciplines are widely believed to employ a shared approach to investigating the natural and physical world, known as *scientific methods* (described in detail later in this chapter). Scientific

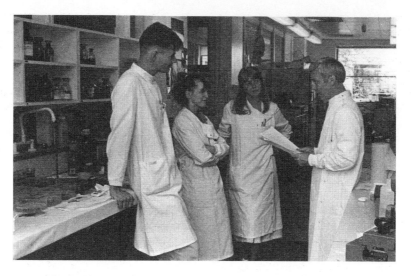

Popular images of scientists and scientific research usually include a laboratory full of complex apparatus, glassware, bunsen burners and chemicals manipulated by people in white lab coats. (Photo: Mike Levers)

methods have, as their hallmark, the systematic study of events that can be observed with the physical senses, and their further investigation by means of measurement and experiment.

The natural and physical sciences enjoy a very high status in industrialised societies. A trivial and commonplace example of this is the appeal to apparently scientific standards of proven effectiveness in the advertising of products as diverse as washing powders and sunglasses. In the field of human health, treatments and methods of preventing illness are generally judged on how closely they conform to some ideal of being scientific.

□ Can you suggest two reasons why the natural and physical sciences have achieved such high status?

■ Perhaps the most convincing reason is that they have proved to be extraordinarily successful at generating benefits for the human species, for example, through medicine and pharmacy, biological improvement of crops and livestock, etc. Despite the serious hazards that modern science has also created, life in a society shaped by scientific knowledge at least lasts a good deal longer than in traditional cultures.[2]

[2]The increasing longevity that accompanies development in modern societies is discussed in *World Health and Disease*. Hazards to human health generated by industrial development are discussed in another book in this series, *Human Biology and Health: An Evolutionary Approach* (Open University Press, 1994).

■ Another possible reason for the high status of the natural and physical sciences is that they appear to be *objective* activities, which 'rise above' the personal and subjective realm of everyday life (but as you will see later, this may be a mirage).

From the seventeenth century onwards, there began to be an interest in applying a scientific approach to the study of human societies and human behaviour and beliefs. In the nineteenth century, a variety of new academic disciplines began to emerge—anthropology, sociology, psychology and economics among them—which, together with already established areas of study such as geography and politics, became known collectively as the **social sciences**.

The relative youth of many of their constituent disciplines may partly explain why the status of the social sciences as truly 'scientific' has frequently been challenged. Practitioners of the natural and physical sciences have tended to dismiss the social sciences as intellectually 'lightweight' and lacking in scrupulous objectivity; the study of human society is easily misrepresented as no more than 'common sense' and politicians have often accused social scientists of being politically motivated and biased in their research.

The principal underlying reason for such devaluation of the social sciences may be that, as yet, they have been less obviously successful at generating knowledge that has enabled people to control aspects of the social world, compared with the demonstrable successes of the natural and physical sciences. A great deal of social scientific research has been driven by the attempt to generate useful knowledge but, as you will see below, the dictates of the scientific methods developed by natural and physical scientists are more difficult for social scientists to follow. Their research subject—humans and their social world—is largely resistant to the rigid controls demanded by laboratory science.

In the rest of this book, we are using the terms 'science', 'scientific' and 'scientist' to relate equally to the natural, physical and social sciences, and to any investigation that uses scientific methods in any academic discipline. For example, in Chapters 4 and 6 you will recognise the use of systematic observation and measurement in disciplines as diverse as *history* (the recording and interpretation of events in human societies of the past) and *epidemiology* (the statistical study of the distribution of disease and disability in human populations). We turn now to a more detailed discussion of the characteristics of scientific methods.

Scientific methods of investigation

The tendency to idealise the natural and physical sciences extends to the description of scientific methods of investigation (sometimes even referred to as *the* scientific method, as though there were no dispute about how science should be conducted). For the moment, we shall set aside the question of how far 'real' science meets the dictates of 'ideal' science (and return to this at the end of the chapter), and describe the principal features of scientific methods on which most scientists would generally agree.

Scientific methods are based on detailed observation and accurate measurement of phenomena that can be detected with the *physical senses* (principally sight and hearing, occasionally touch, taste or smell), where necessary extending those senses beyond human capabilities by using technical apparatus such as microscopes, tape-recorders, X-rays, thermometers, stethoscopes, etc. These investigations are *systematic*, that is, an agreed system for performing those observations and measurements is rigorously followed. The purpose of the system is to minimise the likelihood that the results will be influenced by faults in the apparatus or in the methodology, or by the expectations of the scientist. All the techniques, apparatus and materials used in making the observations and measurements are supposed to be written down in enough detail that another scientist could reproduce, as nearly as possible, the same process.

□ Observations and measurements of the same phenomenon are often repeated several times, perhaps by independent scientists checking each other's results. What is the value of this repetition?

■ A single set of measurements might have been a 'fluke', but if a similar result is obtained on several occasions this strengthens the scientist's confidence that the phenomenon has been accurately recorded. (If you have ever studied statistics, you might also have answered that having a number of measurements of the same phenomenon makes it possible to use a statistical test, which allows the scientist to investigate how confident he or she can be that the measurements are not a fluke. We return to this in Chapter 8.)

The scientist may then conduct an **experiment**, that is a *controlled* and strictly specified *intervention* in the phenomenon under investigation, in which the details of the intervention are recorded as exactly as possible and the outcome is observed and measured. We will look at the meaning of 'controlled' in a scientific sense in a moment, after first considering the *purpose* of the experiment. The intervention made by the scientist is not a random choice, but a carefully selected manipulation of the conditions acting on, or internal to, the subject of the investigation. The selection is often designed to test the validity of an idea that the scientist has had about the phenomena he or she has observed. Alternatively, the scientist may simply be asking 'What happens if...?' rather than testing any pre-formed idea.

Rigorous testing of scientific ideas has long been standard practice, as the following statement from the English physician Edward Jenner, illustrates. In 1796, Jenner devised the method of vaccination against small-pox with fluid taken from the pustules produced by cowpox infection.[3]

> The scepticism that appeared, even among the most enlightened of medical men when my sentiments on the important subject of the cow-pox were first promulgated, was highly laudable. To have admitted the truth of a doctrine, at once so novel and so unlike anything that ever had appeared in the annals of medicine, without the test of the utmost scrutiny, would have bordered on temerity. (Edward Jenner, quoted in Daintith and Isaacs, 1989, p. 208)

---

[3]Vaccination and its effect on the immune system are discussed in *Human Biology and Health: An Evolutionary Approach*, Chapter 6.

Rigorous testing in science generally means that the experiment is 'controlled' in two senses. The first meaning of a **controlled experiment** is that the nature of all (or at least the most important) conditions under which the intervention took place are known to the experimenter, and that he or she is able to keep those conditions 'under control'. For example, adding known quantities of purified chemicals at a certain temperature to a sterile glass test-tube of a certain size can be described as a 'controlled' experiment because all the relevant conditions (as far as they could be determined) are known to the experimenter, and to the best of his or her knowledge no extraneous matter or circumstances are allowed to intrude. The outcome can then be attributed with some degree of confidence to the intervention that the experimenter intends.

Perfect control of *all* the possible variables in an experimental situation is impossible even in the physical sciences, where experiments are usually conducted in the laboratory—an artificial environment specially contrived for the purpose—but it is usually possible to specify the details of most aspects of the experiment and exclude most extraneous matter or circumstances that might influence the outcome.

☐ Control of an experiment in the social sciences—even in this more limited sense of the term—is much more difficult. Can you suggest why?

■ In the social sciences, the subject of investigation is the social world of human beings. It is not possible to make an intervention in such a complex web of interacting phenomena and be certain that other potential influences have been excluded. For example, each person observed has a unique past which may influence their response to an intervention in the present. (Indeed, eliciting and describing the full range of responses to the same intervention may be the purpose of the experiment.) Also, there may be considerable ethical restrictions on what can take place.

The second meaning of a controlled experiment is when the experimenter divides the subjects of investigation into two similar groups: the **test** or **experimental** group (which is exposed to the intervention) and the **control** group (which is not). This method of controlling an experiment is common to all branches of science. In the natural and physical sciences, the subjects in the two groups could be drawn from an enormous range of possibilities: they might be human, but they could also be experimental animals, flasks of chemicals, dishes of bacteria, and so on. In the social sciences, the subjects are always human.

☐ What is the purpose of having test subjects and controls?

■ Since the subjects in both groups are assumed to be similar *before* the intervention takes place, the experimenter can conclude, with various degrees of confidence, that differences between them that are observed or measured *afterwards* are probably due to the intervention that only the test subjects received.

This type of experimental design is most commonly thought of in relation to the natural sciences: for example, *controlled intervention trials* of potentially useful new drugs are carried out on humans or on laboratory animals in this way, as Chapters 8 and 9 will describe. But social scientists use it too. For example, people awaiting an operation might be assigned to a test group in which everyone is given information about what to expect when they come round from the anaesthetic, how long they might stay in hospital etc., whereas a control group of similar people awaiting similar operations might be told nothing at all of this nature. The experimenter then evaluates whether the intervention has had any effect on patients in the test group compared with the control patients. Properly selected control subjects are vital to many branches of experimental science, as you will see later in this book.

The final point to make about scientific methods is that they are supposed to be carried out in a certain frame of mind. The ideal is the *objective* description of tangible phenomena, that is the dispassionate construction of statements about what was observed, undistorted by emotion or personal bias. Various techniques have been developed for assisting the scientist to achieve this goal, for example concealing from the experimenter which of the subjects is in the test group and which are controls, until he or she has observed and recorded the outcome of the intervention. Such experiments are said to be performed 'blind' and are discussed further in Chapter 8. The emphasis on objectivity has had a profound effect on the way in which scientists write up their research in reports for publication, in sharp contrast to the often colourful way they speak to each other in private about their work. We will look more closely at the ideal science of the public arena and the personal science of the private arena at the end of this chapter, and also ask whether the emphasis on objectivity could flow from the predominance of men and hence 'masculine values' in scientific research.

To sum up, the strength of scientific methods of investigation (at least in their idealised form) lies in the scrupulous attention to detail, in the repetition and verification of results, in the publication of the exact activities carried out and in the full specification of any instruments or materials used. Scientific methods are designed among other things to ensure truthfulness on the part of scientists about what they actually observe, to exclude bias and to promote objectivity. However, thus far we have only described *how* scientists are supposed to conduct their work: what scientists 'do with their hands' and the practical reasons for using scientific methods. We turn next to what scientists 'do with their minds'—the underlying purpose of the observations and experiments.

Scientific reasoning

The ultimate purpose of the painstaking exactitude of scientific observations and measurements is to reach an understanding of *why* and *how* the observed phenomena occur and what their *function* or *meaning* is in the natural, physical or social world. Science is about seeking the coherent significance of observable events that in themselves may seem random and chaotic and without a unified function.

There is general agreement among twentieth-century scientists that science is solely concerned with the 'real' world of phenomena that can be observed with the senses. Modern science has nothing to say about imaginary, spiritual or mystical phenomena because they cannot be recorded and measured with the physical apparatus of the senses, even with the help of technologies devised to extend the range of those senses. Many scientists do not deny the existence of this 'world beyond the physical senses' (although some dismiss it), but maintain that it is not a proper subject for scientific inquiry or debate since science has no means of obtaining knowledge about it.

From at least the sixteenth century to the present day there has been a vigorous debate about the extent to which there is a reality beyond human ideas and experiences and—if there *is*—whether science could be used to gain knowledge of it. A detailed discussion of competing philosophies about the limits of science is beyond the scope of this book; however, we can illustrate some important developments in scientific reasoning.

Induction and deduction

The English philosopher and scientist Francis Bacon (1561–1626) was one of the earliest philosophers to have begun to establish the concept of a *material universe*, formed solely from physical matter and governed by physical laws, which could be discovered by scientific observation and measurement. Science, according to Bacon, was the only true source of human knowledge—a

tool so powerful that it could discover the nature of everything in the universe, including human nature and consciousness.

Bacon maintained that the scientist could gain knowledge of universal laws from the observation of real phenomena, by using a form of scientific reasoning known as **induction**, or inductive reasoning. Induction is the process of deriving *general* statements or theories about the laws of nature from the close observation of *particular* phenomena. For example, the Sun has risen each morning of our lives, but when we conclude from this that it will rise again on all our tomorrows because the Earth is revolving around the Sun, we are using induction to derive a 'law of nature' from a simple series of observed events. We have not actually observed the Earth revolving around the Sun. Theories derived by induction go beyond the information contained in the simple observations: they take the scientist into new territory.

Twentieth-century critics of induction have pointed out that this is also its major weakness. For example, the British immunologist and Nobel prizewinner Sir Peter Medawar (1915–1987) argued in a radio broadcast in 1963:

> It simply is not logically possible to arrive with certainty at any generalization containing more information than the sum of the particular statements upon which that generalization was founded, out of which it was woven. How could a mere act of mind lead to a discovery of new information? (Medawar, published 1991, p. 231)

The philosopher Bertrand Russell (1872–1970) dismissed induction as a mere method of making plausible guesses. Curiously enough this is much the same charge Francis Bacon made against the established method of working out universal laws in the seventeenth century, which is known as **deduction**, or deductive reasoning. Deduction is the process of deriving general statements about phenomena on the basis of reasoning *alone*. Theories developed by deduction *may* then be tested against observations, but they can be justified solely by a belief in the power of human reasoning. For example, we might use deduction to construct the following proposition: 'If the price of a single cigarette was suddenly raised to £50.00, then people would quit smoking overnight'. This situation has never been observed and yet an outcome has been deduced. Unlike induction, which begins with observation and measurement of phenomena in the physical world, deduction is a mental process which takes place entirely 'in the mind'. Bacon dismissed it as mere 'armchair speculation'—a view with which sub-sequent generations of scientists have tended to agree, if deduction *alone* is held up as a sufficient method of gaining scientific knowledge.

□ Can you distinguish between induction and deduction?

■ Induction develops general theories about the universe as a result of *first* examining the data obtained by observation and measurement. Deduction *starts* with the general theory developed by reasoning and may then look outward to the universe to see whether the theory fits the observations.

What the advocates of induction and deduction have in common is a view of the universe as constructed at least partly of matter, governed by laws of which knowledge (even if only in some limited sense) may be gained by scientific inquiry and reasoning.

Positivism

From the seventeenth to the early twentieth centuries, the power of induction in scientific reasoning remained extremely influential, despite powerful challenges from leading philosophers. The belief that the natural and physical sciences could discover invariable laws about the material universe was to influence the development of new directions in the *social sciences* in the nineteenth century. The social sciences were based on the belief that 'invariable laws' governing the *social* world could be derived by induction from the systematic observation and measurement of human social interactions.

This philosophy has been called **positivism**, a term derived from the writings of the French philosopher Auguste Comte (1798–1857), one of the founders of the discipline of *sociology*, which he first called 'social physics'. Comte believed that—given time—an ordered society could be constructed, based on the cooperation that would surely follow from the knowledge of 'social facts' about human behaviour, discovered by scientific methods. We should point out that the exact meaning of positivism is the subject of debate amongst philosophers and refer those of you with a greater interest to the Further Reading list at the end of this book. But an example of the approach advocated by Comte and later positivists may help to clarify his influence on scientific reasoning.

When a biologist observes animals in their natural habitats and records the details of their mating displays, he or she does not seek to ascribe emotions or 'inner meanings' to their behaviour. The mating behaviour is considered simply as a response to inbuilt or innate tend-encies in the animal and to measurable external signals such as day length, availability of nesting sites, presence of a mate, etc. Comte and later followers of the positivist approach in the social sciences strive to maintain this same attitude to the study of human behaviour—reasoning that we are simply interacting with others of the same species in response to invariable laws originating in human social organisation. To a positivist, no attention should be paid to 'inner meanings' because even if they exist they cannot be objectively measured. People may *say* that they 'took a mate' because they fell in love, or they sought emotional security, but these states cannot be defined, observed or quantified—they are distractions that the positivist social scientist attempts to ignore.

The 'inner meaning' of these displays is of no interest to a scientist whose approach to investigating the natural or social world belongs to the positivist *tradition. Positivists maintain that the function of the display can be derived only from what can be observed and measured. (Photos:* left: *Marion Hall;* right *Mike Levers)*

The falsifiability of hypotheses

One of the most influential figures in twentieth-century science, Karl Popper, rejected the positivist emphasis on observation and logic as the sole basis for developing theories about the universe. He maintained that developing a theory is a *creative* act, based more on the intuition or inspiration of the scientist than on a painstaking acquisition of 'neutral' facts in which patterns can be discerned and from which theories can be derived. Popper argued that scientific investigation (whether of the natural, physical or social world) is a speculative and creative enterprise, and it doesn't much matter whether a scientist gets his or her ideas about the universe from their observations or their dreams as long as those ideas are *put to the test*.

To Popper, the most important act of scientific reasoning occurs when the scientist formulates an **hypothesis**—a *provisional* explanation for the phenomena he or she has either observed, or reasoned must exist, or simply 'dreamed up'. In fact there will often be several competing hypotheses, which cannot all be correct. The essential feature of a good hypothesis is that it must be formulated in terms that allow *predictions* to be made from it, which can in turn be tested by observation or

Karl Popper, photographed in later life. (Source: Karl Popper) Interviewed in 1992, shortly after his 90th birthday, Popper said: 'The history of science is everywhere speculative.... It is a marvellous history. It makes you proud to be a human being.' (Quoted in Horgan, J., 1992, Profile: Karl R. Popper, the intellectual warrior, Scientific American, *p. 21.)*

experiment. This process allows certain hypotheses to be discarded because the predictions that followed from them turn out to be false when tested. Other hypotheses are strengthened by experimental testing and may lead to more detailed hypotheses, from which more detailed predictions can be made, each capable of yet more detailed testing.

This sequence of scientific reasoning has been termed the **hypothetico–deductive method**. The hypothesis has the status of an inspired guess from which, by reasoning in the mind (deduction), the scientist works out logical predictions that must flow from the hypothesis. Popper insisted that a truly *scientific* hypothesis must be capable of being tested and hence that, if the hypothesis is incorrect, it is also capable of being *falsified*. In practical terms, this means that an experiment can be designed that will show the hypothesis to be false if it is so. For example, the hypothesis 'red blood cells are essential to the transport of adequate supplies of oxygen around the human body' is a scientific statement in Popper's terms because it is capable of being put to the test.

☐ What prediction can be formulated from this hypothesis about red blood cells?

■ It predicts that adequate supplies of oxygen cannot be transported around the human body in the *absence* of red blood cells.

Despite investigation of this prediction, as yet no other naturally-occurring or artificial means of transporting adequate supplies of oxygen around the human body has been detected or devised by scientific experiments (though some are in progress). But according to Popper this does not mean the scientist has been able to establish that the hypothesis is *true*—merely that to date it has not been *disproved*. The hypothesis may indeed be true, but the scientist can never *know* this absolutely. To assume that proof has been established beyond all doubt is to state that every possible line of investigation which might *disprove* that hypothesis has, in fact, been carried out. This is clearly an impossibility. The hypothesis about red blood cells *may* be falsified in the future if some other means of transporting oxygen around the human body is discovered.

Popper argued that scientific hypotheses can never be more than an informed guess about the world and, since they can never be proved to be correct, true scientists should focus on *attempting to disprove* their own hypotheses.

☐ What potential flaw arising from the 'human nature' of scientists might this focus on disproof rather than proof overcome?

■ Scientists may delude themselves into devising only those experiments that have a chance of supporting their 'pet' hypothesis and neglect to carry out those that have a chance of disproving it. The focus on disproof 'protects' scientists from their inevitable vested interest in the outcome of their experiments and encourages the ideal objective detachment required by scientific methods of investigation.

Many critics of the social sciences claim that truly scientific hypotheses (in Popper's sense of the term) cannot be constructed in relation to the human social world because they cannot be adequately put to the test and hence cannot be shown to be false if they are so. Think back to the example given earlier of a controlled trial to evaluate the outcome of giving information to patients awaiting an operation.

□ Using Popper's definition of 'scientific', can you construct a scientific hypothesis concerning the outcome of this trial?

■ 'Patients who are given information about what to expect after surgery will remain in hospital for fewer days afterwards and will need fewer painkilling drugs' is a scientific hypothesis because it makes clear predictions about the outcome, which can be tested objectively.

Another hypothesis about this experiment might be 'Patients who are given information about what to expect after surgery need less aftercare because they feel less anxious'. Using Popper's definition, this hypothesis is *non-scientific* because the existence of subjective states like anxiety are difficult (some would say impossible) to establish and measure objectively. (Many social scientists would disagree and in Chapters 3 and 5 you will be introduced to the methods that they have devised to address this task.) You should note that Popper does not equate 'non-scientific' with 'nonsense': the test of falsifiability simply distinguishes between what he considers to be science and non-science.

However, if the maxim that a scientific statement should contain a testable prediction were to be strictly applied, it would rule out scientific investigation of areas of great interest because they are too complex to allow precise predictions to be made. We cannot predict tomorrow's weather with accuracy, nor the onset of an illness in a particular person at a certain time and place, nor the factors that culminate in war or divorce or any number of aspects of human social relations. Yet these are everywhere considered to be legitimate subjects for scientific investigation. A reaction against a rigid adherence to positivist thinking in science has led to the gradual emergence since the 1970s of a **realist theory of science**, which incorporates both the strict observation and measurement of any phenomena that are amenable to this process, but allows the scientist to postulate the existence of things or states that have not and perhaps cannot be observed.

Reductionist science and holistic science

Complex phenomena are capable of scientific investigation at a number of different 'levels', which can be thought of as a sort of hierarchy: the lowest level is the smallest possible unit that might be involved in the phenomenon (for example, a sub-atomic particle such as an electron), and the highest level would in theory (though obviously not in practice) be the whole universe. Somewhere in between these two extremes come other levels at which the phenomenon might be studied: for example, the cellular level or the level of human social organisation. The natural and physical sciences on the one hand, and the social sciences on the other, have traditionally focused on quite different levels of investigation—although it should be stressed that the division is by no means absolute.

This hierarchy of *levels of explanation* is helpful in making the distinction between *reductionist* science and *holistic* science. The belief that a single unified explanation for complex phenomena can be found within a single level of the hierarchy is termed **reductionism**.[4] Strictly speaking, an explanation such as 'all natural phenomena are the work of God' is reductionist because a single explanation is invoked, but among practising scientists (as distinct from philosophers of science), reductionism is taken to mean the belief that the *ultimate* explanation for natural phenomena can be found in the *lowest* level accessible to investigation. This is usually the level of chemicals or the atoms from which they are constructed. For example, the biomedical scientist observes that the human heart goes on beating even when a person is anaesthetised (an observation at the level of whole organs), but seeks to explain it by focusing on the level below that in the hierarchy (i.e. the cellular level), where it can be demonstrated that the unique properties of muscle cells in the heart give it the ability to continue beating. To a chemist, this explanation could in turn be further 'reduced' to an explanation at the level below

[4]The attempt by René Descartes and his followers to explain everything in the natural world in terms of 'matter in motion' is an example of reductionism; see *Medical Knowledge: Doubt and Certainty*, Chapter 5.

cells (i.e. the chemical level), where it can be shown that chemical reactions inside heart-muscle cells underlie their rhythmic contractions, and so on, until the *ultimate* explanation in terms of the physics of atoms and sub-atomic particles is reached.

The social sciences have usually (but not always) taken a much more **holistic** approach, which claims that complex phenomena can best be understood if they are examined in terms of the *interactions* and *relationships* between *all* the levels involved. Neither the reductionist nor the holistic approach is easy, and both dictate appropriate methods of proceeding with scientific research, which are described later in this book (principally in Chapters 3, 5 and 9). They also tend to drive their advocates towards rather different forms of explanation for complex phenomena.

Reductionist scientists tend to locate the ultimate underlying cause of complex phenomena in the molecules or cells or single events or statements that contribute to the greater whole, and use these 'lower' levels of complexity to explain phenomena that occur at a more complex level of organisation 'higher' up the chain of causality. These have been termed **'bottom-up' explanations**. For example, the ultimate underlying cause of tuberculosis would be traced by a reductionist scientist to the growth of certain bacteria in the body, which in turn explains more complex phenomena such as weight-loss and breathlessness. By contrast, holistic explanations focus on the most complex levels of organisation and proceed to unpack the elements that contribute to it and to specify their interactions and relative weights—these have been termed **'top-down' explanations**.

☐ Can you construct a top-down explanation for tuberculosis?[5]

■ The interaction of social and economic factors in the production of poverty, overcrowded housing, poor nutrition, etc. would be emphasised as the major underlying cause of TB, since these conditions erode physical health to such an extent that the widely prevalent TB bacteria can multiply in the body.

The great strength of reductionism is that it generally allows very complex phenomena (such as the workings of the human body) to be dissected into manageable areas of study. The fruits of reductionist science for human health are all around us, from the aspirin that acts on the

[5]Tuberculosis is discussed in detail in *Medical Knowledge: Doubt and Certainty*, Chapter 4.

nerve-endings which transmit sensations of pain, to the laser technology that burns away blockages in blood vessels serving the heart. However, even among natural and physical scientists, there is a debate about the status of reductionism.

The American psychologist and philosopher, Susan Oyama, has described it as a 'provisional single-mindedness that allows detailed investigation of a mechanism' (Oyama, 1989, p. 7). In her view, the single-mindedness of the reductionist approach should remain 'provisional' so that the small particulars of each experiment can subsequently be reassembled into some approximation of the whole. But a great many natural and physical scientists (perhaps the majority) do not consider reductionism to be a provisional 'act of mind' which helps them to carry out scientific investigations—rather it is a statement of ultimate truth. As Jim Watson, one of the scientists who worked out the structure of DNA, put it in a debate in 1986, '…there are only atoms. Everything else is merely social work.' (quoted in Rose, 1988, p. 161). Conversely, a few influential figures in the natural and physical sciences reject the primacy usually given to reductionism altogether. Steven Rose, a Professor at the Open University, is one.

> When I come into the lab in the morning and begin to plan an experiment with a colleague, or to use a centrifuge, it is clear that the conversation with the colleague would not be possible without the presence in each of us of the DNA, protein and other molecular structures we spend our working lives studying, nor would we be able to use the centrifuge were it not for the properties of the alloys which make the rotors, yet I could not have the conversation, or use the centrifuge, if I ceased to regard my colleague as a person in her own right with her own idiosyncracies, or the centrifuge as a machine, and instead considered each of us as 'nothing but' an assemblage of molecules or even atoms. In our day-to-day life we know better than to try to adopt the philosophical reductionism which many biochemists nonetheless endorse on paper. (Rose, 1988, p. 161)

Biological determinism and relativism in science

A special form of reductionist reasoning is involved in the philosophy known as **biological determinism**—the view that, if everything can be traced back to its smallest components, then human behaviour can ultimately be attributed to the activity of human genes. Popper ridicules this view ('Determinism means that if you have sufficient knowledge of chemistry and physics you can predict what Mozart will write tomorrow', quoted in Horgan, 1992, p. 21), but others see a more sinister side to it. To the biological determinists, juvenile crime can be attributed to genes for wickedness, in much the same way that having blue eyes can be attributed to certain genes. It is the rationale of the Eugenics movement, which began in the nineteenth century and led to attempts to breed a 'master race' and the extermination of 'inferior stock' in Hitler's Germany. It also has a more familiar expression in popular axioms such as 'women are naturally more nurturing and therefore make better nurses, whereas men are naturally more decisive and hence make better doctors'. Wherever nature is invoked to justify the social order, you can be sure that biological determinism lies below the surface of the statement (a subject we revisit in Chapter 9).

In the social sciences, practitioners espouse a much wider range of views about the status of human knowledge. At one end of the spectrum, positivists (few remain in the 1990s) maintain that knowledge can be gained of objective 'facts' about the human social world. At the opposite extreme, the *relativists* hold that there is no single system of ideas that is privileged above others in its access to the truth: the validity of all knowledge depends upon the specific social or historical context in which that knowledge was formulated.[6] In practice, most social scientists in the 1990s would adopt a position somewhere in the 'middle ground' between the strict dictates of positivism and relativism.

Ideal science and 'real' science

The philosophy of relativism leads us to question the extent to which the rigorous principles of scientific, dispassionate methods of investigation are an ideal, distant from the reality experienced by the men and women who go to work as scientists. Science is a human activity, influenced by the culture in which it takes place. It has a social and an historical context, yet modern scientists tend to present an idealised version of what they do to outsiders. This ideal is the 'dominant culture' within science. We have chosen to illustrate the cultural relativity of science in two ways: first by an examination of the language and format of scientific research articles, especially those published since the 1950s; and second, by discussing the view that revolutions in scientific thinking betray the extent to which scientists work within a framework imposed by their own scientific culture.

[6]Relativism was discussed in *Medical Knowledge: Doubt and Certainty*, Chapters 2 and 7.

Scientific language

There is a *genre* of scientific research writing every bit as developed and mutually understood as say science fiction or historical romance. Modern research papers published in scientific journals tend to be written in what we might call 'scientific language'—emotionless, motiveless, self-effacing and impersonal—in stark contrast to the rich use of imagery and speculation in the writing of scientists in previous centuries,[7] and indeed to the 'popular science' written by scientists for the general reader as opposed to their scientific colleagues. Unlike their modern counterparts, earlier generations of scientists also promoted their *individuality* in writing about their observations. Consider this description of his investigation of the structure of air by Robert Boyle (1627–1691), the Irish physicist and chemist, writing in 1670.

> Of the structure of the elastical particles of the air...one may think of them to be like the springs of watches, coiled up and still endeavouring to fly abroad. ...One may also fancy a portion of air to be like a lock or parcel of coiled hairs of wool; which being compressed...may have a continual endeavour to stretch themselves out, and thrust away the neighbouring particles. ... I remember too, that I have, among other comparisons of this kind, represented the springy particles of air like the very thin shavings of wood, that carpenters and joiners are wont to take off their planers... (Boyle, 1670, quoted in Hall, 1965, p. 381)

Boyle and his contemporaries used rhetoric and the power of their personal advocacy in their scientific writing to persuade the reader that the 'facts of the matter' had indeed been discovered. By the middle of the twentieth century, the style of the research article had become very different. Imagery and metaphor had disappeared, along with the personal pronoun and most traces of the scientist's excitement in discovering something new. 'I found that...' has been replaced by the self-effacing 'It was found that...', which tends to create the impression that the scientist is simply describing the neutral facts of a reality that he or she has passively observed.

Published scientific work frequently now has more than one author (in the natural and physical sciences, five

[7]For example, consider the description of a tuberculous lung by Laënnec in 1819, which likens the damaged tissue to millet and hemp seed and to cheese, in *Medical Knowledge: Doubt and Certainty*, Chapter 4.

or more collaborators is commonplace), but they do not 'speak' as individuals. An extensive list of references to previously published research, much of it supportive of the present work, is further evidence of the modern scientists' apparent desire to melt into the crowd. Moreover, the sequence of events laid out in the published report of a scientific investigation often bears little relationship to the sequence of events that actually took place, as Peter Medawar pointed out in his 1963 radio broadcast 'Is the scientific paper a fraud?' He began by describing the traditional structure of the scientific article.

> First, there is a section called the 'introduction' in which you merely describe the general field in which your scientific talents are going to be exercised, followed by a section called 'previous work' in which you concede, more or less graciously, that others have dimly groped towards the fundamental truths that you are now about to expound. Then a section on 'methods'—that is OK. Then comes the section called 'results'. The section called 'results' consists of a stream of factual information in which it is considered extremely bad form to discuss the significance of the results you are getting. You have to pretend that your mind is, so to speak, a virgin receptacle, an empty vessel, for information which floods into it from the external world for no reason which you yourself have revealed. You reserve all appraisal of the scientific evidence until the 'discussion' section, and in the discussion you adopt the ludicrous pretence of asking yourself if the information you have collected actually means anything.
> (Medawar, published 1991, p. 228–9)

He went on to argue that in reality 'scientific work of an experimental or exploratory character *starts* with some expectation about the outcome of the enquiry' (p. 231, our emphasis). The hypothesis is the *inspiration* for the work that follows, not—as the formal structure of the scientific paper would have us believe—the *consequence* of work that went before.

The effect of the conventional structure and language of the scientific paper is to enhance the claim that scientific research is about the objective discovery of 'facts' and to conceal from the public gaze the reality that it is conducted by human beings who make mistakes, follow hunches, compete with each other for fame and funding, get bored and occasionally fake their results. In other words, scientific research is a social activity which is often 'dressed up' to look as though it isn't.

Revolutions in science

An important contribution to the recognition of science as a social activity was made by the American physicist and philosopher of science, Thomas Kuhn (born 1922), in his book *The Structure of Scientific Revolutions* (published in 1962). Kuhn's philosophy tends towards the relativist tradition, for he considers scientific knowledge to be formulated within a particular 'world view' (he called it a *scientific paradigm*), which dominates whatever is considered to be scientific knowledge for a time.[8] The culturally-relative nature of the scientific paradigm is revealed by the fact that it is periodically subject to fundamental revolutions, which destroy the very nature of what was formerly agreed to be valid scientific knowledge. Kuhn called this a **paradigm shift**.

> □ What was the medical paradigm that dominated ideas about blood before William Harvey's experiments led to the circulatory system becoming widely accepted?[9]

> ■ The earlier medical paradigm was humoral theory, derived from the writings of the Greek physician Galen: blood was seen as a vital force, consumed in the body to give energy and recreated as one of the four 'humours'.

The dramatic paradigm shift in medical knowledge that (belatedly) followed Harvey's discovery might be dismissed by modern positivist scientists as no more than 'Galen got his facts wrong, but Harvey discovered the truth'. Kuhn argued the relativist position that one paradigm is simply replaced by another which is accepted as a statement about the real world *at that time*, but which may in its turn be supplanted. In any period in which a particular scientific paradigm has become universally accepted, most scientists find it very difficult to work *outside* the framework of that paradigm because to reject it might be to label oneself a heretic.

For example, the dominant scientific paradigm in biology in the 1990s revolves around the structure and function of DNA (deoxyribonucleic acid). In the reductionist tradition, all roads of inquiry ultimately lead back to DNA as the source of instructions for the working of

---

[8]The construction and erosion of medical paradigms is discussed in *Medical Knowledge: Doubt and Certainty*, Chapter 3.

[9]Harvey's experiments are described in *Medical Knowledge: Doubt and Certainty*, Chapter 5.

living cells, the 'programming' of the characteristics of the whole organism, and the transmission of characteristics from one generation to the next and hence the whole of evolution. Even for biologists who refuse to 'reduce' every biological explanation to DNA, it is literally unthinkable to deny its central role in all living things. Yet the structure of DNA was only made clear in 1953 and it is an act of faith to assume that this paradigm will still dominate biology by 2053.

Kuhn argued that the dominant scientific paradigm of the day profoundly influences the selection of subjects for scientific research, the questions that scientists ask and the results that are accepted for publication. It becomes impossible for most scientists to think outside that paradigm, and any that do are liable to be ridiculed by their colleagues and have their scientific articles rejected. There is an elite 'club' within all branches of the sciences, with its own systems of patronage and glittering prizes, which tends to promote an idealised version of the current paradigm. In the 1990s, it is well represented by the scientists working on the billion-dollar Human Genome Project, which aims to 'map' the exact location and function of the hundred thousand (or more) genes contained in human cells.[10]

This project illustrates another aspect of the Western scientific paradigm, which has been attacked by feminist scientists in both the natural and social sciences: namely the pursuit of objectivity. The map of human genes has been heralded as the greatest scientific venture ever undertaken, but it will not tell us how it *feels* to be human. Many times in this chapter we have stressed that a hallmark of idealised scientific methods is the dispassionate sifting of observable 'facts' and the exclusion of subjective feelings. Feminist writers have argued that this merely reflects the dominance of 'male' values and attributes in scientific research, which have not (until recently) been challenged because elite scientific careers have been almost wholly reserved for men. This proposition turns on its head the frequently-heard jibe that women don't get on as scientists because they cannot think objectively. To the feminist scientist, women excel at bringing together subjective and objective ways of investigating the world, but this approach to scientific research has been excluded by a masculine 'closed shop'.

Kuhn predicted that, over time, evidence slowly accumulates that challenges the dominant scientific paradigm of the day and this begins to create anxiety in the scientific community. A period of crisis follows in which the possibility is faced that the accepted paradigm may be inadequate to explain new knowledge; it may even be fundamentally wrong and careers that have been built upon it may be in ruins. But the pressure for change becomes irresistible and a revolution in scientific thinking occurs: the new paradigm is accepted because it seems capable of reconciling the uncomfortable 'facts' that the old paradigm could not incorporate. The new paradigm has its day, but it may one day be challenged in its turn.

Kuhn's ideas about paradigm shifts draw attention to the fact that the dominant paradigm of a particular scientific age is either 'policed' or 'undermined' by scientists themselves, particularly those leading men (and infrequently women) who belong to a scientific elite. As the twentieth century draws to a close, a feminist reconstruction of scientific research may yet emerge with enough force to challenge the emphatic insistence on objectivity which has characterised masculine science hitherto. As you read the chapters that follow in this book, bear in mind that the methods, perspectives and conclusions presented there—whether from the social sciences (Chapters 3 and 5), history (Chapter 4), epidemiology (Chapters 6–8) or biology (Chapter 9)—are influenced by the current paradigms in scientific thinking and the present members of scientific elites.

[10]You will meet the Human Genome Project again in *Human Biology and Health: An Evolutionary Approach*.

OBJECTIVES FOR CHAPTER 2

When you have studied this chapter, you should be able to:

2.1 Describe what is meant by 'ideal' science and scientific methods of investigation, demonstrating an understanding of the terms 'systematic' and 'controlled' in relation to scientific experiments.

2.2 Discuss important approaches to scientific reasoning, distinguishing between: induction, deduction and the hypothetico–deductive method; positivism, relativism and realism; and reductionism and holism in scientific explanations—commenting where appropriate on the advantages, limitations or consequences of these approaches.

2.3 Demonstrate some insight into ways in which cultural factors affect the status of scientific knowledge and the conduct of scientific research, including the traditional manner of reporting and publishing results and the theory of paradigm shifts in science.

QUESTIONS FOR CHAPTER 2

Question 1 (*Objectives 2.1 and 2.2*)

In 1928, the Scottish bacteriologist Alexander Fleming was growing bacteria in dishes of nutrient jelly to test their susceptibility to destruction by a protein that occurs naturally in human saliva, tears and nasal secretions (he had isolated this protein—called lysozyme—in 1922). Fleming noticed that one of his dishes had clear patches in the carpet of bacteria where the bacteria had died and, on closer inspection, he found a mould growing in those areas of the dish.

(a) Construct a scientific hypothesis arising from Fleming's observation, and explain why it would satisfy Karl Popper's definition of 'scientific'.

(b) Is the process you used in (a) to construct an hypothesis closest to induction or deduction, and why? Having constructed the hypothesis, did you arrive at a testable prediction by induction or deduction?

(c) In general outline, how would you set about devising a *controlled* experiment to test your hypothesis? Why are controls an important feature of experimental science?

Question 2 (*Objective 2.1*)

Which aspects of the popular version of Fleming's discovery of penicillin (given above) fit the 'ideal' method of scientific research discussed in this chapter?

Question 3 (*Objective 2.2*)

Read the following extract from a speech given by Patrick Jenkin, then Minister for Social Services, in 1980. What tradition in scientific thought does it exemplify?

> Quite frankly, I don't think mothers have the same right to work as fathers. If the Lord had intended us to have equal rights to go to work, He wouldn't have created men and women. These are biological facts, young children do depend on their mothers. (Quoted in Rose, Lewontin and Kamin, 1984, p. 6)

Question 4 (*Objective 2.3*)

According to Peter Medawar, in what sense is the scientific paper a fraud?

3 Qualitative methods in sociology and anthropology

You will be asked to listen again to the first audiotape of this course, entitled 'Why me? Why now?', as you study this chapter. Frequent reference is made to examples of sociological and anthropological research described in Chapters 2, 7, 8 and 9 of Medical Knowledge: Doubt and Certainty, *which is therefore important background reading for a full understanding of this chapter.*

Introduction

The social sciences of social anthropology and sociology have two broad purposes: to *describe* the way of life of social groups, and to *explain* the dynamics and development of human societies. Thus a sociologist might seek to discover whether medical consultations are patient- or doctor-centred by going into doctors' surgeries and tape-recording consultations. This would be an attempt at description. To seek to find out *why* patient-centred consultations are popular, or whether one form of consultation is more successful than another in satisfying people, is to attempt explanation.[1] Some social scientists say that explanation involves the discovery of *cause–effect relationships*. Such relationships are then expressed in the form of generalisations: rules that are held to be true across a variety of settings.

Compared with natural and physical scientists, social scientists have on the whole found it very difficult to construct successful generalisations of this kind. Frequently, the generalisations made by social scientists are limited to only a few settings, or contain incomplete accounts of causes. The main reason for this is the

---

[1]A sociological view of medical consultations is given in *Medical Knowledge: Doubt and Certainty,* Chapter 9.

different nature of the subject matter of the two types of science. Molecules, cells, pieces of tissue, do not think. Unfortunately for the social scientist, people do. People think about their relationships, they argue about the future course of their affairs, they discuss with each other their preferences for different types of medical consultations and they read research reports written by social scientists. As a result, they may change their behaviour and so undermine the validity of generalisations about the reasons for their behaviour.

Social scientists have dealt with this awkward fact of human consciousness in different ways. The methods described in this chapter involve delving into peoples' subjective worlds in order to understand how groups of people behave. This can often involve asking people to describe how they think, to explain their behaviour, to allow the researcher insight into the personal *meaning* that events have for them. It can also involve using written documents, tape-recordings of talk or even visual images produced by the people studied. Data in this type of research generally consists of words rather than numbers, or **qualitative data** rather than *quantitative data*. Max Weber (1864–1920), an early contributor to sociology, described this type of science as being that of *verstehen*, which roughly translates into *understanding* the meanings that people share, and through which they communicate. **Symbols** are often important in qualitative social science, as these are objects that have acquired important meanings in a culture, an understanding of which can help in explaining the way of life of its people.

☐ Can you think of a common symbol of medical status in the United Kingdom?

■ One example is the white coat traditionally worn by doctors in hospital settings. Everyone knows that this 'means' that the wearer is a doctor and acts accordingly. Stethoscopes and black bags are also medical symbols.

However, symbols can change their meaning. There is an increasing tendency for people who are not doctors—laboratory staff, ward clerks, receptionists—to don white coats in hospital settings. Hospital consultants often do *not* wear white coats, leaving this to their juniors. The status that the white coat indicates, then, may be a lower one than in times past.

Focus of the chapter

This chapter will first describe the methods of **ethnography**, a word that originally described the writing down (-*graphy*) of facts about groups of people (*ethno*-). Although the groups studied by ethnographers were originally the 'primitive' peoples described by early anthropologists, their methods have increasingly come to be used to study any human group, including people in modern health-care settings such as hospitals. The method used in most ethnography involves the researcher joining in with the daily life of the group studied, and recording what he or she sees, hears or experiences. This is known as *participant observation*. However, some groups cannot be studied in this way, and *qualitative interviewing* may then be used. The discussion of interviewing is followed by sections on the analysis and reporting of qualitative data and the ethical issues raised by the ethnographic approach.

As you read this chapter, we will help you to assess the general strengths and weaknesses of qualitative research. In particular you should become more able, when reading research reports that have used qualitative methods, to assess how rigorously authors have grounded their conclusions in adequate evidence.

Participant observation

People's actions may often contrast with their accounts of what they do and why they do things. In its extreme form this is commonly thought of as *hypocrisy*; these are people whose words contrast with their actions because their words are untrustworthy ('actions speak louder than words'). The link between the language of intentions and the world of human action is often tenuous. The social scientist interested in meaning will often, therefore, want to observe people as they go about their daily lives, and gain some understanding of the relationship between peoples' expressed intentions and what they really do.

Participant observation combines such observation with the gathering of peoples' own accounts.[2]

This method originated in the discipline of anthropology, which itself grew out of an earlier tradition of tales told by travellers about foreign lands and peoples. Bronislav Malinowski (1884–1942) is usually regarded as the founder of anthropological field work, as he collected information about the social groups he studied (largely the Trobriand Islanders in what is now Papua New Guinea) by living among them for long periods of time, learning their language and becoming immersed in their way of life. Previously, most investigators of 'primitive' social groups had visited for brief periods only, collecting a few artefacts for museums, and remarking—sometimes disparagingly—upon the 'primitive' groups' customs. From a view that 'savages' were superstitious, or inferior to the observer, alternative accounts emerged that were more sympathetic to the world-view of the people studied. The anthropologist suspended his or her way of thinking, and made a sustained effort at understanding the meanings shared by people in social settings. Increasingly, sociologists have used the method to study a variety of social settings, including many familiar in everyday life such as hospital clinics.

The modern participant observer proceeds as far as possible by joining in the daily life of the community being studied. By recording and analysing observations of what people do and say over a period of time, regular patterns may be identified, and the explanations that people give for their actions may assume a certain consistency. Observations are recorded as soon as possible after they are made, and notes should be as complete as possible, ideally containing verbatim accounts of conversations, rather than the researchers' own summaries which might subtly distort the content.

☐ Try to think of some examples of research studies that have used this method.[3]

[2]There is a related approach known as *ethnomethodology* in which the focus is on speech itself as a form of action. This is not covered here but is described more fully in Silverman (1985).

[3]Several are described in *Medical Knowledge: Doubt and Certainty*, Chapters 2, 7 and 8.

■ You may have suggested some of the following. Horacio Fabrega summarised the work of a number of anthropologists who studied societies with 'elementary' systems of medical thought. Sociological work that involves this method is represented by Paul Atkinson's study of bedside teaching in Edinburgh and the work of Pearl Katz and Nicholas Fox in operating theatres.

In fact, ethnographers do not *exclusively* collect qualitative data. They may also *count* the incidence of certain actions and statements. Julius Roth, in his study of a TB hospital (Roth, 1957)[4] did this, in addition to collecting qualitative data.

☐ What did Julius Roth quantify and why?

■ He counted the number of times different grades of hospital staff wore protective clothing in order to discover the ritual and symbolic meaning of such items in a medical setting.

Roles and relationships in the field

A spectrum of roles is available to the participant observer, ranging from complete participant to complete observer, with shades in between where the researcher participates some of the time and observes at others. Paradoxically, in both the complete participant role and the complete observer role, the presence of the researcher is often secret. An example of a complete participant role would be that of the researcher who puts on a nurse's uniform and pretends to be a nurse in order to observe medical settings. In complete observation, the researcher watches or listens to people without them knowing that the research is going on, perhaps through remote surveillance by camera or tape, or use of a one-way window which allows the researcher to see the people being observed without being seen by them. Such secrecy has the obvious advantage of maximising **naturalism**. The people observed will behave in their usual manner, without reacting to the presence of the observer. The researcher may be able to investigate groups who would not be willing to cooperate.

However, secrecy involves considerable problems. Ethically, and indeed legally, it may be unacceptable—masquerading as a doctor is punishable in law. In some circumstances, a participant observer, researching a setting where violence can occur, may be in some physical danger, and secrecy may increase this risk. Secret participation may also mean that the researcher is constrained in the settings to which he or she has access. Someone pretending to be a patient in a hospital, for example, may have only limited access to meetings between hospital staff where treatment is discussed. Further, observing people at a distance, or through a one-way window, makes it impossible for the researcher to ask questions of the people studied.

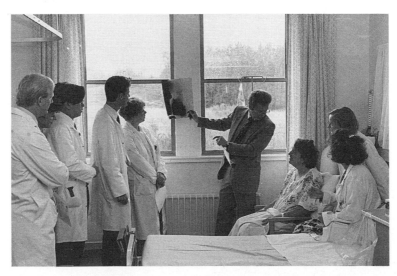

Participant observation often involves some degree of secrecy. Which one is the participant observer here? (Photo: Mike Levers)

[4]This study is described in *Medical Knowledge: Doubt and Certainty*, Chapter 7.

In fact, most participant observation involves a continuing process of negotiation about the role of the researcher in the setting, with different degrees of secrecy in different contexts. Here is Paul Atkinson describing how he managed his role in his study of bedside teaching in a medical school.

> It was a general condition of the access that I negotiated to the hospital wards that the patients should be made aware of my identity by the medical staff. But in the event this rarely happened. Although I was an 'open' observer as far as the doctors and medical students were concerned, I was inadvertently acting as a 'disguised' observer vis-a-vis the patients. This was not a deliberate strategy, but was forced on me by the circumstances, since control over the teaching was in the hands of the doctors and it normally would have been most disruptive had I interrupted proceedings to introduce myself.
> (Atkinson, 1977, p. 106)

In the course of participant observation, relationships with particular people in the setting may develop so that they become special informants. Published ethnographic research has many examples of such characters, who for a variety of reasons become involved in the research process, so that they take on some of the researcher's objectives, and assist in the collection of information. As well as sometimes having access to settings and information which the researcher is denied, such people may also act as *sponsors*, introducing the researcher to new people, and helping to build up trust.

The 'underdog' perspective

The views of people in positions of power and authority are usually readily accessible, often in accounts that are made publicly available in newspapers and television programmes. Modern ethnographers, on the other hand, have often been interested in discovering the views of the 'underdogs' in social settings, who generally have less access to official means of promoting their views. Demonstrating the reasonableness of the underdog perspective often calls into question the rationality of competing 'official' views.

In the 1930s in the University of Chicago (shortly after the time of Al Capone), a group of sociologists (known as the *Chicago School*) specialised in studying the way of life of a variety of 'deviant' or disadvantaged people. The lives of those involved in organised crime, of hobos, prostitutes and the like, were investigated by sociologists who either joined such people for periods of time, or interviewed them extensively.

It is not uncommon, in sociological accounts of medical settings, for patients to be portrayed as underdogs, whose rationality is denied by professional health workers. One example of this arises in the study of when and how patients follow advice given to them by doctors.

> ☐ Doctors sometimes complain that patients do not follow their advice. This is known as *non-compliance*. How does the medical view of non-compliance differ from people's own explanations?[5]

> ■ Sociological research suggests that some people regard non-compliance as part of a strategy to assert personal control over their illness, and adjust medical regimes to the demands of everyday life.

While this sociological interest in the views of 'underdogs' continues, more recently sociologists have developed an interest in describing the perspective of those who have power and authority, and in showing the means by which this is sustained in a variety of social settings.

Bias and naturalism

A central issue in qualitative research is the problem of **bias**. Ethnographers are often challenged by those used to the methods of the natural and physical sciences. They ask, for example: how is it possible to have an objective science based on an exploration of subjective meaning? Surely the ethnographer, or any social scientist, will influence the behaviour of the people studied? How will we know that the account produced by the sociologist does not reflect his or her own preconceptions and prejudices?

One answer to this last question is to examine the contrast between journalism and social science. Some tabloid journalists make their living from producing lurid, impressionistic accounts, that may deliberately distort what they describe so that readers' feelings are inflamed. Issues are presented in a way that maximises the sense of conflict. Stories may be chosen according to their closeness to the themes of sex, violence and forbidden behaviour. Social scientists are not immune from the desire to shock and titillate, since they too must sell their wares to an audience, but they also have other pressing concerns. In particular, they have a need to justify their academic discipline against competing claims for status and funds from natural science, which is commonly characterised as objective and value-free in the popular

[5]See also *Medical Knowledge: Doubt and Certainty*, Chapter 2.

imagination (as you saw in Chapter 2).[6] Thus the professional motivations of social scientists are likely to be different from those of many tabloid journalists. They will have an investment in identifying sources of bias, and may seek to persuade readers that they have done everything possible to eliminate it. The personal biases of researchers will be dealt with in more detail in later sections of this chapter.

Another concern that some researchers have is about the danger that people who know they are being studied will alter their behaviour as a result. This tendency to change behaviour is called **reactivity**. In interviews, for example, people may wish to present a good account of themselves to the interviewer, especially if they think other people may get to know what they said. The sociologist Jocelyn Cornwell's study of families in London's East End distinguished between *public* and *private* accounts as a way of explaining this.[7]

□ How did Jocelyn Cornwell distinguish between the two types of account?

■ Public accounts reflected what people believed might be acceptable to the interviewer, or to some image of 'society at large'. Private accounts were more likely to contradict the acceptable view, and required a degree of trust in the interviewer before they could be shared.

Some qualitative researchers take the view that private accounts, where people are no longer presenting a public *front*, are more authentic or true, and suggest that participant observation minimises this source of bias by studying people in their natural setting, observing them over a period of time and in different contexts so that discrepancies between words and behaviour are often revealed. The ethnographer using this method is generally careful about placing too much reliance on information gained in interviews, preferring to rely as much as possible on what people say when engaged in their normal activities. Thus the great strength of participant observation is said to lie in its naturalism and in its minimisation of reactivity. Howard Becker, a sociologist from the University of Chicago, emphasises this aspect of

the method, contrasting it with interviews and other forms of social research in which the people studied are removed from their usual social settings:

> [The people studied are] enmeshed in social relationships important to them…. The events they participate in matter to them. The opinions and actions of the people they interact with must be taken into account, because they affect those events. All the constraints that affect them in their ordinary lives continue to operate while the observer observes. (Becker, 1970, p. 46)

□ Could Jocelyn Cornwell have used participant observation in her study?

■ She was interested in investigating people's beliefs about many aspects of their lives and social relationships over a number of years. It would not have been possible to join their lives for such a period of time. She had to rely on interviews in which she asked them to describe what happened in the past.

There are important differences between *positivist* social scientists[8] and ethnographers like Howard Becker. Most notable is the fact that the positivist view regards only the study of observable behaviour as providing *objective* data about the social world; whereas Becker and others with a similar approach to Max Weber's (look back to the discussion of qualitative data at the beginning of this chapter) are interested in the *subjective* meanings of the people studied, as well as in what people do.

Some qualitative researchers, however, go further than this, suggesting that a concern with bias and error reflects a limited view of what constitutes knowledge. The philosophical root of this position is *relativism*. Here, the search for some single, unbiased truth is seen as fruitless, since either it does not exist, or we cannot know it in any meaningful sense, or there are in fact multiple contradictory truths. The task of the qualitative researcher, from this point of view, is therefore to treat the impressions that people try to create for each other and for the observer as valuable sources of data in themselves, often revealing a great deal about the motives of the person studied. The focus of the researcher is then upon the social setting in which the research takes place, rather than using the accounts gained through research to explain behaviour in settings where the researcher is *not* present. This approach is illustrated at the end of the following discussion of qualitative interviewing.

[6]See also *Medical Knowledge: Doubt and Certainty*, Chapter 2.

[7]Her work is described in *Medical Knowledge: Doubt and Certainty*, Chapter 2. It is also featured in the first of the television programmes associated with these books, entitled 'Why me? Why now?', and in the audiotape of the same name.

[8]Positivism is described in Chapter 2 of this book (as is the contrasting position of relativism).

Often a qualitative interview is tape-recorded and then transcribed.
(Photo: Mike Levers)

Qualitative interviewing

We will examine this ethnographic method by focusing on a particular interview: the account of events leading up to her hysterectomy given by a woman interviewed by Jocelyn Cornwell.[9] Before considering the interpretation of this interview, let us see how the researcher approached her task.

Doing the interview

The aim of **qualitative interviewing** is to allow the person interviewed (sometimes known as the **respondent**) to expose his or her way of seeing things, without imposing the preconceptions of the researcher. John Lofland has described such interviews as aiming 'to find out what kinds of things are happening, rather than to determine the frequency of predetermined kinds of things that the researcher already believes can happen' (Lofland, 1971).

To this end, **open-ended questions** rather than **closed** or **pre-coded questions** are asked. An example of a closed question about a person's health would be 'Would you say that your health for your age is excellent, good, fair or poor?' Here, the respondent is only offered four answers, which the researcher has constructed already. Often the interviewer will circle a number on the interview form corresponding to the chosen answer.

[9]At this point you will find it helpful to re-play the audiotape 'Why me? Why now?', associated with *Medical Knowledge: Doubt and Certainty.*

□ What might an open-ended question on the same topic be?

■ Examples are: 'How would you describe your health?' or 'Please tell me about your health.'

The open-ended question might, in practice, be answered with a response like 'excellent' or 'fair,' but might equally receive a detailed account of recent health-related events in the person's life. Alternatively, the respondent might say 'My health gives me great satisfaction, all things considered'. This would be a cue for the qualitative interviewer to probe with a question like 'How do you mean, all things considered?' in the hope of eliciting more about the respondent's views about the meaning of the word 'health'. In qualitative interviewing the interviewer follows up leads given by the respondent, often exploring topics that could not have been predicted at the start. The result is a mass of words, often transcribed from a tape-recording, which may then be analysed with a coding system that is constructed to fit the data that has emerged. (We discuss coding systems later.)

What follows is a transcript of Jocelyn Cornwell's speech during her interview with Wendy. Each statement or question has been given a number so that it can be readily identified in the subsequent analysis.

Jocelyn Cornwell's speech during her interview with Wendy

1   Let's start off now by talking about what's happening to you now. You're living in the same place as you were before.

2   How old are the children now?

3   Are they still at home?

4   You told me that between the times we'd seen each other that you'd been in hospital and had had an operation.

5   Can you tell me about that? Take me back to the beginning—what happened—were you unwell? What happened?

6   What was the bleeding about?

7   You went to see the GP because you were bleeding.

8   And you decided to go to the doctor about that.

9   Did you, did you talk to anyone about it before you went to see the doctor?

10   No one at all.

11   Did you talk about anything of that kind with either Sandra or your mother?

12   Or with your friends?

13   And did they talk about that sort of thing or not?

14   So you went to see the doctor and she sent you to the hospital.

15   Who was it who first mentioned having a hysterectomy then—you or them?

16   You.

17   How old were you?

18   What made you think of that as an option? You were given other options. Were you given the option of being sterilised or anything like that?

19   Right.

20   I think a great many people would find it shocking that you chose that as an option.

21   Have you ever had any idea about why you always bled so much—why your periods haven't ever been regular?

22   So she actually refused to prescribe unless you stopped smoking.

23   Did she give any explanation for why you needed to stop smoking that was connected to whether or not she would prescribe the pill?

24   Getting older, taking the pill and smoking.

25   Right.

26   And what's the consequence of this been? You had the operation about a year ago.

27   Has it made any difference to your sense of yourself?

Jocelyn knew Wendy and her family from previous visits, and one of the claims that she makes for her method is that private accounts were given to her because of the trust that repeated visits had built up.

☐ Which statements are largely concerned with building and reinforcing trust rather than eliciting information?

■ She starts the interview by referring to the fact that she has known Wendy in the past, and is doing this interview in order to catch up on events, as one might do with a friend whom one has not met for a while. Statements 2 and 3 reinforce this feeling, and are of the nature of polite enquiry before business begins with 4. The researcher indicates that she is listening and attending closely to Wendy with 'Right' at 19 and 25. (In fact the tape also contains many 'mm's and 'yes's which have the same purpose but which are not in the transcript above.) Her statements at 22 and 24 in summarising what Wendy has just said are also of this reinforcing nature. Statement 22 is specifically supportive of Wendy's dislike for the way her doctor treated her.

With statements 4 and 5, Jocelyn defines the type of interview that she would like to see: one where Wendy takes her through the story of her hysterectomy from 'the beginning'. Once Wendy has picked up this cue, and begun the story, the purpose of most of Jocelyn's statements and questions is to encourage the flow of the narrative, sometimes focusing on particular aspects of events that are of interest to the researcher.

☐ What aspects of Wendy's account does Jocelyn enquire particularly closely about?

■ Statements 9 to 13 are all about the extent to which Wendy talked with other people about her condition, with 14 cueing Wendy to resume the story. At 15, 16 and 18 Jocelyn appears concerned to establish exactly where the decision to have a hysterectomy came from, and her underlying concern at 18 with the extent to which doctors offered Wendy information is taken up again at 23.

This focusing by Jocelyn suggests that she is pursuing an agenda. This fits the view that qualitative research proceeds by progressively focusing on areas of interest, as theories develop from an initial sorting through the data. Interviewing can be informed by these emerging concerns while still allowing respondents to provide a substantial input of their own concerns. Jocelyn may have been exploring concerns about the extent of lay referral and consultation, or about the power of doctors to control behaviour through withholding information.

However, at one point (20) Jocelyn proposes that the world at large would find Wendy's account 'shocking'. It may surprise you to see such an evaluative statement here. If the purpose of qualitative interviewing is to elicit the respondent's way of seeing things, surely it would make sense for the interviewer to reinforce, empathise and support what Wendy has to say? The answer to this lies in the quality of Wendy's answer. She flatly contradicts Jocelyn, and in so doing reveals more clearly than anywhere else her view of her body:

> Well no, not really. I've got my children, if you want to look at it that way. That's what the womb is for. The womb is for reproduction. I've done my bit; I've got my two, I didn't want any more. So it was fine for me to have it taken away. It's not an organ that can be transplanted into someone else—I did ask about that actually. I said, if there's nothing wrong with it, can't you give it to someone else? But it's the wrong type of organ; it can't be done. But I didn't see the point in keeping it.

Sufficient trust has been built up so that the respondent feels free to disagree with the interviewer; an evaluative statement from the interviewer has led to valuable material.

You may wish to note that what *we* have just done is to analyse a piece of qualitative observational data on *interviewer* behaviour. We constructed a rough category system by which statements were ordered according to their purpose in the interaction. A theory has been proposed: that, in qualitative interviewing, statements that evaluate respondents' views negatively *can* lead to valuable data, if sufficient rapport has been achieved.

Feminism and qualitative interviewing

Feminist researchers have often claimed the qualitative interview as being of special value. This arises from a concern with inequality in the relationship between researcher and researched in other forms of data collection. Janet Finch, describing her experience of interviewing women who ran playgroups, tells the following story:

> I arrived at one interviewee's home…only to find she was being interviewed by someone else. This seemed like the ultimate researcher's

> nightmare, but in the end proved very much to my advantage. The other interviewer was…ploughing her way through a formal questionnaire in a rather unconfident manner, using a format which required the respondent to read some questions from a card ('Do you receive any of the benefits listed on card G?', and so on)…I recorded in my fieldnotes that the stilted and rather grudging answers which she received were in complete contrast with the relaxed discussion of some very private material which the same interviewee offered in her interview with me. My methodological preferences were certainly confirmed by this experience. (Finch, 1984, in Hammersley, 1993, pp. 167–8)

A non-hierarchical relationship between the two parties in research is seen as desirable by many feminist researchers, with the researcher under an obligation to expose her own thinking to the subjects of research.

This is seen first as an ethical issue, an obligation for those committed to exposing inequalities to do so from a position of equality with their respondents, rather than a position of power. Additionally, a non-hierarchical relationship is seen as leading to more authentic accounts of women's experiences, less subject to the distorting effect of a male-dominated culture. Feminist sociologists are critical of the value traditionally placed on objectivity in social research, which is seen as constraining respondents to answer pre-coded questions that are largely a reflection of the researcher's preconceptions.

The interview as a topic and resource

The feminist view of the interview as described above distinguishes between more or less 'authentic' accounts. This involves seeing the interview as, at least in some respects, a *resource* for the researcher to build into a larger picture of beliefs and actions. The validity of each account can be checked against, say, the actions of the respondent. This may be contrasted with a more radical, relativist view that treats the words that are spoken in an interview as a *topic* of interest in their own right. The issue at stake here is whether the language used by the person interviewed can be regarded as describing life outside the interview setting (i.e. the interview as a resource for the researcher), or whether it should be analysed purely as an event in its own right, in which the person interviewed uses the opportunity largely for their own purposes, for example to display himself or herself in an advantageous way (i.e. the interview as a topic).

☐ What, in Wendy's speech, suggests that she was concerned to display particular qualities of character during the interview?

■ She presents herself as actively choosing between doctors, manipulating them to her own ends, since she has the moral right to determine what happens to her own body.

To the researcher concerned to treat this interview as a resource, such self-reporting would be troubling as it may not represent what really happened in the consultations that Wendy had with doctors. To the researcher interested in regarding the interview as a topic, Wendy's presentation of herself as strong and powerful in relation to doctors is of interest in its own right. Such a researcher might be concerned to see whether this presentation is given in a variety of settings in which Wendy finds herself, or whether some other presentation is substituted. No single presentation would be regarded as more or less authentic than any other.

Thus some qualitative researchers would argue that although qualitative interviewing is a method that may result in more private accounts, the quest for the one authentic account that will somehow be the 'true' one is something of a chimera. All accounts are given in particular social settings and are the products of those settings. People are always speaking to a particular audience, even in their private thoughts where changes of mood can result in different *internal* 'audiences'.

The researcher who is concerned to use respondents as a resource for information needs to take into account, when choosing people to interview, the fact that different people may have different types of knowledge about a setting. A student nurse, for example, will have a very different perspective on the reasons for wearing surgical masks from that of a senior doctor. When assessing whom to interview, and how to interpret the account gathered, the researcher—and the reader of a research report—should constantly be aware of these characteristics of interview data.

Analysing qualitative data

Through means such as participant observation or qualitative interviewing, then, the qualitative researcher builds up a quantity of **field notes**, largely containing accounts of what people say and do in the setting observed, some also perhaps being based on verbatim transcripts of tape-recordings. These can sometimes become voluminous, and it is important that the researcher works on organising field notes as they are gathered. This is done by *coding* them.

Coding observations

Coding involves inventing and applying a category system. Sections of the researcher's notes are allocated to topics that reflect the researcher's emerging concerns. An example of how this is done is provided by William Foote Whyte, in the account of his study of an Italian-American inner-city neighbourhood in the 1930s:

As I gathered my early research data, I had to decide how I was to organise the written notes. In the very early stage of exploration, I simply put all the notes, in chronological order, in a single folder. As I was to go on to study a number of different groups and problems, it was obvious that this was no solution at all.

I had to subdivide the notes. There seemed to be two main possibilities. I could organise the notes topically, with folders for politics, rackets, the church, the family, and so on. Or I could organise the notes in terms of the groups on which they were based, which would mean having folders on the Nortons, the Italian Community Club, and so on. Without really thinking the problem through, I began filing the material on the group basis, reasoning that I could later re-divide it on a topical basis when I had a better knowledge of what the relevant topics should be. (Whyte, 1943, 1981 edition, p. 308)

Whyte sorted his notes into physically separate files. Others conduct the process by means of code letters or numbers in the margins of field notes, indicating that certain sections of writing in the notes fit into a particular category. A single chunk of text may fit into more than one category, and as the researcher's thinking develops, category systems may be modified, and earlier sections of field notes will have to be re-coded. It is particularly helpful if field notes are entered into a computer, where programmes designed for the purpose can be used to extract segments of information (or *data* as we should perhaps now be calling it) with the same code.

Coding is a creative process, reducing the mass of words in the field notes, and marking patterns and similarities which the researcher has identified. These patterns are the beginnings of *generalisations* that the researcher seeks to make about the setting that he or she has observed. These *generalisations* may eventually reach a sufficient degree of sophistication to acquire the label of *theory*.

Developing theories

An example of a theory generated from field notes can be seen in the work of two researchers, Barney Glaser and Anselm Strauss, who observed hospitals where dying patients were cared for. This theory arose from instances in field notes where nurses spoke about the death of patients, examples of which are shown below.

Nurses talking about patients who have died

One that upset me was here when I came. He was the hardest for me to see die—he was young and not only that—such a wonderful fellow. Even as sick as he was, he was always kind and courteous.

…I found it so hard to talk to him, and he, of course, knew enough about medicine to realize what his condition was … [Interviewer asks: 'He was close to your age?] Yes, he was, I think this was part of what made me feel so badly.

…He was a young boy who had everything to live for.

…[Referring to a 14 year old girl] I felt badly about it, you know, here was a young girl and just to see her lying there, and there really wasn't too much you could do for her, you know, only to keep her comfortable and then she wasn't even aware of that. I think more than anything, it's just a helpless feeling, sort of a loss feeling, you just don't know what to do and you couldn't do too much in this particular case.

(Glaser and Strauss, 1966, pp. 130, 238–9, 244, 247)

□ What aspects of the patients seem to trouble the nurses in these extracts?

■ Largely, their youth, but also in the first case their manner ('wonderful…kind and courteous').

In such instances, Glaser and Strauss found, nurses could be very upset about a death. In addition to the patient's age, if the person had young children, or had aspirations to fulfil a social role of high status (for example, to become a doctor) the nurses would explain their distress with reference to these characteristics. If the person was old or of low social status, the nurses' composure would be less ruffled when he or she died.

First, then, the field notes in this study would have been coded according to whether they described a nurse speaking about the death of a patient, or described some other aspect of life on the wards. The segments of data relating to a death would then have been separated into instances where composure was lost, and those where it was not. Each of these would then have been sub-divided according to the different characteristics of the person who had died which were mentioned by nurses as important in assessing the social loss represented by the person's death (class, age, etc.).

The full theory generated from these field notes is summarised in Box 3.1. The substantive theory was developed in relation to the care of dying people (the *substantive* or specific setting in which the original research was carried out), but in their proposal of it as a *formal* theory, Glaser and Strauss are suggesting that it may apply to *other* settings where there is interaction between experts and their clients. For example, teachers might calculate the value of their students in this way, or

---

Box 3.1   A theory about the calculation of social loss

Elements of theory	Type of theory	
	Substantive theory	**Formal theory**
Category	Social loss of dying patients	Social value of people
Properties of category	Calculating social loss on basis of *learned* and *apparent* characteristics of patient	Calculating social value of person on basis of *learned* and *apparent* characteristics
Hypotheses	The higher the social loss of a dying patient (1) the better his care, (2) the more nurses develop loss rationales to explain away his death	The higher the social value of a person the less delay he experiences in receiving services from experts

Source: Glaser, B. G. and Strauss, A. L. (1967) The Discovery of Grounded Theory, *Aldine, Chicago, p. 42.*

social workers their clients. Observation of teachers and social workers would be needed to see whether the theory was useful in explaining their behaviour.

As you have seen, Glaser and Strauss developed this theory (and others) by the systematic coding of field notes as they were collected. Their developing ideas led them to seek out settings in which nurses reflected on the deaths of patients in order to collect further instances, and to see whether the developing theory held true (a process which they called **theoretical sampling**). This interplay between data collection and reflection upon its meaning is typical of good qualitative research. It involves a critical attitude to emerging ideas, their testing by further episodes of data collection, and the systematic consideration of all parts of the data, rather than the impressionistic selection of a few that support the researcher's preconceptions.

☐ How might bias nevertheless have crept into the account given by Glaser and Strauss?

■ The hospitals they studied may not have been typical of all hospitals. The nurses observed may not have been typical of other nurses.[10]

Because of their approach to the creation of theory from data, Glaser and Strauss have described their work as proceeding through *grounded theorising*. This they contrast with the *hypothetico–deductive* method that you were introduced to in Chapter 2, and which Karl Popper proposes as the appropriate model for science. Although the distinction between these two is not always as clear in actual research practice as Glaser and Strauss suppose, this does provide a useful way of thinking about differences between an approach intended to *generate* theory, and an approach intended to *test* theory. In their view, the ethnographer should enter the setting with as few preconceptions as possible (difficult though this may be), and record everything he or she sees. Gradually, categories of interest begin to be apparent, and tentative theories emerge which suggest further lines of data collection. The theory thus generated is therefore grounded in the data. This is different from the approach of some other social scientists who generally work with *quantitative* (numerical) data, often seeing their primary purpose as being to test the theories that others have generated. The methods of these other social scientists will be discussed in Chapter 5.

[10]The importance of studying representative samples is discussed in Chapters 5 and 7 of this book.

Reporting qualitative data

Data analysis for the qualitative researcher proceeds in tandem with data collection. Researchers doing participant observation code their notes into categories that may change over the course of fieldwork, and they plan their data-collection activities on the basis of emerging ideas. The qualitative interviewer proceeds similarly—indeed, to an extent the conduct of a qualitative interview will be influenced by what the researcher thinks about what has just been said, and these thoughts are the seeds of data analysis.

However, a crucial part of any piece of research is the production of a *report*, usually in written form. A key problem in reporting qualitative data lies in showing the reader how the analysis has been done, so that the reader may assess the influence of the writer's views on the account that is given. Ensuring that coding is comprehensive can help with this, and here computer software that ensures that all segments of data in the relevant category are made readily available to the writer is a help. In addition, a process of searching for instances in the field notes or interview transcripts that *contradict* the emergent theories is useful in testing the robustness of the researcher's generalisations. This 'search for negative instances', as it is known, is a form of theory testing, and can be related to Karl Popper's idea that science proceeds towards truth when the scientist deliberately attempts to disprove hypotheses.

☐ Imagine that Glaser and Strauss had come across a few instances of nurses who said in interviews that *every* time any patient died they experienced a sense of profound loss, regardless of the patient's age or social circumstances. Would this refute the theory given in Box 3.1?

■ Not in itself, since what is said in an interview may not describe what nurses feel in the ward setting, but it would have alerted the researchers to the possibility that the theory was wrong, and guide further data-collection activities, perhaps focusing on these nurses to discover if their actions support this claim.

The researcher may also provide what is known as a **reflexive account** of the research process. This basically involves telling the story of how the research was done, and the way in which the ideas of the researcher developed over the course of field work. Some assessment is made of the way in which the people studied may have tailored their behaviour for the researcher, and the researcher's own preconceptions are described as honestly as possible. Information is given about the decisions made on whom to interview or observe, which lines of enquiry to pursue in data collection and which to reject. This can help the reader assess how the researcher's own views and actions have influenced the account given, and is perhaps a technique from which research done in the quantitative tradition (see Chapter 5) would benefit as well.

□ Identify elements of reflexive accounting in the material you have read so far in this chapter.

■ Paul Atkinson provides an account of his relations with the people he studied; Janet Finch describes what lay behind her choice of interviewing method; William Foote Whyte gives an account of how his ideas developed about what was important in the setting, and how this process was reflected in the organisation of his notes.

It is unlikely to be feasible to present all the data collected to the reader. If the researcher has interviewed fifty people, how can the reader know that the writer has selected a fair and representative collection of quotations for the report? Perhaps the writer has just selected a series of *anecdotes*, unrepresentative accounts that support his or her personal prejudices? The writer should show how the selection was made. However, there is always a tension in qualitative research between on the one hand placing weight on an event because it happened a lot of times, and on the other using the researcher's judgement that some infrequent events or quotations supply unusual levels of insight.

Giving an account of how categories and concepts used in the report emerged from the data can also help reassure readers about the validity of the account. Here is an example of this from Howard Becker and his colleagues' study of medical school students in the 1950s:

I first heard the word 'crock' applied to a patient shortly after I began my fieldwork. The patient in question, a fat, middle aged woman, complained bitterly of pains in a number of widely separate locations. When I asked the student who had so described her what the word meant, he said that it was used to refer to any patient who had psychosomatic complaints. I asked if that meant that Mr X—a young man in the ward whose stomach ulcer had been discussed by a staff physician as typically psychosomatic, was a crock. The student said that that would not be a correct usage, but was not able to say why.

Over a period of several weeks, through discussion of many cases seen during morning rounds with the students, I finally arrived at an understanding of the term, realising that it referred to a patient who complained of many symptoms but had no discoverable organic pathology. I had noticed from the beginning that the term was used in a derogatory way and had been enquiring into this, asking students why they disliked having crocks assigned to them for examination and diagnosis. At first, students denied the derogatory connotations, but repeated observations of their disgust with such assignments soon made such denials unrealistic. Several students eventually explained their dislike in ways of which the following example is typical: 'The true crock is a person who you do a great big workup for and who has all these vague symptoms, and *you really can't find anything the matter with them.*' (Becker and Geer, 1957, p. 29)

Here, you can see the researcher testing a theory (that 'crock' meant 'psychosomatic') by asking questions of people in the setting. The contrast between students' words and deeds became clear, in a way that it might not have done in a study based on qualitative interviewing alone. Quasi-statistical statements such as 'many cases' and 'several students' are used to indicate how common the term was. A single quotation, judged to be typical of many others, is chosen for presentation to the reader. Elsewhere in this study, Becker makes it clear that searches for *negative instances* (in this case, presumably, examples where the treatment of such patients was welcomed by students) were done during the analysis of field notes.

Qualitative data analysis is thus an interaction between creativity and restraint. Creativity is involved in the generation of categories and theories that organise the data, but restraint is exercised in the testing of these during data collection and analysis.

Ethics and marginality

All participant observation, and indeed qualitative interviewing, is, by its very nature, secret to some extent. It is never possible to explain to the people studied exactly what will be done with the material that the researcher is collecting. This is partly because qualitative research is creative, and what will emerge from the data cannot be predicted in advance. All the researcher can do is give the best account of his or her intentions at each stage in the research process. It is often possible to reassure the people studied that their identities will not be revealed in any subsequent report. One further strategy is to show drafts of reports to the people studied, for them to read and comment upon before publication.

However, Howard Becker makes the comment that 'a good study…will make somebody angry'. This is because, as he explains,

> Unless the scientist deliberately restricts himself to research on the ideologies and beliefs of the people studied and does not touch on the behavior of the members of the community or organization, he must in some way deal with the disparity between reality and ideal, with the discrepancy between the number of crimes committed and the number of criminals apprehended. A study that purports to deal with social structure thus inevitably will reveal that the organization or community is not all it claims to be, not all it would like to be able to feel itself to be. (Becker, 1964, p. 332)

In considering the ethical aspects of reporting, the researcher needs to take account of any bargains that were struck with the people studied during the research process, but it will always be a matter of fine judgement as to the correct place to draw the line between the reporting and the suppression of results. On the whole, the reporting of facts that are unnecessary to the overall argument is avoided, if they are likely to cause suffering to the individuals involved. But this has to be balanced against the gain in making the facts public. To some extent this may depend on who the researcher sees as his or her own 'moral community'. A researcher studying the actions of employers discriminating against people with AIDS might feel more justified in reporting material embarrassing to the employers than one studying women's views of contraceptive services who found material embarrassing to the women.

Ethical issues are at the heart of the problem of the **marginality** that social scientists doing this type of research may often feel. A sense of being a marginal person arises from the fact that the process of ethnographic research usually involves some emotional attachment to the people studied; to get good information, friends are made. Even when reporting relatively harmless findings, there can be a sense of betrayal in the fact of joining a group of people for an ulterior motive. Janet Finch expresses such feelings about the women she interviewed:

> I have…emerged from interviews with the feeling that my interviewees need to know how to protect themselves from people like me. They have often revealed very private parts of their lives in return for what must be, in the last resort, very flimsy guarantees of confidentiality…it was principally my status and demeanour as a woman, rather than anything to do with the research process, upon which they based their trust in me. (Finch, 1984, in Hammersley, 1993, pp. 173–4)

The human desire to feel friendship and a sense of common purpose with people is challenged by adopting the role of researcher. The emotional stress of maintaining this role can be considerable.

Conclusion

The strength of qualitative research lies in the capacity to study people in their everyday settings. Because the methods involve a sustained effort at describing behaviour in such settings, and understanding the meanings that people use in arranging their lives, the qualitative approach appears to minimise the influence of the researcher's own biases.

However, qualitative research also has weaknesses. The first of these is that, in spite of all the efforts which may be put into reassuring the readers of a research report that the researcher has tried to give a full and fair account of the setting, the reader can never really know how honest the researcher has been. The reporting of qualitative data is itself a process of 'impression management', with the writer seeking to present the best possible image of methodological rigour to his or her audience. Although this is true to some extent of any type of scientific writing (as you have seen in Medawar's account of the scientific paper discussed in Chapter 2), with qualitative research the problem is particularly acute as the data is not in a form that can be easily summarised in a short space.

A further weakness is that it is often hard to know how representative the study is. For example, Becker and his colleagues found medical students talking disparagingly about 'crocks' in one medical school in America in the 1950s. Does this mean that medical students everywhere behave like this now? Qualitative research is often very labour-intensive, and it may only be possible to study a small number of cases.

In Chapter 5 you will learn about quantitative methods, the advantages and disadvantages of which are in some ways a mirror image of those of qualitative research. Quantitative methods are generally strong on representativeness and weak on naturalism. With qualitative methods, one may always suspect that two researchers studying the same setting might come up with very different results. With quantitative research, it is possible to replicate the methods of study used in one piece of research, and be more confident that any variation in findings is due to variation in the setting studied rather than to the particular interests of the researcher.

OBJECTIVES FOR CHAPTER 3

When you have studied this chapter, you should be able to:

3.1 Describe how data in social science may be influenced by the impressions people wish to give to the researcher and other audiences.

3.2 Assess the strengths and weaknesses of participant observation and qualitative interviewing.

3.3 Assess whether conclusions in qualitative research reports are supported by adequate evidence.

QUESTIONS FOR CHAPTER 3

The following interaction was recorded in a hospital clinic.

> A paediatrician is speaking to a mother wanting to adopt a baby and to the social worker who has accompanied her. He has just carried out the necessary examination of the baby and completed the adoption form for the magistrate. 'I certainly think everything's all right…I can't find any abnormalities so it'll be through by the end of January…'. After they have left he comments to the researcher, 'That was a difficult one. I'd have been a lot happier if she'd reacted to the rattle and lifted her head up earlier. She did it in the end but I felt she could have done it earlier. One has also got to take into account that she is an Indian baby; they might be slower to develop. Negroes, of course, are faster. There's also the reason why she's adopting this baby. She may be one of those people who have a thing about under-privileged children. I would like to see her again in two or three months time perhaps, but as she seems to be so set on this thing, I won't implant the doubt in her mind. She seemed a pretty lively thing.' (Strong, 1979, pp. 174, 175)

Question 1 (*Objective 3.1*)

People often alter their behaviour to suit their audiences. Who is the doctor's audience here, and how might his behaviour have altered as a result?

Question 2 (*Objective 3.1*)

What does this extract show us about the trustworthiness of official documents, such as adoption records?

Question 3 (*Objective 3.2*)

How could we tell whether this paediatrician's behaviour is typical of other paediatricians?

Question 4 (*Objective 3.3*)

Imagine that Philip Strong, who collected these data, wanted to put forward a theory that the paediatricians in this setting used racial stereotypes to guide their assessments of babies. What further work would need to be done to make this case persuasive?

4 Historical research methods

This chapter makes some references to Chapter 6 on Hysteria in **Medical Knowledge: Doubt and Certainty,** *and to the associated Reader article by Mary James entitled 'Hysteria and demonic possession'.*[1]

Theory and practice in the history-making process

What is history? It sounds like a very simple question to which most people might immediately suppose they know the answer. One might reply, for instance, 'it is the study of past events'.

This is part of the definition given in the *Concise Oxford Dictionary*. The full definition given there is

> **1** a continuous, usu. chronological, record of important or public events. **2 a** the study of past events, esp. human affairs. **b** the total accumulation of past events, esp. relating to human affairs or to the accumulation of developments connected with a particular nation, person, thing, etc.... **3** an eventful past... **4 a** a systematic or critical account of or research into a past event or events etc. **b** a similar record or account of natural phenomena. **5** a historical play. (Allen, 1990, p. 559)

Already we can see that the study of history is not a simple or straightforward activity. Historians will differ, for instance, as to what constitutes 'an important event', and give different interpretations of complex human behaviour and motives. The kinds of history that are written depend upon the different approaches and methods used.

[1] *Health and Disease: a Reader* (Open University Press, revised edition, 1994).

In this chapter we will look at how the types of historical *method* adopted by historians determine not only what they find out about the past, but also how they select which 'facts' are relevant to their task—the quotation marks are a reminder that so-called facts are not necessarily value-neutral, but may contain the value judgements or biases of their compiler. Consequently historians need to be sensitive to the purposes served by recording 'the facts' in the first place.

All method implies an underlying *theory* and consequently historical research methods cannot be studied in isolation from the theory that shapes the historian's work. In historical terms, we will take 'theory' to mean the set of assumptions that form the historian's point of departure. Before examining how historians set about their work the question of theory must be considered. Let us take a brief look at what this involves.

Different styles of research represent different *theoretical positions,* not only with regard to *how* history is studied, but also as to *what* is studied. The historian might, for instance, focus on the economic, political, social, biographical or any other aspect of the past. In this series of books, for instance, we focus on the history of health and disease. However, irrespective of the field of historical inquiry, how the historian delineates the subject, and which of its features are incorporated in the work, depends upon the theoretical stand-point he or she has adopted. Although historians may be neither aware nor explicit about theory, their point of view will nevertheless provide the theoretical framework that shapes the project and will impinge very much upon their choice of research methods.

Some historians of medicine, for instance, focus their attention on describing the *evolution* of ideas about illness and its treatment over the centuries. This type of general history is usually based on an underlying theory of *linear progress in medicine.* It tends to strike an optimistic note by emphasising scientific achievements. There is much historical evidence to support this point of view and such an historian can easily gather information on what have been seen as major scientific advances, for instance the discovery of anaesthetics, the development of antibiotics, and the growth of surgical techniques such as organ transplants.

This type of history, which often emanates from within the medical profession, is largely characteristic of the history of medicine until the 1960s. It is known as **Whig history** after the reforming political party that dominated British politics for almost the whole of the eighteenth century, the time when Britain itself grew to be the most powerful country in the world. The Whig party, the old version of the Liberal party, was fundamentally concerned with presenting a picture of continuous and coherent historical development with an emphasis on progress. Thus Whig history is the sort that is written by the confident and the successful to reinforce the picture of past 'triumphs' from the perspective of the writer's own time.

However, Whig history (to which we will return) has, since the 1960s, provoked various critical responses, informed by altogether different theoretical positions. Examples of theoretical positions which have taken the place of historical Whiggery are explored later in the chapter. Their titles give an insight into the underlying theory which influences the historians who adopt these approaches: critical intellectual history; social and political history; and feminist history.

Historiography is the study of history-writing and is included in this chapter to help to illuminate how different kinds of history are produced in terms of both theory and practice. The types of histories that are written vary considerably because they are the product not just of a theoretical position (which, as you have seen, reflects the concerns of the writer), but also a *process of selection* of what to include.

On the one hand, this process is influenced by the kinds of *sources* of historical data that are available. These, however, may take such a variety of forms that this chapter can provide only a flavour of their richness. On the other hand, selection is determined by the personal choices of individual historians. Consequently the selection process inevitably entails a strongly subjective component. As we said at the outset, what constitutes an 'important event' is not objectively defined.

Furthermore, since our knowledge of the past is processed by the particular mind that attempts to reconstruct it, it will reflect the attitudes, interests, concerns and so on of the historian's own time and place. After all, ideas do not arise in a vacuum, but are unavoidably influenced by the context in which they take shape. However, the time and culture-bound nature of historical writing does not correlate in a fixed or uniform way with the period in which it is produced. History-writing is shaped by a variety of elements and, even at the same time, histories are often written from opposing points of view. For example the obvious differences in perspective between Nazi and Soviet historians' accounts of the same political events highlight the significance of the particular vantage point of the historian.

In this chapter we will consider how different historians, irrespective of the period in which they are writing, can draw on the same sources and yet reach quite different conclusions. This means that history, like all other branches of knowledge, is always changing and varying and is open to different readings.

However, this is not to suggest that, since all history involves personal judgements and points of view, any history is as good as another. Much will depend upon how the historian sets about discovering 'the facts', but also on the sensitivity and rigour with which these are subsequently interpreted and assembled into a coherent and plausible account. By combining a methodical and systematic approach with interpretive and imaginative skills, the history-making process can not only provide insights into past events, but may also facilitate better understanding of present practices and explanations.

Approaches to history

There is no general agreement as to how historians should carry out their studies and many approaches are possible. Different *source materials* and different methods are needed to tackle different problems. Often the most exciting history may use more than one method and draw on a wide variety of sources. Indeed it is this broadness of range that can facilitate historical understanding. However, the nature of the issues the historian wishes to investigate is crucial because it will suggest the particular form the history will take. This may, for instance, be *narrative* history or *analytical* history.

Narrative history is usually concerned with specific people and events. It entails a chronological recital of 'the facts', to unfold a *story*. The facts are drawn from any information pertinent to the subject matter that the historian can acquire, and constitute the raw material from which the narrative history is framed. By carefully interpreting and piecing together those details most relevant to the inquiry, the historian may illuminate the meaning and significance of past human behaviour and events. This approach to history tends to be literary rather than statistical and as such is the product of **qualitative methods** very similar to those described in Chapter 3 for social research in present-day settings.

Analytical history is more concerned with discovering historical *trends*. Once various co-existing trends have been identified, the relationships between them can be analysed to provide historical insights. For instance the relationship between age at marriage, wages and crop yields over a particular period might be examined to show the impact of their inter-relationships upon health, fertility or other aspects of past societies.

Analytical history is based upon the systematic collection of data from sources such as the Public Record Office, the Office of Population Censuses and Surveys, and their equivalents in other countries, and other official statistical departments founded to record population numbers and movements. Using statistical methods, this information can be processed to reveal general patterns of events. These may come from a wide variety of fields, such as data on infant mortality or the impact of infectious diseases on different sections of the population. The term **quantitative methods** is used to describe this sort of mathematical or statistical approach to the study of history.[2]

The quantitative approach to history

Statistical methods are commonly used in economic history and are also central to **demography,** the study of populations. Demographical studies are based upon the *vital statistics* of births, marriages, deaths, diseases and so on as a means of examining the conditions of life of a community. In Chapter 6, demography is discussed further in the context of present-day population statistics.

Medical historians using a demographic approach may accumulate data from various sources. Hospital records, for instance, often provide details about patients such as occupation, marital status and diagnosis of the disorder. The minutes of health authority meetings, hospital reports, newspaper articles, government documents and so forth, may also prove useful and may contain data that are quantifiable.

If this material covers a sufficiently broad span of time, general trends in the history of medicine may be calculated and stated in numerical terms. However, the further back in time one goes, the less likely it is that detailed records were accurately compiled and are still in existence. For instance, the first British census was taken in 1801, but the system of civil registration of births,

deaths and marriages did not begin until 1837. This means that reliable material is rather recent, and it is always limited by the ways the information was elicited.

☐ What sources of bias might be inherent in the records?

■ Data are often gathered to serve a particular political agenda. Records are kept, usually, by those in positions of authority, and consequently may reflect the various and sometimes contradictory interests of officialdom. Furthermore the records may contain inaccuracies and omissions and so not be representative.

There is considerable potential for using quantitative methods in the history of medicine. Some topics lend themselves easily to quantification, such as certain characteristics of patients and their social backgrounds, the duration of treatment, the number of readmissions and so forth. At the other extreme are areas that are much less suitable for this approach. A historical study of doctor–patient interaction, for example, could not be carried out in numerical terms alone. Sometimes, however, quantitative and qualitative methodologies may combine to provide complementary insights into a subject, as in the interpretation of standards in patient care.

Even though the historian may in some instances make considerable use of quantitative methods, because of the complexity and variety of human society, non-numerical, i.e. qualitative methods, will always have an important role to perform in the historian's task of reconstruction. Furthermore the *interpretation* of data inevitably entails a subjective component, since personal judgement must be exercised in this process. This means that the conclusions of quantitative history, although intended to be objective, can never have the certainty of mathematical proof. However, although historical numerical data may not be totally valid and reliable (a criticism that may also apply to contemporary data), they may nevertheless serve important illustrative purposes.

Historical demography: a case study

An example of analytical history using quantitative methods is the demographic study entitled *Population History of England 1541–1871*, by E. A. Wrigley and R. S. Schofield. This work, which was published in 1981 after many years' research, sets out national demographic patterns extending over several centuries. It provides the basis for an examination of the relationship between economic and demographic changes, such as the rapid developments that occurred in the course of the Industrial

[2]In Chapter 5 you will read about quantitative methods used in social science.

Revolution in the late eighteenth and early nineteenth centuries.[3]

Anthony Wrigley, Professor of Population Studies at the London School of Economics and Political Science, and his colleague Roger Schofield are members of a school of historical demographers based in Cambridge, known as the Group for the History of Population and Social Structure. This group, established in the 1960s, has produced several works covering a sample of all the parishes of England.

The aim of the group is to foster interest in the numerical study of past society in order to illuminate long-term social change. They are concerned with collecting data on, for instance, the size of families, age at marriage, the mobility of individuals both geographically and socially, and information on certain types of disease. By analysing these data, they seek to identify general trends in, for instance, population size, fertility and mortality and to provide broad explanations for these phenomena.

Wrigley and Schofield theorise that *biological* occurrences (birth, disease, death) affecting population movements are not only determined by biological factors such as nutritional levels and micro-organisms, but by complex cultural choices. Cultural factors influence, for instance, the social distribution of resources, customary patterns of marriage and so on, and hence affect the health and fertility of a population. However, these socio-cultural factors cannot easily be summarised in numerical terms: demographic history therefore involves qualitative as well as quantitative methods.

In order to trace demographic changes over the period 1541–1871, Wrigley and Schofield focused primarily on English **parish registers**. These are church records of baptisms, marriages and burials of people of the Anglican faith. (An example is shown in Figure 4.1, *overleaf.*) They were first required to be kept in the 10 000 or so ancient English parishes in 1538; however, few registers survive from that date. Furthermore, the recording of events was rarely found to be complete over a continuous period of time. Breaks in registration or periods when registration was defective occurred in almost all registers. In particular, periods of religious and political crisis, such as the Civil War, 1642–9, affected the level of registration. Also in times of plague and famine entries were less likely to be made, leaving the record blank just when it was most important, from the historical demographers' point of view, that it should be complete.

However, breaks and oversights did not only occur during crises. The priests and parish clerks responsible for

registration were not always attentive to this task. After all they did not have in mind the aims of the historical demographer! It is probable that even in the best-kept records there are inaccuracies and omissions.

Wrigley and Schofield devised a statistical method to identify and deal with short breaks and periods when registration did not break down entirely, but was incomplete. This method was systematically implemented. However, despite this, a substantial proportion of registers remained unusable for a variety of reasons. For instance, some entries were too uninformative to allow analysis. Where a break was prolonged the simplest course for the demographers was to exclude the parish from their sample. Nevertheless, because England has several thousand parish registers beginning before 1600, even after the process of elimination the demographers still had an extremely rich source of data to draw on.

In order to determine which parish registers were suitable for their purposes, lists of possibilities were drawn up county by county. An appeal was then made to local historians with an interest in this field, for help in enumerating the relevant details. As a result of these historians' work, a total of 404 registers were located that passed the various tests devised to ensure reliability of information. The registers identified dated back to 1541 and furnished Wrigley and Schofield with a total of 3.7 million entries of Anglican baptisms, burials and marriages. These form the basis of almost all the demographic description and analysis presented in the book.

□ Demographers base many of their calculations on counts of the total numbers of births, marriages and deaths occurring in an area. What problems do you envisage in obtaining these data from what is recorded in parish registers?

■ There are two main ones. First, the registers record only the ceremonies of baptism, marriage and burial of those of the Anglican faith. Thus births, deaths and marriages of non-Anglicans are (usually) not recorded. Second, the timing of baptisms and burials may not match the timing of births and deaths closely enough.

Although most burials occurred within three days of death, and so may be a fairly accurate reflection of this vital event in predominantly Anglican communities, the case is different for baptism and marriage. Baptism might be delayed for months, or even years after birth. Some infants may not have been baptised at all, especially if they survived only for a short period. At times clandestine marriages were common. Also couples might live out of wedlock.

[3]The work of Wrigley and Schofield is discussed further in *World Health and Disease*, Chapters 5 and 6. The Industrial Revolution is discussed in Chapter 5 of the same book.

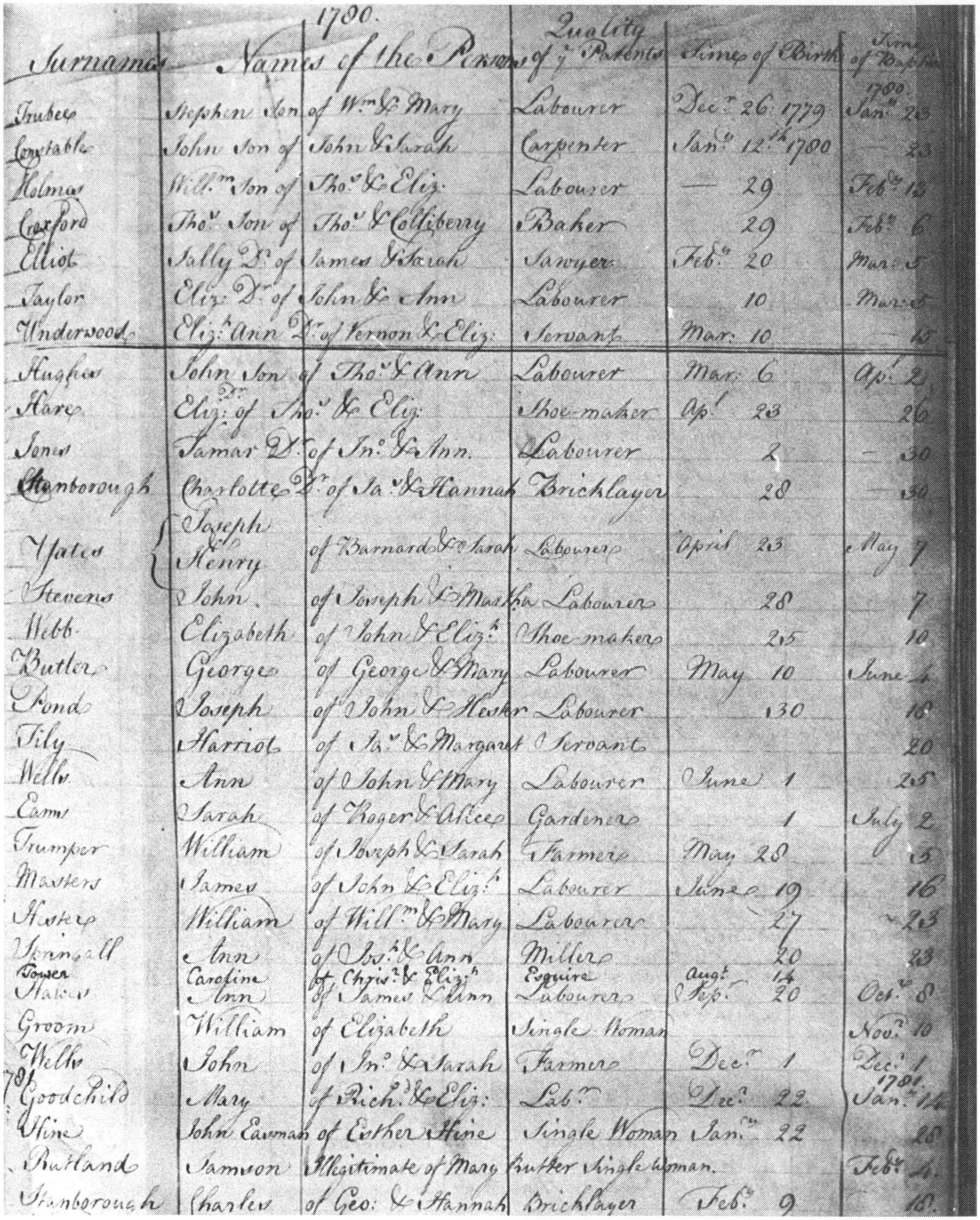

Surnames	Names of the Persons (1780.)		Quality of ye Parents	Time of Birth	Time of Baptism 1780
Trubee	Stephen Son	of Wm. & Mary	Labourer	Decr. 26. 1779	Janr. 23
Constable	John Son of	John & Sarah	Carpenter	Jany. 12th 1780	23
Holmes	Willm. Son of	Thos. & Eliz.	Labourer	— 29	Feby. 13
Carford	Thos. Son of	Thos. & Colliberry	Baker	29	Feby. 6
Elliot	Sally Dr. of	James & Sarah	Sawyer	Feby. 20	Mar. 5
Taylor	Eliz. Dr. of	John & Ann	Labourer	10	Mar. 5
Underwood	Eliz. Ann Dr. of	Vernon & Eliz.	Servant	Mar. 10	15
Hughes	John Son of	Thos. & Ann	Labourer	Mar. 6	Apl. 2
Hare	Eliz. Dr. of	Thos. & Eliz.	Shoe-maker	Apl. 23	26
Jones	Tamar Dr. of	Jno. & Ann.	Labourer	2	— 30
Stanborough	Charlotte Dr. of	Jas. & Hannah	Bricklayer	28	— 30
Yates	Joseph & Henry	of Barnard & Sarah	Labourer	April 23	May 7
Stevens	John	of Joseph & Martha	Labourer	28	7
Webb	Elizabeth	of John & Eliz.	Shoe-maker	25	10
Butler	George	of George & Mary	Labourer	May 10	June 4
Pond	Joseph	of John & Hester	Labourer	30	18
Tily	Harriot	of Jas. & Margaret	Servant		20
Wells	Ann	of John & Mary	Labourer	June 1	25
Eams	Sarah	of Roger & Alice	Gardener	1	July 2
Trumper	William	of Joseph & Sarah	Farmer	May 28	15
Masters	James	of John & Eliz.	Labourer	June 19	16
Hester	William	of Willm. & Mary	Labourer	27	23
Tonnsall	Ann	of Jos. & Ann	Miller	20	23
Bowser	Caroline	of Chris. & Eliz.	Esquire	Aug. 14	
Hawes	Ann	of James & Ann	Labourer	Sep. 20	Oct. 8
Groom	William	of Elizabeth	Single Woman		Nov. 10
Wells	John	of Jno. & Sarah	Farmer	Dec. 1	Dec. 1
1781 Goodchild	Mary	of Richd. & Eliz.	Labr.	Dec. 22	1781 Jan. 14
Hine	John Cawman	of Esther Hine	Single Woman	Jan. 22	28
Rutland	Samson	Illegitimate of Mary Butler Single Woman.			Feb. 4
Stanborough	Charles	of Geo. & Hannah	Bricklayer	Feb. 9	18

Figure 4.1 *Extract from the Iver (Buckinghamshire) parish register of births and baptisms, 1780. (Source: Bucks County Record Office)*

The registers thus posed a number of problems of both reliability and interpretation. Wrigley and Schofield employed various techniques to overcome most of these problems, and the strategies they adopted are set out in the first part of their book. Nevertheless, as Wrigley stated in an earlier work on historical demography: 'This study is now, always has been and always must be a matter of approximation' (Wrigley, 1966, p. 4).

Because of the formidable size of the *data set* (3.7 million entries) and the complexity of the operations required to be carried out upon it, the historians had to rely heavily on computers. Furthermore, unlike narrative history which is usually a solitary activity, their study was based upon the collaborative effort of many workers collecting and analysing the material.

The qualitative approach to history

Historians using a qualitative approach obtain their information from a wide variety of sources, often very different from those used by Wrigley and Schofield.

Oral sources

In order to get to the grass roots level, that is to say to the level of ordinary people whose point of view is not usually heard, historians in modern times have shown a growing interest in compiling *oral history*. This method entails recording the spoken recollections of events made directly to the historian. You will notice here a similarity to the technique of *qualitative interviewing* described in Chapter 3.

Oral history is a personal, one-to-one approach, allowing the interviewee to talk at length. For this reason it is a particularly valuable method for historians of medicine concerned with patients' experiences. Furthermore, because this technique can be both informal and free-ranging, it offers the possibility of exploring in detail many controversial and unusual topics which the more formal accounts produced by the medical profession do not usually include. A brief extract from an oral history of health care in London before the establishment of the NHS follows.

> I had diphtheria as a child. I was sent to Hither Green Hospital. I was very ill and they think that's what left the kidneys weak. It was terrible really. I was in hospital for quite a long time. There were several children up the road who caught it, and they were trying to find a carrier. They said there was a carrier about and they did find her in the end; a foreigner. They really thought I was going to go you know with the diphtheria.

> They found all this diphtheria had left me weak, so I had to wear these leg irons. I was in Bayland Street Hospital and they were ever so kind. They used to take all of us children in those old-fashioned wheelchairs through the gardens, they'd lovely gardens, and mulberry bushes, you know. It used to be lovely there.
>
> (Nellie Carroll, in Schweitzer, P. (ed.), 1985, p. 27)

One important drawback to the oral history approach is that interviewees may fail to remember accurately the events of years gone by, or else may feel inclined to tell 'the story' they think the interviewer would like to hear. Consequently, oral history may be an unreliable source of information, but since cross-checking is often possible this need not be a serious impediment. Although this method is restricted to living memory, it has the major advantage of providing historians with the opportunity to ask questions.

Personal documents

Personal documents, diaries and letters can shed light on the personal lives of individuals, both past and present. Historians who explore these sources of information need to be sensitive to the author's motive for writing and the possibility of self-censorship.

☐ Why is it important to gauge the motives of those who produce the material?

■ The motive influences what is (and is not) recorded. If a diary or letter has been written in the expectation of publication, the material it contains may be tailored to that market. It may therefore be less than entirely candid. Consider the diaries of politicians or public figures when they write about their time in office.

The Goncourt Journals: a case study

The brothers Jules and Edmond Goncourt kept a journal documenting their life in Paris in the late nineteenth century. The Goncourts were well-known literary men at that time and their four-volume journal, entitled *Mémoires de la Vie Littéraire 1879–1890*, was written for publication. This was the period when the prominent French physician and neurologist Jean-Martin Charcot was at the peak of his career and had become one of the great public figures of his time.[4] An initially trivial

---

[4]Charcot's work in relation to hysteria is discussed in *Medical Knowledge: Doubt and Certainty*, Chapter 6, and in the article 'Hysteria and demonic possession' by Mary James, in *Health and Disease: A Reader* (revised edition, 1994).

misunderstanding between Charcot and the Goncourts escalated into bitter enmity and the brothers used their journal to ridicule and discredit Charcot professionally and personally.

Charcot was portrayed by the Goncourts as an ostentatious, pompous and ill-mannered hypochondriac. They accused him of tyranny and corruption at the Paris Faculty of Medicine. Even Charcot's physical appearance was the subject of derision. They said he shaved his temples to make himself look like 'a great thinker' (Goncourt, journal for Thursday 14 June, 1888). Indeed, the entire Charcot household was dismissed as 'a veritable family of crackpots' (Goncourt, journal for Friday 8 March, 1889).

For the historian studying Charcot, the Goncourt diaries have to be treated with caution. They can undoubtedly provide valuable insights into the nature of Parisian society, but they are too unremittingly hostile to be accepted without reservation. The generally pejorative tone of their remarks, however, can prompt the historian to investigate what personal interests they wanted to further, and to raise such questions as the importance of 'reputation' in medicine. Insights resulting from such inquiries can themselves be helpful to the history-making process.

Although personal documents can reveal fascinating historical details of the minutiae of everyday life, they are not always either an appropriate or an available source of information. Diaries, as highly personal and subjective documents, are often intended by the diarist to be private and confidential. Consequently, delving into this source may raise ethical questions for the historian. It is because of the possible embarrassment that may be caused to the writer's family and associates that, at least during the period of living memory, the historian must acquire permission from the family or the archivist (the person in charge of the collection of documents) before private sources can be used.

Documents of any sort have to be approached with a critical eye. As the example of the Goncourts' journal shows, the value of the historical document may not lie in what it actually says, but in the reader's sensitivity to the purpose it sets out to achieve. Sometimes one document contradicts another. This might appear to be confusing and frustrating. However, this inconsistency can itself be an important discovery, helping to illuminate the issue more fully. M. G. Murphy described this in his book *Our Knowledge of the Historical Past* (1973) in the following way, 'differences are not "errors" to be eliminated, but functions of the social and cultural characters of the observers' (Murphy, 1973, p. 59).

Artefact sources

Historians are not concerned exclusively with the written or spoken word. Anything that facilitates insight into the subject may be examined, and in this context the term 'document' takes on a much broader meaning. It may signify, for instance, paintings (see the frontispiece to this book), photographs, medical instruments (see Figure 4.2) and artefacts of many kinds. Close scrutiny of these can cast light on past practices, attitudes, interests and so on. Thus museums, galleries and private collections, as well as libraries and archives, often supply the historian with valuable sources for the qualitative approach.

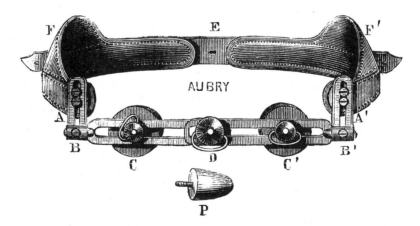

Figure 4.2 *Ballet's apparatus for compressing the ovaries. This illustration, taken from Richer, P. (1881)* Etudes Cliniques sur l'Hystéro-Epilepsie ou Grande Hystérie, Delahaye et Lecrosnier, Paris, *shows a belt to be worn by hysterical women. Conical objects like that labelled P were attached at C and C' to apply external pressure to the ovaries. The aim was to reduce the severity of hysterical attacks. It was claimed that Ballet's apparatus was superior to previous forms of ovarian compressor because it was easier to use and could be hidden under the clothing. (Source: Royal Society of Medicine Photographic & Film Unit)*

The process of selection and interpretation

Historians tend to approach their subject initially by visiting the establishment that either specialises in the field or promises to offer a fruitful point of departure. By starting with the most readily available documents, and consulting *bibliographies* (lists of books or articles by a particular writer or on a particular subject) and earlier scholarship, the researcher may be steered towards other less obvious sources to follow up elsewhere. Each book or article may contain references to other relevant literature.

Usually the main problem for historians is not how to find useful information, but how to cope with an overwhelming supply of pertinent and fascinating material. Not all the evidence can be used since research must be kept within manageable bounds. Consequently each historian must make choices to which neither method nor material can really provide a solution.

The selection process should be guided by the scrupulous examination and careful weighing of evidence to ensure that the history constructed does not merely confirm the historian's preconceptions. The findings of other studies must also be borne in mind to avoid replication. Chapter 3 described how sociologists and anthropologists minimise distortions by constantly checking the initial aims and intentions of the study against the evidence brought to light. History, too, may profit from this approach. Although for both historians and social scientists, underlying theory may influence the choices made, too rigid a theory should not be allowed to cloud their vision or blind them to possible biases inherent in the 'facts'.

Whereas the historian's task entails, first and foremost, the discovery and examination of evidence, this must then be compiled into a coherent form, accessible to the reader. It is not just a question of finding and classifying important facts, but of using experience and imagination to construct these into a meaningful account. Ultimately it is the *interpretation* of the evidence that is the prime task of the historian. However, this must always be problematic to some extent because interpretations can never be final. They are always open to debate. At the level of interpretation the existence of 'the truth' is an unresolved problem.

☐ How do the methodological problems and approaches of the historian resemble those of the ethnographer (as described in Chapter 3)?

■ The ethnographic method highlights the individualistic nature of observation and raises the question as to how far different observers will observe the same things. The historian and the ethnographer share the common objective of attempting to penetrate into the complexities of human meaning, even if these can never be grasped in their entirety.

Hysteria—a case study

The Reader[5] in this series of books includes an article by Mary James entitled 'Hysteria and demonic possession'. This is an example of narrative history. In order to gain a clearer idea of how the process of selection is actually put into operation, we are now going to examine how this account was constructed.

First a wide variety of both *primary* and *secondary* literature was used. **Primary sources** are original texts dating from the period under investigation. **Secondary sources** are those written subsequently, by other authors, in order to explain, interpret or supplement the original texts in some way. These texts were located initially by consulting the subject index at the British Library and the Wellcome Institute for the History of Medicine, and then following up those bibliographical references that related most closely to the subject.

Amongst the most important primary texts were J.-M. Charcot's collected works, including transcripts of the formal weekly lectures he delivered to his students. Most of Charcot's works were translated during his lifetime into several languages, and these translations are also regarded as *primary* literature. Contemporary scientific and medical journals were another primary source. These were a powerful way for the scientific community to express itself, and so contain copious information on the major neurological and psychiatric issues of the time.

The *Iconographie Photographique de la Salpêtrière*, produced by two of Charcot's colleagues and published in three volumes between 1877 and 1880, also constituted a vital source for the study. It documents in detail the case histories of Charcot's hystero-epileptic patients on the wards at his hospital, the Salpêtrière in Paris. These vivid accounts helped to illuminate the doctor–patient relationship. Also of interest in this connection was the photographic illustration of the patients' case histories included in this source (an example appears as Figure 4.3, *overleaf*).

[5] *Health and Disease: A Reader* (revised edition, 1994).

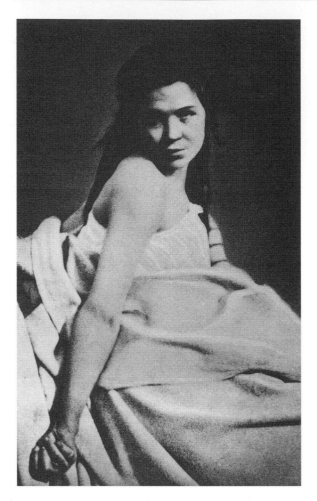

Figure 4.3 *A photograph of a woman diagnosed as hysterical in the 1870s in the Salpêtrière hospital in Paris. From the* Iconographie Photographique de la Salpêtrière. *(Source: British Library)*

The primary literature was found in various locations, most importantly the Charcot library at the Salpêtrière and the Bibliothèque Nationale in Paris, which houses a copy of all works printed in France. Several libraries also offered a vast array of secondary literature on the subject. Much of this helped to cast light on the socio-cultural climate in which hysteria was nurtured.

Although various libraries provided access to the published works on hysteria, *unpublished* material was also important for a deeper understanding of the issues. For instance, considerable information on Charcot's patients was obtained from the administrative and medical records of the hospital and from the registers of admission kept at the Archives de l'Assistance Publique in Paris.

The subject was also approached through artefacts in museums and exhibitions. For example, an exhibition held at the Musée de l'Assistance Publique in Paris in 1986 brought together an impressive range of items. These included paintings, sketches and photographs as well as interesting scientific and personal articles illuminating Charcot's work.

Even this cursory glance at some of the sources reveals just what a minefield the processes of selection and interpretation can be. Consider how the historian sorted the evidence in this specific case.

Stage one entailed setting up a card index. The index itself was divided into two main sections, one for listing authors, the other subject headings. The author index, filed in alphabetical order, was compiled by systematically noting onto a card the name of each author consulted and all the relevant bibliographical details, including where the text was located, its class number, the date of first publication and so forth. This meant that all the documentary sources were on record and were easily retrievable if further information was required.

The subject index was created by methodically recording onto separate cards each new relevant subject as it arose from copious reading of the various source materials. This process was similar to the coding of field notes described in Chapter 3. Headings such as 'Science and religion', 'Demonic possession', 'Women in the nineteenth century', and 'Hysteria—diagnostic signs' were set up as signposts to the main themes. These cards were also used to record a brief summary of what each author had to say on the subject and was cross referenced with the author index.

Other information such as page numbers for pertinent quotes was also stored in this way. Often lengthy hand-written notes were made while reading and the card would be used as a reminder that these had been taken, with a folder number to indicate where they had been filed.

As the card index grew, patterns began to emerge from the data collected. Some of the 'facts' were often repeated so that it became clearer, for instance, which phenomena of demonic possession were most relevant to Charcot's description of hysteria. Once a substantial amount of information had been collected for each of the main headings, it was possible (as stage two of the process) to sift through it and assemble profiles of specific topics of interest. It was then a question of framing this material into a narrative, by using qualitative methods. The literary style of narrative history was appropriate for this study, to illustrate the nature and history of medical knowledge of hysteria. The complex and subtle issues of human culture, psychology and behaviour were not amenable to quantification.

Historiography

By now it should be clear that historians are never merely passive observers. In this section we will look more closely at some examples of how the various perspectives that shape historians' work are intertwined with the basic concerns of their own time and place. In looking at the *manner* in which history is written by historians, we are taking an **historiographical approach**.

Whig history of science and medicine

To explore the complexities of historiography we will look first at a form of historical writing mentioned earlier, namely *Whig history*. This has been described as history that 'studies the past with reference to the present' (Carr, 1971, p. 41). That is to say Whig historians look back to the past through the prism of a self-satisfied present and tell the story of how success was achieved. This approach to science and medicine, (as to any other field of activity that has met with success), constructs the 'heroes' and 'great men' of the age who are seen as contributing unproblematically to the course of *progress*. A tone of untroubled certainty is struck by selecting, from the infinitude of facts, only those which seem to confirm these ideas.

☐ What do you think the Whig approach to the history of science and medicine might leave out?

■ This way of writing history leaves unexamined what appear to be false starts and dead ends. By focusing only on successful individuals, it ignores all the others working in the same field. It also leaves out the broader context of social, economic and political factors, which shaped the times and the thoughts of those who created scientific medicine. Feminist historians have argued that the Whig history of medicine omits certain characteristic male attitudes towards women.

Once again, the history of hysteria provides us with examples. In sharp contrast to the Goncourts' journals, mentioned earlier, some accounts of Charcot's career cast him in the role of 'great hero of science'. This worshipful attitude is known as **hagiography** (from the Greek *hagios* meaning holy). This is because it can be equated with the style of writing of the lives of the saints, the authors of which are known as *hagiographers*.

Charcot, as the leader of the powerful Salpêtrière School, gained a following of loyal disciples.[6] These men

[6]Charcot's influence is discussed in *Medical Knowledge: Doubt and Certainty*, Chapter 6.

not only acquired their medical training through Charcot, but also relied upon his patronage for the furtherance of their careers. The hagiographic tradition that has grown up around Charcot stems from their reminiscences and uncritical accounts of 'the master'. They had an interest in raising his status, for it would indirectly do the same for theirs.

Sigmund Freud, for example, coloured the historical portrayal of 'the great man' through his recollections of his momentous encounter with 'the Maître Charcot' during his brief spell of study in Paris in the winter of 1885–6. This is how Freud described the effect of Charcot upon him at the time.

> I believe I am changing a great deal. Charcot, who is both one of the greatest of physicians and a man whose common sense is the order of genius, simply demolishes my views and aims. Many a time after a lecture I go out as from Notre Dame, with new impressions to work over. But he engrosses me: when I go away from him I have no more wish to work at my own simple things. My brain is sated as after an evening at the theatre. Whether the seed will ever bring forth fruit I do not know; but what I certainly know is that no other human being has ever affected me in such a way. (Quoted in Jones, 1977, pp. 173–4)

Initially most of the accounts of Charcot's work were not only produced by former students, but were written to mark important occasions in his honour. They were, therefore, predisposed towards taking the most uncritical and flattering tone. Subsequently, the masses of literature generated by his 1925 centenary celebration continued to draw a picture of 'the great Charcot' who rose systematically from strength to strength. Such works, by the very nature of the circumstances in which they are produced, contain no appraisal of the *actual* extent of the progress nor of the historical *context* in which it took place.

Once the hagiographic tradition has been set up, it tends to become self-perpetuating and to enter into Whig accounts of history. The view of Charcot's disciples, for instance, was continued by their own students in their turn. In 1955 when Georges Guillain, a former pupil of two of Charcot's followers, came to write a biography of Charcot, he drew his material from the types of sources that have just been described, namely from the accounts and recollection of Charcot's one-time collaborators. Needless to say the biography focuses on Charcot's 'brilliant years', that is the period during which his most notable neurological discoveries were made.

Consequently Guillain's account resonates with the contemporary construction of Charcot's image, perpetuating this as historical reality.

Guillain was of course aware that by his own day hysteria was no longer understood according to Charcot's model, and the emphasis of the book, which devotes just one brief chapter to this subject, serves to minimise the problems that Charcot's approach entailed.

Late twentieth-century history-writing

The Whig approach to history of any kind, by concentrating on successes and achievements, is ultimately something of a propaganda exercise, although not crudely so. However, despite its limitations, this type of history has brought together much pertinent material of use to later medical historians. We will end this chapter by examining the *manner* in which history-writing has changed in the late twentieth century. In this *historiographic* analysis, we will contrast Whig history with some other approaches to the study of hysteria that have been carried out in more recent years.

In the 1960s and 1970s the historical study of science and medicine was transformed by the emergence of keen academic interest in women's studies, social history and the sociology of science. The rapid development of these new fields alerted historians to a range of non-scientific factors shaping past medical theory and practice. Many external influences, (social, religious, political and so on), as well as class and gender divisions, became part of the new approaches to the history of science and medicine. Studies of hysteria dating from this period are, for instance, often concerned with the cultural and interpersonal aspects of the disorder (i.e. those involving the relationships between people) which went largely unexamined in the earlier accounts.

Critical intellectual history of medicine

Many *intellectual histories* of various aspects of medicine have been written. These are accounts of medical *ideas* of the past. Often they have taken the form of a chronological (*linear*) narrative account of medical theories as they have been recorded in published works through the ages. The first writings of this kind, reviewing a range of medical opinions, appeared in the eighteenth and early nineteenth centuries and generally presented a Whig interpretation.

However, since the 1960s intellectual history has adopted a less Whiggish approach. The aim of **critical intellectual history**, as this approach is now known, is to examine ideas within the context in which they took shape. Earlier work is not dismissed as 'wrong', but is understood in terms of its own internal logical

framework. An example of a critical intellectual history is Ilza Veith's *Hysteria: The History of a Disease*, published in 1965, which provides a century-by-century chronicle of the major relevant works. Veith sets out to examine hysteria as it was explained at different times in the past; she makes no attempt to evaluate the disease concepts of the past by those of her own day. Her focus is upon the changing approach of physicians as they strove to understand this baffling ailment.

This type of history of ideas has been criticised by social historians who note that it pays little attention to the social and cultural aspects of the subject. Indeed it has become *de rigueur* in recent years to denigrate linear intellectual histories as Whiggish and old fashioned. For example, Veith's closing assumption that, with the advent of psychoanalysis, the definitive understanding of hysteria had been achieved might well be regarded as somewhat Whiggish. Nevertheless, where there is a high degree of intellectual analysis and the story is told in an accessible style, this approach can be interesting and informative.

Social and political history of science and medicine

Since the 1960s there has been a burgeoning of interest in **social history**. This relatively new focus may be due to the increasingly complex social tensions of Western industrial society, in the years after World War II. The problems facing industrial society have made social questions a major preoccupation of the late twentieth century. Historians have responded to these problems by shifting the focus of historical study on to a wide range of social issues such as those associated with demography, the nature of the family, and the position of women and children in society. Since the late 1980s, historians of medicine have been deeply concerned with the social construction of disease categories. Theories of disease may be mediated by gender, class, race or other non-scientific or social factors.[7]

☐ What sources of evidence would social historians use? (Think back to the sources we discussed earlier in this chapter.)

■ Social history depends upon a great range of records. Diaries, letters, personal memoires and artefacts of various kinds might provide useful sources of information. Parish registers contain material that is quantifiable for a demographic

[7]This is illustrated in relation to TB and hysteria in *Medical Knowledge: Doubt and Certainty*, Chapters 4 and 6.

approach to the topic. Social historians of medicine might use hospital records and patient's case histories. Sometimes oral histories might be appropriate, where the subject of interest lies within living memory.

A pitfall facing social historians has been the tendency to drift into descriptive accounts of how people in the past lived their lives, with little or no attempt to analyse the broad social, political and economic influences shaping their attitudes, activities and so on. However, this tendency has been mitigated by applying sociological concepts and theories to social historical material to give it greater rigour. By moving away from simple description, a more analytic orientation has made social history a complex and intellectually stimulating discipline that has become increasingly prominent in the 1990s.

Social historians of science and medicine, by adopting a sociological orientation, focus on those aspects of the data that reflect prevailing social and cultural conditions. They may, for instance, demonstrate the social and political functions played by past scientific or medical theories and practices, or emphasise the covert social and political agendas of science and medicine.

The social and intellectual historian, Jan Goldstein, for example, in *Console and Classify* (1987), has formulated a specifically political interpretation of hysteria in late nineteenth-century France. Using sociological concepts for her analysis of Charcot's theory of hysteria, she shows how medical ideas were used to strengthen the hand of the French republican government of the time in its actions against the power of the Church. Note that the approaches of social history and intellectual history are not incompatible, as demonstrated in Goldstein's work.

Feminist history of science and medicine

The feminist perspective on the history of science and medicine originated in the 1960s with the rise of the women's movement. This orientation has joined in turn with intellectual history, social history and psychoanalysis. Not surprisingly, hysteria, the quintessentially female malady, has been the subject of considerable analysis, in what has come to be known as **feminist history**.

The feminist literature explores hysteria from the point of view of themes of gender and sexuality. It may, for instance, focus on the doctor–patient relationship as a confrontation driven to a large extent by gender roles, or examine the extent to which the medical view of hysteria reflected cultural stereotypes of women. How the social context of the time shaped the lives, thoughts and experience of women is also of central concern. (Mary James'

case study of hysteria in the Reader is an example of a feminist medical history incorporating each of these themes.)

Although the feminist perspective is concerned with the relationship between hysteria and gender, feminist history-making contains considerable diversity of approach and interpretation. Some feminist writers, for example, have conceptualised hysteria as an objectively 'real' disease which might arise in any time or place regardless of culture. Others, while not denying the reality of the suffering involved, have viewed hysteria as a social construction.

In the 1970s a number of feminist historians, dealing specifically with hysteria, emphasised the way in which women were victimised by the male medical establishment. Drawing on gynaecological textbooks and fictional and autobiographical writings as their chief historical sources, these feminist writers understood hysteria as a stereotyped female role that served to maintain the social and sexual status quo.[8]

This interpretation has been criticised from within the feminist camp. In 1972, Carroll Smith-Rosenberg's article, 'The hysterical woman: sex roles and role conflict in nineteenth-century America' shifted the focus away from the medical definition of women, emphasising instead the secondary gain of the *sick role*.[9] She argued that this allowed women to resist the prescribed gender roles of wife, mother and daughter. Throughout the 1970s, Smith-Rosenberg's attenuation of the 'male oppression model' was increasingly reflected in the feminist literature.

Elaine Showalter's feminist social history of psychiatry, *The Female Malady* (1987) takes into account both the social and medical context in which women were defined and diagnosed as hysterics in the nineteenth century. She interprets their behaviour as a direct response to the educationally and intellectually stifling circumstances of the time. In order to construct this account she drew on sources such as women's diaries, memoires, novels and accounts from the patients' point of view. By this means her perspective on 'the female malady' reflects the views of those who were more often the subjects of medical opinion than its theorists and shapers.

[8]Feminist histories of this period are discussed by Micale, 1989.

[9]The sick role was discussed in *Medical Knowledge: Doubt and Certainty*, Chapter 8.

Conclusion

If you allow that the historical perspective will vary according to the social and historical position of the individual historian, then there can be no such thing as *the* definitive interpretation of the past. In the final analysis, irrespective of the methods used, the art of history remains always the art of constructing a plausible, articulate and accessible account.

Nevertheless, the type and quality of history produced will depend upon certain fundamental procedures. First, historians must decide on the focus of their inquiry. Next comes the gathering of data and relevant information. Necessarily implicit within this is a process of selection. Much will depend upon *how* the historian decides what to include and what to leave out. To a certain extent the criteria for selection will relate directly to the nature of the inquiry itself.

Once the raw material has been accumulated from libraries, archives, museums and so on, the historian must interpret it. This may mean using either quantitative or qualitative methods, or a combination of both. Here we again come back to the unavoidable psychological involvement of the historian in any understanding of the past. Nevertheless, historians who are sensitive to their particular vantage points can minimise prejudice and avoid reading the past as a justification for the practices of the present. Historians who are scrupulous in their methodology and who keep a critical awareness of the issues, can produce valuable insights into the past. After all, although they can never be immune to the influences of their own socio-historical situation, it is still historians alone who 'make history'.

OBJECTIVES FOR CHAPTER 4

When you have studied this chapter, you should be able to:

4.1 Describe the range of sources of evidence available to historians and comment on their strengths and limitations.

4.2 Use examples to illustrate both qualitative and quantitative methods of historical research.

4.3 Say what historiography is and give examples.

QUESTIONS FOR CHAPTER 4

Not long after her first rest cure in 1904, Virginia Woolf read and reviewed *A Dark Lantern* [a novel by Elizabeth Robins, in which the heroine has a successful rest cure]: 'I have been reading Miss Robin's (*sic*) book all the evening, till the last pages. It explains how you fall in love with your doctor, if you have a rest cure. She is a clever woman, if she weren't so brutal.' [The quotation is from *The Letters of Virginia Woolf*.] Although Woolf's doctor was George Savage, by then a stout clubman in his sixties, she did not make fun of Robins's plot as we might expect. Even Gilman, linking the husband with the physician in 'The Yellow Wallpaper', acknowledged a kind of eroticism in the rest cure. For Woolf as for Gilman, however, the the romantic implications of this quasi-courtship were overshadowed by its intrusions. She resisted even the mild rest cure that Savage imposed upon her after her father's death. Under his orders she was sent to stay with an aunt in the country. 'I have never spent such a wretched 8 months in my life,' she wrote to Violet Dickenson, 'and yet that tyrannical and as I think, shortsighted Savage wants yet another two…. Really a doctor is worse than a husband.' Alice James, too, found the condescension of her doctors to be one of the worst burdens of her neurasthenia [a nervous disorder commonly diagnosed in the late nineteenth century, involving a 'deficiency in nervous energy']: 'I suppose one has a greater sense of intellectual degradation after an interview with a doctor than from any human experience,' she confided to her diary in 1890. (Showalter, 1987, pp. 243–4)

Question 1 (*Objective 4.1*)

Describe and assess the sources Showalter has drawn on. Which type of history do they exemplify?

Question 2 (*Objective 4.2*)

Say whether a qualitative or a quantitative historical method has been used and why it is appropriate.

Question 3 (*Objective 4.3*)

Provide an historiographical interpretation of the text.

5 Quantitative methods in social science

Introduction

Aspects of human life, such as birth, death, health and illness, crime or even happiness, can be measured by turning these qualitative experiences into numbers. This process is known as **quantification**. Particularly in Northern European countries, in the early nineteenth century, the enumeration of the lives of citizens became intricately bound up with methods of government. Large bureaucracies, devoted to the collection and reporting of statistical facts about the population, took the place of small-scale recording such as the parish registration you read about in Chapter 4. A new way of thinking about human affairs, and of maintaining social order, emerged that was based on the concept of *statistical normality*. Thus the citizen could be measured in terms of degrees of deviation from a statistical average.

☐ What sorts of statistical averages do we use to assess our health?

■ There are many examples, so here are just two. The weight, height and physical development of infants are closely monitored by health professionals and by parents in terms of deviation from a statistical average, with a 'normal' range about the average. Normal blood pressure is defined in a similar way. Extreme deviations from the norm may indicate pathology.

Alongside quantification, and the increasingly widespread application of the idea of statistical normality, came a new way of thinking about future events. Increasingly, the likelihood of events (such as the occurrence of illness, suicide or crime) became a matter of calculable *chance*. A science of **social statistics** arose that, in the twentieth century, permeated the thinking of governments and other experts, as well as influencing the population at large, to think of their actions in terms of *risk*. These days, we are well schooled in the art of thinking about what we eat, the exercise we take, the

'stress' we put ourselves through, and so on, in terms of the risk these actions hold for our future state of health.

This chapter concerns the application of this way of thinking in the social sciences, and in particular, sociology. This discipline arose from desires to discover *laws*[1] that determined social affairs. Such laws, for early sociologists, were based on the identification of statistical regularities, such as the association of crime or suicide with particular social groups in the population.

Methods of quantification, of turning qualitative experience into numbers, are discussed first since such techniques precede the construction of laws. Ways of measuring health, as well as events in people's lives that are thought to influence health, will be used to illustrate the techniques involved in such measurement. This is followed by a discussion of the modern *social survey*, and of the design of questions and questionnaires. The importance of studying groups of people who *represent* larger groups to whom results will be generalised (i.e. to whom the 'laws' discovered are thought to apply) is then discussed. Finally, you will be introduced to some of the ideas behind the *analysis* of quantitative data, a topic with which the following chapters of this book are centrally concerned.

The main purpose of this chapter is not to equip you fully to go out and do quantitative social research. It is to help you assess whether the conclusions of particular pieces of quantitative research are based on adequate evidence.

Measurement: from quality to quantity

Quantitative social research depends on it being possible to assign numbers to the characteristics of people or of social settings. For some things this is easier than others. For example, take the *concept* (idea) of educational level. Suppose we want to measure how well educated a person is. It might seem at first glance to be appropriate to take

[1]The word 'laws' is being used here in a similar sense to that in phrases like 'laws of nature' or 'laws of physics'.

the number of years a person spent in full-time education to 'indicate' their educational level. In this case, the indicator (number of years' education) is an *indirect* or **proxy measure** of the underlying concept (educational level) since this cannot be measured *directly*—unlike, say, the measurement of volume, which can be measured by the amount of water in a measuring jug. Establishing links between concepts and their indicators is known in social science as **operationalisation**.

□ How might the idea of 'health' be operationalised? (i.e. what indicators of health or the lack of health can you suggest?)

■ There are many indicators of health. We might ask a person to rate their health on a scale of one to ten; we might ask their doctor to report on illnesses from which they have suffered; we might discover how often a person has consulted a doctor in the past year, and so on.

It is important to ensure that an indicator is **valid**; that is, that it corresponds closely to the concept it is supposed to operationalise. The validity of **concept–indicator links** is always open to question, and the social scientist constructing an indicator of a certain concept must always do the best he or she can to prove that the links made between the two are plausible.

Take the example of educational level that was introduced earlier. It is not difficult to find flaws in the idea that this can be measured by years in full-time education. Some people spend many such years, learn very little and get no qualifications. Others catch up in later life through part-time study. So should the concept of educational level, then, be indicated by the number of qualifications gained? Unfortunately, some people are good at passing exams and then forgetting everything a day later, so this indicator also has its problems. Examination passes, however, may correspond better to the concept of educational level than the number of years at school.

On the face of it this seems plausible; arguments such as the ones being described here are sometimes known as arguments about **content validity**, since they depend on logical analysis of whether the *content* of a complex concept like health or educational level is adequately measured by the indicators proposed. The researcher would be expected to 'think through' the strengths and weaknesses of the indicators he or she has used, and make them plain in reports of the research.

□ Think of objections to the measurement of health by counting visits to the doctor.

■ A lot of ill-health does not come to the attention of doctors, for many reasons.[2] People may visit on behalf of others (for example, for children) or for preventative treatment or check-ups when they are not ill.

We will come back to the question of validity later.

The measurement of health

The objection raised to using certain indicators as proxy measures for particular concepts often rests on the problem of variations in *meaning*. For concepts whose meaning is commonly agreed, measurement can be fairly straightforward. For example, the concept of age can be indicated fairly uncontroversially by counting the number of years since birth. The meaning of other concepts, however, may vary from one setting or one person to another, and are therefore more difficult to measure. *Health* is an example of such a contested concept. The following example illustrates some of the difficulties researchers face in measuring health.

In a survey of health and lifestyles done by the sociologist Mildred Blaxter (1990),[3] 9 003 respondents were asked to answer the following question:

At times people are healthier than at other times. What is it like when you are healthy?

This is an example of an open-ended question designed to gather qualitative data, although here it is being used in a large-scale *social survey*. Some of the answers are shown below.

1 I don't know when I'm healthy, I only know if I'm ill.
2 I'm never healthy so I don't know.
3 You don't have to think about pain—to be free of aches and pains.
4 Health is when you don't have a cold.
5 There's a tone to my body, I feel fit.
6 I can do something strenuous and don't feel that tired after I've done it.
7 Being healthy is when I walk to my work on a night, and I walk to school to collect the grandchildren.

[2]The concept of the *clinical iceberg* is relevant here. This is discussed in *Medical Knowledge: Doubt and Certainty*, Chapter 2.

[3]Featured in the first television programme, 'Why me? Why now?', associated with this series of books.

8   Health is being able to walk around better, and doing more work in the house when my knees let me.

9   Emotionally you are stable, energetic, happier, more contented and things don't bother you so. Generally it's being carefree, you look better, you get on better with other people.

10   Well I think health is when you feel happy. Because I know when I'm happy I feel quite well.

(Blaxter, 1990, pp. 20–30)

Two hundred of the questionnaires were used to construct a category system into which all or most of the replies to open-ended questions like this could be placed (a process known as *coding*, already described for qualitative data in Chapter 3). After all the comments on the 9 003 questionnaires had been placed in these categories, they were then given numbers, and the data entered into a computer. Table 5.1 shows the categories used to quantify the qualitative data that were gathered in response to the question about health.

The ten answers listed above fall into all five of the main categories (excluding 'other') in Table 5.1.

Table 5.1   Categories of answers given to the question 'What is it like when you are healthy?', by age and gender (percentages)

Age/years	Males 18–39	40–59	60+	Females 18–39	40–59	60+
	%	%	%	%	%	%
unable to answer	16	12	10	11	7	8
never ill, no disease	14	17	16	12	10	10
physical fitness, energy	39	27	12	41	32	16
functionally able to do a lot	22	26	43	22	36	34
psychologically fit	31	40	36	48	52	44
other	5	6	10	6	8	12
number of individuals replying (=100%)	1 668	1 240	997	2 150	1 596	1 352

The percentages in each column add up to more than 100 because some individuals gave more than one reply. (Source: Blaxter, M., 1990, *Health and Lifestyles,* Tavistock/Routledge, London, Table 3.2, p. 18)

□ See if you can assign answers 1–10 to the categories given in the table.

■ Answers 1 and 2 fall into the category 'unable to answer'; 3 and 4 fall into the category 'never ill, no disease'; 5 and 6 fall into 'physical fitness, energy'; 7 and 8 fall into 'functionally able to do a lot', and 9 and 10 into 'psychologically fit'.

This shows that people describe their health in different ways. If the measurement of health is to be based on people's *own* views of health, this needs to be taken into account. As well asking people to say whether their own health was excellent, good, fair or poor, Mildred Blaxter measured four other aspects of people's health. These were:

unfitness/fitness, based on physiological measurements made by the (medically trained) interviewers, such as respiratory function, blood pressure and the degree of being overweight;

disease/disability, based on self-reported, medically-defined conditions and the degrees of disability which accompanied them;

illness, based on people's reports of any symptoms they suffered, such as pain;

psycho-social health, based on their reports of psycho-social symptoms such as depression, sleeplessness or feelings of strain.

People who reported high levels of disease or disability did not necessarily have high levels of psycho-social malaise. One man of 71 in Blaxter's survey defined his health as 'excellent', and yet had several chronic medical conditions, was wheelchair-bound and required assistance with many activities in his daily life. Conversely, it was possible to be measured as very fit, and yet report a number of symptoms. Blaxter concludes:

Health is not, in the minds of most people, a unitary concept. It is multi-dimensional, and it is quite possible to have 'good' health in one respect, but 'bad' in another.... An implication of this multi-dimensionality is that health status is unlikely to be susceptible to measurement along one linear scale. (Blaxter, 1990, pp. 35–6)

Thus Blaxter's answer to the problem of variation in the meaning of health was to use a variety of different indicators, each one operationalising a different aspect of the concept. More faith can be placed in a measurement strategy such as this than one that relies on only a single indicator of a concept.

Measuring life events

Another useful distinction to make when measuring the meaning that concepts or events have for people is the distinction between *respondent-based* and *researcher-based* measures. To ask a person 'Is your health for your age excellent, good, fair or poor?' is to put the meaning of those terms in the hands of the respondent. The researcher is faced with the outcome of numerous assessments where different individuals will have meant different things by 'good' or 'poor' in their replies. One solution to this, albeit a time-consuming one, is to put the judgement of meaning into the hands of the researcher, who can apply a series of rules for each case.

This was done by George Brown and Tirril Harris when measuring the severity of adverse *life events* in a study which sought to relate these to the onset of depression in women (Brown and Harris, 1978). Examples of life events are the death of someone close, moving house, losing a job or even happy events such as falling in love or being promoted at work. All of these can have a disturbing psychological effect on the person experiencing the event. Brown and Harris wanted to measure life events on a scale of severity, so that they could be ordered according to the level of distress they might be expected to cause. A respondent-based measure might have asked people themselves to rate the severity of the event on, say, a 10-point scale ranging from not being at all upsetting, to being extremely upsetting.

> ☐ What problems of interpretation would this have caused?

> ■ This would have been subject to variation in people's understanding of the meaning of the word 'upsetting'. One person recording a level of five, say, might have had a very different level of disturbance from another person who also recorded five.

Brown's interviewers gathered qualitative data, asking the women they interviewed to describe events in their lives. No attempt at quantification was made at this stage. The women's accounts of events were then examined separately from their reports of the emotional impact of the events. A group of researchers read the transcripts and made their own numerical ratings of the severity of particular events in people's lives, basing their judgements on their own views of how the events might have affected the people interviewed. Through discussing and comparing different case histories, the researchers built rules and precedents that determined subsequent ratings,

and ensured some consistency in the meaning of the numerical scale.

> ☐ Did Blaxter use respondent or researcher-based measures when measuring the meaning of the concept 'health'?

> ■ She used both. Asking people whether their health was excellent, good, fair or poor is a respondent-based measure. Asking them to describe what they meant by health, and then making a category system to code replies is a researcher-based measure.

Reliability and validity

Most of the discussion about measurement so far concerns ways of improving concept–indicator links so that the **validity** of measures is ensured. There are a number of ways of checking whether this has been successful. Content validity was described earlier, but another common way of establishing validity is to see whether the measure gives the same result as some *other* measure of the *same* concept. Preferably there will be some reason for believing that the second measure is also a good one. This type of validity is known as **criterion validity,** as the second measure is the criterion for judging the first. An example would be where a researcher has constructed a series of questions designed to produce a score that measures depression. The researcher would apply the questions to a group of people, and compare the results of this exercise with ratings of depression made by clinical psychologists in interviews with the same people. If the two ways of measuring depression gave the same results, the questionnaire would be said to have criterion validity.

There are other ways of assessing validity that are beyond the scope of this book. It is important always to be aware that validity is a potential problem in measurement, and thus to assess whether researchers have done enough to show their measures are valid tests of the concept under investigation.

However, it is also important that measurement is done in a **reliable** way. This means that the same result must be obtained if the measure is repeated again and again. It is no good having a weighing machine that gives a different result each time (unless the person's weight has actually changed!). One way of assessing reliability is to ask the same questions twice to see if respondents answer the same way each time. A measurement can, however, be reliable but not valid. It is possible for a weighing machine to give a result that is quite consistently five kilograms below true weight. The relationship between reliability and validity is shown in Figure 5.1.

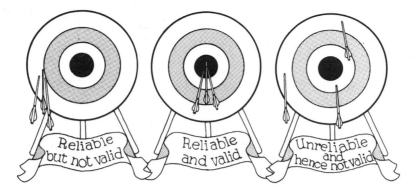

Figure 5.1 *Reliability and validity. (Source: Open University, 1979,* Classification and Measurement, *DE304, Block 5, The Open University, Milton Keynes, p. 68)*

To conclude this section on measurement, here is a summary of what has been covered so far. Turning qualities into quantities is a matter of establishing good concept–indicator links. An important concern for any reader of a research report based on quantitative measurement is to assess the validity of such links. This can be done by assessing whether, on the face of it, the indicators chosen genuinely reflect various aspects of the concept. The reader can also look for evidence that the researcher has tested validity more formally, for example by assessing criterion validity. A further consideration is to assess whether the complexity of concepts that have a contested or variable meaning (such as health) has been adequately represented, and here the distinction between researcher-based and respondent-based measures can be helpful.

Now we can turn to perhaps the most common method of collecting quantitative data in social science: the social survey.

The social survey

The origins of the modern **social survey** lie in the work of Victorian social reformers and philanthropists who were concerned with the problem of poverty. The Victorian British had a passion for collecting and enumerating things of all sorts, as witness the great museum collections, and this approach was applied to social problems as well. To this end, in the 1830s and 1840s, statistical societies sprang up in towns and cities throughout the land, consisting of well-meaning local citizens who saw fact gathering as an essential part of the process of reform.

The activities of these societies declined after the Government set up the General Register Office in 1837, in part as a response to lobbying by representatives of local statistical societies. Thus there were links between the activities of early social scientists and the interests of national government. Such links are maintained to this day in the social survey tradition, which in practice is frequently used to formulate and investigate matters that are of concern to policy-makers and others in positions of power.

You can see an example of an early questionnaire in Figure 5.2 (*overleaf*), which is part of the form used in an enquiry by a statistical society into living conditions in the Parish of St George's in London's East End in 1845.

The key feature of a such a questionnaire is that exactly the same information is gathered from each **unit** surveyed. The unit of analysis in a social survey is most frequently an individual. We are all familiar with postal questionnaires coming through our letterboxes, in which we are asked for our views of some product or service. You may have been stopped by market research interviewers in the street and asked your opinion of some social issue. But social surveys can take groups of people as the unit of analysis: a household, a family, a business, a health centre, a geographical region or a country.

☐ What is the unit of analysis in the questionnaire in Figure 5.2?

■ It appears to be the family, although it could be the house or the street as well.

For a long time—indeed until after World War II—the subject matter of social surveys concerned the living conditions of the working classes and the poor, to the extent that one early textbook on the social survey defined it as:

…a fact-finding study dealing chiefly with working class poverty and with the nature and problems of the community. (Wells, 1935, p. 13)

Name and Condition of Street or Place.	Number of House.	Number of Families in the House.	Number in Family.	Male Children, under 16.		Female Children, under 16.		Able-bodied Males above 16.		Able-bodied Females above 16.		Aged and Infirm Males.		Aged and Infirm Females	
1. Height of Houses, in Stories. 2. Length and Width of Place. 3. Open or not at each end. 4. Paving and Lighting. 5. Cleansing. 6. Sewerage. 7. Supply of Water.				Well.	Ill.	Well.	Ill.	Well.	Ill.	Well.	Ill.	Well.	Ill.	Well.	Ill.

Age of Father when first Child born.	Age of Mother when first Child born.	Present Age of Mother.	Number of Children she has had.	Number now living.	Occupation and Weekly Earnings of head of Family.	Occupation and Weekly Earnings of others than the head of the Family.	Weekly Earnings of the whole.	Number of Times that the Family has Animal Food in the Week.

Figure 5.2 *Part of the questionnaire from an enquiry into the Parish of St George's in London's East End, 1845. (Source: Statistical Society of London (1848) Report of an investigation into the state of the poorer classes in St George's-in-the-East,* Quarterly Journal of the Statistical Society of London, **II**, *p. 194)*

However, this narrowness of scope is now no longer the case. The growth of market research and the interest in information on all sorts of topics by government and academic social planners has widened the scope of social surveys immensely, so that today, most importantly for this book, they are often used to investigate health-related issues.

Although the unit of analysis need not be the individual person, what *is* important in the social survey is that the *same* items of information are collected for each unit. Such information may be gathered by means of questioning individuals with a questionnaire, by asking organisations to fill in returns on specially designed forms, by examining officially published statistics indicating, say, the level of health-care activity in different countries, or by almost any means, as long as the same information is gathered for each unit. Items of information are known as **variables**, as these are the things on which the units in a survey vary. Thus people may vary in their gender (male or female), their opinion of their doctor (excellent, good, fair or poor) or almost anything that they are asked about.

☐ What are the variables in the questionnaire in Figure 5.2?

■ There are a large number, but examples are the number of times the family has animal food (meat) in the week, the weekly earnings of the head of family, and the age of the father when the first child was born.

The essential characteristic of the *modern* social survey is not that it is restricted to a particular topic, such as poverty, nor that it is restricted to a particular unit of analysis such as the individual. The social statistician Catherine Marsh, who wrote extensively about the history of the survey method, provided a definition that is sufficiently encompassing:[4]

A survey refers to an investigation where…systematic measurements are made over a series of cases yielding a rectangle of data…the variables in the matrix are analysed to see if they show any patterns…the subject matter is social. (Marsh, 1982, p. 6)

Thus a modern definition of a survey is in terms of its product: a **data matrix**. You can see a small data matrix in Table 5.2.

[4]She used the word 'case' to refer to what we have been calling a 'unit' of analysis.

Table 5.2 A data matrix

| Cases (Units) | Variables | | |
	Sex	Age	Employed
Case 1	M	66	No
Case 2	F	34	Yes
Case 3	F	25	Yes
Case 4	M	14	No
Case 5	M	78	No

☐ What patterns can you see in this data matrix?

■ The men are all either past retirement age or too young to have left school, and are not employed. The women are of working age and are employed.

☐ Is Table 5.1 (on page 51) a data matrix?

■ Although it does contain a rectangle of numbers, it is not a data matrix, rather the product of analysing one. The original data matrix would have contained 9 003 units of analysis (or cases—the total number of people surveyed) and several variables (age, gender and descriptions of health).

The fact that all units are asked the *same* questions, or to put it in a more technical but also more general way, are *measured on the same variables*, is an essential point distinguishing the quantitative social survey from much qualitative interviewing and ethnographic work. In qualitative research, units—which may be individuals or social settings—are all explored as unique instances. The researcher may follow *different* lines of enquiry with each one. The search is not so much for common factors between units, as for moments of insight into the unique characteristics of each person or setting studied.

Questionnaires and interviews

It follows from the definition given by Marsh that a great variety of methods can be used to collect the sort of data used to construct a data matrix. Perhaps the first thing that people think of when considering how to collect social survey data is the **questionnaire**. These are either administered by post (**self-completion** or **postal questionnaires**) or by face-to-face questioning (**structured interviews**).

☐ Think of some other ways of collecting numerical data in health-care settings, suitable for inclusion in a data matrix.

■ The analysis of medical records and counts of verbal interaction in medical consultations are two ways.[5] Official statistics, such as counts of births and deaths, are also often used.

The social survey researcher is firmly committed to treating the interview (or questionnaire) as a *resource* rather than a *topic*.

☐ Look back to the section on qualitative interviewing in Chapter 3. What does the distinction between topic and resource mean?

■ Examining how respondents use the interview setting to create impressions for the researcher is to treat the interview itself as the *topic* of the research. To treat the interview as a *resource*, however, the researcher assumes there is some correspondence between what the respondent says in the interview, and their behaviour in other settings.

In fact, a researcher in the social survey tradition may have a rather different view from qualitative researchers about respondents tailoring their accounts to suit the interview setting. For the qualitative researcher, this effect may be a source of useful information about the sort of 'fronts' that people like to present to authority figures. For the quantitative researcher such effects are considered to be *bias*, distorting the true account that would otherwise be gained.

A number of methods are used to control such bias. First, efforts are made, in designing questions, to ensure that the *language* used in the questions has a commonly understood meaning among the sort of people who will take part in the study. This may be done by conducting preliminary, open-ended, qualitative discussions with potential respondents, and using their words to help make up questions that will be in the survey questionnaire that is eventually used (regardless of whether it is self-completed or filled in by an interviewer). We will look at question design in more detail in a moment. Once questions have been designed, they are asked in the same way, and in the same order, with every respondent. In structured interviews, the views of the interviewer are kept secret in case they influence the replies.

[5]See the work of Klim McPherson and colleagues described in *Medical Knowledge: Doubt and Certainty*, Chapter 7, and of David Tuckett and his colleagues in Chapter 9 of the same book.

Interviewers sometimes undergo extensive training to minimise this last source of bias, even to the extent of videotaping practice interviews so that non-verbal cues prompting the respondent to answer in a certain way are eliminated from interviewers' behaviour. Figure 5.3 shows a page from a structured questionnaire intended to be completed by the interviewer, who would use it to conduct a structured interview. Interviewers were expected to speak the words exactly as written on the questionnaire, and not to substitute their own in case the meaning of the question was changed. If a respondent asked 'What do you mean by that question?' the interviewer said something like 'Whatever it means to you', rather than supplying their own interpretation. Interviewers were sometimes allowed to probe further into what respondents have said, but in a controlled manner, using neutral phrases like 'Could you say more about that?'. It was unacceptable for the interviewer to evaluate what the respondent said, or to reveal what he or she thought of the topic in any way.

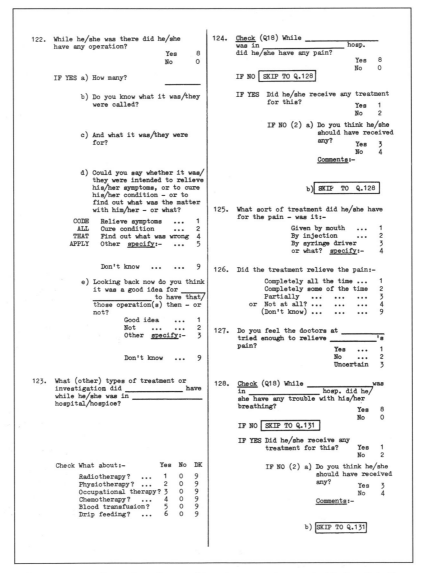

Figure 5.3 *An extract from a structured questionnaire enquiring about symptom control in hospital. (Source: used in a study described by Cartwright, A. and Seale, C., 1990,* The Natural History of a Survey, *King's Fund, London)*

□ What criticisms might a qualitative researcher have about these attempts to control for bias?

■ Even though the conditions in the interview are the same for each respondent, the sort of data gathered on these occasions may still reflect people's desire to impress the interviewer with a particular account, rather than containing true reports. The questions give respondents little chance to raise matters that might be of concern to them, but that were not thought of by the researchers. The pre-coded items (for example, questions 125 and 126) require respondents to answer in terms set by the researchers rather than expressing their views in their own way.

The problem with qualitative interviewing, however, is that it is hard to judge how widespread a particular phenomenon is, since everyone may be asked different questions. Respondents in qualitative interviewing are also free to create impressions for the interviewer.

Question wording

Such objections to highly-structured interviews or self-completion questionnaires are probably relevant when considering the measurement of contested concepts (such as health) or attitudes, where the discrepancy between words and deeds may be strongest. Much social survey work, however, depends on the accurate collection of simple factual data, whose meaning is not particularly variable across different social settings, or among different social groups.

There are a number of well-established principles to follow in designing questions about such matters. Aspects of question wording that can result in inaccuracy have been summarised by the social statisticians Sir Claus Moser and Graham Kalton (1971). These concern, for example, questions that are insufficiently specific, too complex, ambiguous, vague, leading, hypothetical or embarrassing. Not all of these can be illustrated here, but a few examples will suffice to show the sort of care that should be put into question wording.

A classic example of a question that is too complex is the following, taken from a government social survey from the 1950s:

Has it happened to you that over a long period of time, when you neither practised abstinence, nor used birth control, you did not conceive? (YES/NO).

An example of ambiguity, which may not initially be obvious, is the question 'Do you have a television set?'. The ambiguity concerns the word 'have'. Does it mean personal ownership, renting or just viewing rights?

An example of vagueness is to ask 'What kind of house do you have?'. The respondent could answer according to whether it is semi-detached or in a terrace, whether it is painted white or green, or big or small. This question also assumes that the respondent lives in a house rather than a flat, caravan or street.

Perhaps the most commonly recognised error in question design is that of the leading question, where respondents are encouraged to answer in a certain way by the wording of the question. Phrases such as 'Shouldn't something be done about...?' or 'You don't think...do you?' create this effect. However, leading questions can sometimes be used creatively in structured interviews, to get respondents who make a particular point of opposing what is socially acceptable to identify themselves. Such people are often of great interest.

Embarrassing questions present particular problems for social survey researchers, and a variety of techniques have been developed to deal with these. Guarantees of confidentiality, of course, can help, but the respondent might still be ashamed to admit to misdeeds to an interviewer. Sometimes the use of self-completion questionnaires may help, by reducing the respondent's embarrassment. Alcohol consumption is normally under-reported in social surveys; estimates derived from surveys of self-reported consumption are lower than those that would be expected from records of alcohol sales. One researcher got around this problem by counting the empty bottles in people's rubbish bins, comparing this with what they said at interview.

Questions involving memory are notoriously prone to error as, for a variety of reasons, recall of events may be imperfect. One way of getting around this is to ask people to record events in a diary as they happen.

When considering the results presented by social survey researchers, it can be very important to know the way in which questions were worded, as this can often influence the responses reported. Consider, for example, the problem of estimating whether usage of alternative medical therapies has risen between two time points. In 1986 an opinion polling agency (Gallup, 1986) reported that 3 per cent of a random sample of adults in the United Kingdom said they had used homeopathy, and 7 per cent had used osteopathy. In 1989 MORI reported that in a similar poll, these figures were now 11 and 10 per cent respectively.

Overall, there *appeared* to have been a large rise in use between 1986 and 1989. However, a close look at the questions used to establish these facts is revealing. The 1986 question was

Have you or any members of your family ever consulted an alternative medical practitioner? If yes, which of the following alternative medical practitioners have you or your family consulted?

Practitioners that the respondent had themselves consulted were counted. The 1989 question asked:

> There has been a lot of talk recently about alternative forms of medicine to drugs and surgery. Which, if any, of these alternative forms of medicine would you seriously consider using, and which have you personally ever used?

The results were based on answers to the respondents' personal use of the therapy.

□ How might the question wording have affected the results?

■ The 1986 question requires that people actually consult a practitioner before being counted as using the therapy. The 1989 question is less exclusive. Homeopathic remedies can be bought in health food shops, without the need to consult anyone. If people received osteopathy from a medical doctor who had had additional training, they might not have counted themselves as consulting an alternative practitioner in the 1986 survey, whereas they might have included this treatment in answering the 1989 one.

This example serves to underline the importance of knowing the methods by which data have been collected, in order to judge whether conclusions based on the evidence are justified. A research report should provide information about the method of data collection that is sufficient for the reader to make such judgements.

Sampling and response rates

There is another aspect of social survey work that can be very important in influencing our judgements of the validity of conclusions. This concerns the extent to which the sample of people surveyed can be truly said to represent the wider population to whom it is hoped the conclusions will apply.

In a survey a data matrix must be created, consisting of units and variables. Most of the discussion so far has been about how to collect data about each unit, in other words how to fill in the variables on a data matrix. We now turn to the way in which units are selected for study, otherwise known as **sampling**.

□ How are units selected in ethnographic research and qualitative interviewing (Chapter 3)?

■ On the grounds that they might provide data that will illuminate, extend or test the researcher's emerging theories. This is called theoretical sampling.

The main disadvantage of this method of sampling is that readers of the ensuing report often do not know whether the settings or individuals studied are *representative* of others to which the researcher hopes the findings will be relevant. The ability to generalise results is the great strength of quantitative social survey work, provided proper sampling procedures are followed.

In the early days of the social survey it was assumed that, if one wished to discover the distribution of a variable in a population, it was necessary to know about the circumstances of *every* member of the population. Charles Booth, a rich Liverpool ship owner, spent 17 years between 1886 and 1902 surveying one part of London after another to discover the extent of poverty. He interviewed school attendance officers and other local officials about the circumstances of households street by street, so that by the end of his great labour he was able to conclude that 30.7% of the population lived below his 'poverty line' (Booth, 1886–1902). In 1902, Seebohm Rowntree did the same in York, this time interviewing members of households directly, with teams of interviewers (Rowntree, 1902).

Clearly, adopting such an approach was extremely costly and time-consuming, amounting indeed to a **census** (complete coverage) of the populations concerned. The great breakthrough came with the work of A. L. Bowley, professor of statistics at the London School of Economics and Political Science, who in the early part of the twentieth century applied **sampling theory** to the social survey.

Without going into the details, the essence of sampling theory lies in the notion of **sampling error**. The calculation of this depends on the fact that a sample of units has been taken in a *random* way, so that each unit in the population has a known chance of being selected. (In this context the units in the populations are known as *sampling units* or *sampling elements*.) What is found out about the sample can then be generalised to the whole of the relevant population, and the likelihood of errors or discrepancies of various sizes in doing this can be precisely calculated.

For example, a researcher might be able to predict on the basis of findings in a sample of 1 000 people that 20 per cent of the population from which the sample was drawn live in poverty. The degree of certainty about this can be quantified. A standard estimate of this suggests that the size of the sampling error will be plus or minus

2.5 per cent. This means that although one cannot be certain that *exactly* 20 per cent of people in the population live in poverty, one can be confident (to a quantifiable degree) that a true estimate lies between 17.5 per cent and 22.5 per cent. Because of his application of sampling theory, Bowley was able to do a study of poverty in five towns for far less effort than that made by Booth or Rowntree (Bowley and Burnett-Hurst, 1915).

Sampling error can only be calculated if everyone in the population from which the sample is drawn has a known chance of being selected for the study. This means that the *researcher* must select the people (or sampling units, be they people, households, organisations or some other grouping). It is no good asking for volunteers to come forward, as this is a self-selected sample and likely to be unrepresentative of the population. To sample in this way, a **sampling frame** is needed, which is a list of all the sampling units.

□ Can you think of listings of people that are available for use as sampling frames?

■ You may have thought of some of the following: the telephone directory, the electoral register, the records of patients kept by a health centre, the national register of birth and death certificates, the Medical Register (a list of qualified doctors in the country).

Most sampling frames are incomplete in some way and are therefore not fully representative; some people do not register as electors, for example, and these tend to be people with shared characteristics that are different from those who do register. For some studies it is impossible to find a good sampling frame.

□ For what sort of studies might it be hard to find a good sampling frame?

■ People engaged in activities that they are concerned to hide from officialdom. For example, studies of injecting drug users are rarely able to show how representative the people studied are.

If a sampling frame is found for a study, sampling units must be selected from it at *random*. Every person on the list must have a known chance of being selected. There are a number of ways of selecting random samples. The most straightforward is the **simple random sample**, which is analogous to a blindfolded person sticking a pin into a map to choose a place to visit. In this case everyone listed has an *equal* chance of being selected.

But there are other ways: if the researcher is interested in people with particular characteristics, and there are not many of them in the sampling frame, these people might be *weighted* so that they have a greater chance of being selected, albeit still at random. Geographical areas can be randomly selected first, and then within those areas people to interview can be selected at random in order to reduce travelling costs for interviewers. The calculation of sampling error must be adjusted for special random samples of this type, but the basic principles remain the same: as complete a listing as possible of the population from which the sample is to be drawn should be found, and units selected from this in such a way that all have a known chance of being selected.

Unfortunately, too often proper sampling procedures are not followed. When you read reports of social surveys, always assess the sampling methods. There is little point in giving much weight to research whose findings are only relevant to the small sample of the population that happens to have been studied. In addition, a research report should give an indication of the actual *numbers* involved when calculating percentages. If a percentage is based on a very small number of units (for example, the findings applied to 50 per cent of a sample of only 4 people), less weight can be placed on the finding than if it were based on a bigger number (for example, 50 per cent of a sample of 100). If the sampling methods are poor, a convincing case needs to be made by the researcher that the findings might be expected to hold true for other groups of people.

□ Look at the following extract from the Reader article by Ursula Sharma.[6]

The sample was largely obtained by inviting readers of the local newspaper to volunteer their experiences of alternative medicine. We cannot draw any conclusions about the representativeness of such a self-selected sample in terms of demographic or socio-economic characteristics, but this was not the purpose of the research. (Sharma, 1990, p. 130)

What bias in her sample of people might be introduced by her sampling procedure?

[6]Sharma, U. M. (1990) Using alternative therapies: marginal medicine and central concerns, reprinted in *Health and Disease: A Reader* (Open University Press, revised edition 1994).

■ Since the respondents were self-selected, they may have been users of alternative medicine who were special in some way.

One of her conclusions was that users of alternative medicine were not 'marginal' people, by which she meant that they were not people whose lifestyles in other respects suggested that they were on the 'fringe' of main-stream society. The sampling problem, however, under-mines this conclusion. Perhaps people who are more 'marginal' in respects *other than* their use of alternative medicine would be *less* likely to respond to such a news-paper advertisement, thus reducing the likelihood of their being represented in the study. Sharma's main conclusion would then be false, as it would simply be a consequence of her sampling procedure.

Of course, it is easy to think up methodological criticisms of most pieces of research. There is some onus on the critic to come up with plausible counter-arguments to researchers' conclusions, and you may consider that the criticism made of Sharma's study is not very plausible. It may have been the best that could be done in the absence of a suitable sampling frame. Doing research is harder than pulling it apart afterwards. But, as you have seen, there are sampling techniques that, if followed, minimise the possibilities for criticism.

Non-response

Once a sample has been drawn and the method of data collection decided upon, the people or organisations in the sample are approached, perhaps to be interviewed, or they are sent a questionnaire. It is at this point that some people may refuse to take part in the study.

This is a matter of concern since such **non-response** can make the results unrepresentative. This can happen if the people who do not take part are special in some way that is important to the purpose of the study. For example, a study might aim to find out about the health-care needs of elderly people living in private households. This would be unrepresentative if old people living on their own were more likely to refuse to allow an interviewer into their homes than people living with others. Old people living alone are likely to have different health-care needs.

People refuse to take part in surveys for a host of different reasons, and survey researchers have exercised great ingenuity in trying to minimise non-response. Follow-up letters are sent, phone calls to remind people are made, sometimes people are even paid to take part. In particular, willingness to respond to surveys is increased if people feel that the results will be treated confidentially, with individuals' replies not being shown to people who have nothing to do with the research project. It also helps

if respondents know that reports will be written up in such a way that identities are not revealed. Such guarantees of confidentiality are often given to potential respondents, and trust is often enhanced if the researcher comes from a prestigious institution, or is accompanied by guarantees from people the respondent knows and trusts, such as their GP.

An account of a survey should contain a report of the **response rate**, that is, the number of people who actually responded, expressed as a percentage of the number who were sent the questionnaire or asked to give an interview. If possible, the reasons for any non-response should be given. Sometimes it is possible to investigate the charac-teristics of non-responders. Ann Cartwright and Clive Seale, for example, did a study in which the relatives of people who had died were interviewed about the last twelve months of the deceased person's life. It was some-times not possible to find anyone to interview, or a refusal was given, resulting in an overall response rate of 80 per cent of those in the original sample. However, it was usually possible to discover from neighbours and others something of the circumstances of people for whom no interview was obtained. Some of the resulting data are shown in Table 5.3.

Table 5.3 Data on whom the deceased person lived with, classified according to whether an interview with relatives was obtained

The person lived:	Deaths for which	
	no interview	interview
	%	%
alone	35	26
in institution	11	16
with others	54	58
number of deaths (=100%)	133	629

Information on whom the deceased person lived with was not obtained in relation to 28 deaths where no interview was obtained and 10 deaths where an interview was obtained. (Source: Cartwright, A. and Seale, C., 1990, *The Natural History of a Survey*, King's Fund, London, Table 9, p. 83)

□ What does the table show about differences between cases where an interview was not obtained, and cases where it was? What are the consequences of this for results arising from the survey?

■ The most marked difference is that in over one third (35 per cent) of those deaths where no interview was obtained, the deceased person lived alone, compared with 26 per cent of deaths where an interview was obtained. This implies that, if a deceased person had lived alone, an interview with a relative was less likely to be obtained, than if they had lived with others. Any results are therefore likely to underestimate the needs of people living alone.

Data analysis

The product of data collection by social survey is a data matrix, usually much larger than the one shown in Table 5.2, typically consisting of as many units as there were people who answered a questionnaire, and as many variables as there were questions on the questionnaire. The survey by Cartwright and Seale, for example, consisted of 639 units (people) and about 800 variables, resulting in a data matrix of over 500 000 numbers. This was small by the standards of government-sponsored surveys such as the General Household Survey, where information from 12 000 households and 33 000 people is collected every year.

Such data are normally entered onto a computer and analysis can then proceed. Data analysis will be the subject of later chapters in this book, but a few points can usefully be made here. You will recall from the introduction to Chapter 3 that social scientists try both to *describe* and to *explain* the way of life of social groups.

☐ What is the difference between the two?

■ Explanation, unlike description, requires statements about cause and effect.

Description was a major aim for both Booth and Rowntree in their surveys of London and York: they wanted to describe the extent of poverty, and the circumstances of the poor. Data analysis for descriptive purposes is pretty simple: you need to know the percentage of people with a certain characteristic, perhaps breaking this down according to some other variable such as age or sex.

Explanation, however, is much more demanding because it involves attempting to prove that one thing causes another. Both Booth and Rowntree attempted some explanatory analysis in their surveys. Booth, for example, discovered that many wage earners lived in poverty, and concluded that poverty was caused not solely by vice and idleness (as many Victorians had believed) but also by low wages. But such cause–effect statements are often very difficult to sustain. This is because of two main reasons: the relationship claimed may later be proved *spurious*, or the *causal direction* may be unclear.

Imagine, for example, that a researcher does a survey in which an association is found between poverty and ill-health. That is to say, a greater proportion of people who are poor are unhealthy than people who are rich. The researcher claims that this proves poor people cannot afford to lead healthy lifestyles; they cannot, for example, afford healthy food. A critic might claim two points. First, some other factor may be causing both poverty and ill-health. Perhaps it is lack of education, which restricts people to poorly-paid jobs, and leads to ignorance in how to look after their health. This casts doubt on the claimed association between poverty and health, which may be **spurious**.[7] Second, a critic might claim that it is equally likely that ill-health leads to poverty. When people fall sick, they sometimes lose their jobs. This is a reversal of the assumed **causal direction**.

It is possible to counter these criticisms to a greater or lesser extent with further data analysis, or a different study design, and indeed these have been done by researchers interested in the links between inequality and health.[8] Proving that one thing causes another involves a sustained effort at constructing an argument based on evidence. Consider the following examples.

☐ A researcher finds that storks live in areas where there are also a lot of babies. Does this prove that storks drop babies into mothers' laps from the sky, or might the relationship be spurious?

■ Storks live in rural areas. Perhaps country people tend to have large families. If so, the relationship is spurious.

☐ Studies in some Third World countries have found that families who own a television set are less likely to experience child mortality. Does this prove that watching television protects children against disease?

■ No. The television-owning families are likely to be relatively well off, and hence more likely to be able to feed their children well and look after their health. The association between owning a television set and low child mortality is spurious.

Explanation is very difficult in social science. Special types of research design or special types of data analysis, that we have not covered in this chapter, may be needed to establish causality. These topics will be covered in later chapters of this book, particularly in Chapter 8.

---

[7]Technically, it is said that the effect of poverty is *confounded* with the effect of lack of education. This is discussed further in Chapter 8.

[8]You can learn more of these studies in *World Health and Disease*.

OBJECTIVES FOR CHAPTER 5

When you have studied this chapter, you should be able to:

5.1   Describe what is meant by a data matrix, units of analysis and variables.

5.2   Define what is meant by operationalisation, validity, concept–indicator links, and reliability, and use examples to illustrate their meaning.

5.3   Assess the advantages and disadvantages of structured interviews, compared with qualitative interviewing (as discussed in Chapter 3).

5.4   Demonstrate an understanding of the principles of interviewing technique and question wording for survey research.

5.5   Demonstrate an understanding of the importance of representative sampling and high response rates to surveys.

QUESTIONS FOR CHAPTER 5

Question 1

A local authority social services department is planning to develop a home-help service. They want to assess how many of the elderly people living alone in the borough might need such support and what type of support they need most.

(a) (*Objective 5.1*)
They decide to collect quantitative data using a social survey. What would the units be, and what would the variables consist of?

(b) (*Objective 5.3*)
What would be the advantages and disadvantages of choosing either qualitative interviewing or structured interviews as a means of collecting the necessary data?

Question 2 (*Objective 5.2*)

A group of researchers have decided to measure how independent the old people they are interviewing are. Comment on some of the difficulties they may face in operationalising the concept of independence, and how they might try to overcome these difficulties.

Question 3 (*Objective 5.4*)

An imaginary questionnaire on smoking and related topics included the following questions:

A   Are you a smoker? YES/NO.

B   What type of smoker are you?

C   What action do you think the Government should take to attack the evil of tobacco? (Choose one option.)

   Increase tobacco tax

   Ban tobacco advertising

   Ban smoking

   Imprison those who sell cigarettes to children

On what grounds can these questions be criticised?

Question 4 (*Objective 5.5*)

Alfred Kinsey and his colleagues surveyed the sexual practices of American adults in the 1950s, obtaining their sample by advertising for volunteers in a local newspaper. The resulting books were called *Sexual Behaviour in the Human Male* (Kinsey *et al.*, 1948) and *Sexual Behaviour in the Adult Female* (Kinsey *et al.*, 1953). Why are these titles misleading about the representativeness of Kinsey's sample?

6 *Analysing numerical data*

Looking for patterns in numbers

You saw in the last chapter that the products of social science research include numerical data. You will be aware that research in many other disciplines relevant to the study of health and disease involves counting and measuring things, and therefore involves dealing with numerical data. The purpose of this chapter is to introduce some of the basic ideas and principles involved.

Everyone has been faced with the problem of dealing with numerical data. It is not easy to survive in our society without some skill at dealing with numbers, and even hard-bitten statisticians have been known to blanch at the prospect of extracting the right numbers to enter on an income tax return from a pile of crumpled papers in the bottom of a drawer. At any level, and in any context, interpreting numerical data amounts to looking for *patterns* in the numbers—looking at how all the numbers are related to each other. There *are* complicated methods of data analysis, but they are not the concern of this book. Any data interpretation, however complicated it might turn out to be in the end, will typically begin by looking for straightforward patterns in graphs and tables of data. In many cases, simple graphs and tables are all that is needed.

For example, here are some numerical data. If you have children, you may well be concerned about their physical development. Are they growing properly? You might have done what many parents do—measured their height at regular intervals.

Table 6.1 gives the height of a girl on four of her birthdays. When she was two, she was 81 cm (about 2 ft 8 in) tall; by the time she was five, she had grown to 96 cm (about 3 ft 2 in).

Table 6.1 Julie's height

Age/years	Height/cm
2	81
3	87
4	93
5	96

☐ Can you see any patterns in these data?

■ One obvious pattern is that the older Julie gets, the taller she gets. Slightly less obviously, you may have noticed that she put on 6 cm in height between her second and third birthdays, and another 6 cm between her third and fourth birthdays, but only 3 cm between her fourth and fifth. That is, her growth seems to have slowed down. This pattern might be important to Julie and her parents if they are anxious about whether her growth is normal.

This answer indicates that the *kind* of pattern you might look for in data depends on the kind of questions you want to ask. Julie's parents want to know if she is growing properly—so they look at the data to see how fast she is growing.

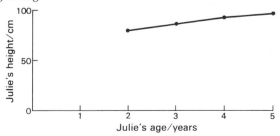

Figure 6.1 *Julie's age and height.*

Finding patterns in data is not always as straightforward as in Julie's case: usually, the data have to be put into a form where the pattern is easier to see, and this may involve drawing a diagram like Figure 6.1, for example. This kind of diagram is called a **graph**. In Figure 6.1 the slowing in Julie's growth is perhaps more obvious than it was in the original table. The pattern can be made yet more obvious if the graph in Figure 6.1 is redrawn as in Figure 6.2. The scale of height, going up the side of the graph, starts at 70 cm instead of zero to get rid of a lot of blank paper and make the slowing down in growth easier to see. However, a quick, uncritical glance at Figure 6.2 might give the impression that Julie's height had more than doubled between the ages of two and five, which of course is wrong. So diagrams can clarify patterns—but they need to be viewed critically because they can mislead!

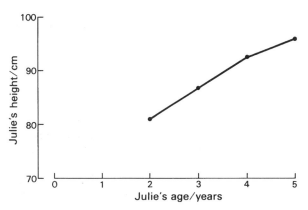

Figure 6.2 *Julie's age and height shown with the height scale starting at 70 cm, and 'stretched' in comparison with Figure 6.1.*

Tables, pie charts and histograms: analysing births

Much of the rest of this chapter is concerned with data about births; the intention is *not* that you should learn in detail about aspects of birth, but instead that you should see from the examples the kind of techniques that can be used to deal with numerical data from any context. We will show you ways of looking for patterns in data in tables, including two different ways of converting numerical data into diagrams that can make the patterns easier to find.

One factor in determining the kind of maternity care a mother-to-be will receive is her age. The importance of the mother's age to the health of mother and child is not a simple matter. Obstetricians generally consider that

women who are expecting their first child at a relatively late age are subject to a higher risk of things going wrong during birth than are rather younger mothers. Mothers who are particularly young may be considered to be at high risk as well. Therefore, people who are concerned with planning the provision of maternity care may well need to take into account the age of mothers in their area. Let us look at some data on the age of mothers, and develop ways of presenting the data that make any underlying patterns easier to see. Here is an example of the type of issue that can be investigated.

Are British mothers younger than Dutch mothers?

How might one go about answering this question? All births in the United Kingdom have, by law, to be officially registered. Among the information collected by the Registrar is the mother's age, and her usual place of residence. So, in the offices of the Registrar-General for England and Wales (in London), the Registrar-General for Scotland (in Edinburgh) and the Registrar-General for Northern Ireland (in Belfast) are huge numbers of records of birth registration. Information based on these records is regularly published by Her Majesty's Stationery Office (HMSO). Similar registration and recording systems are in operation in other industrialised countries, including the Netherlands, and data from different countries are collated and published regularly by international agencies such as the United Nations and the World Health Organisation. These data show that in 1989 there were 777 285 live births[1] to mothers living in the United Kingdom, and 188 979 to mothers living in the Netherlands; a total of 966 264 births in the two countries.

In terms of mother's age, the 966 264 births in the United Kingdom and the Netherlands can be split up into 659 838 in which the mother was aged under 30, and 306 426 in which the mother was 30 years or older.

☐ Can the data presented so far be used to answer our question about the age of British and Dutch mothers?

■ No, they cannot. We have not yet told you how many of the *Dutch* mothers were under 30, for instance.

However, a partial answer to the original question can be found from Table 6.2.

---

[1]'Live births' is the term used when the baby is born alive, even if it subsequently dies.

Table 6.2 Number of live births in 1989 in the United Kingdom and in the Netherlands, classified by the mother's age

Mother's age when child was born/years	Mother's country of residence		row totals
	United Kingdom	Netherlands	
under 30	547 027	112 811	659 838
30 and over	230 258	76 168	306 426
column totals	777 285	188 979	966 264

Data from United Nations (1992) *1990 Demographic Yearbook*, United Nations, New York, Table 10.

This table shows that, for example, there were 547 027 live births in 1989 to mothers under 30 resident in the United Kingdom, and there were 76 168 live births to Dutch mothers aged 30 and over. The main part of the table has two horizontal *rows*, corresponding to mothers under 30 and mothers 30 and over, and two vertical *columns*, corresponding to the two categories of the mother's country of residence. The table also includes some figures referred to as 'row totals' and 'column totals'. As the name indicates, each of these is just the totals of the figures in the corresponding row or column of the main part of the table. For instance, the first row total is calculated by adding *along* the row as: 547 027 + 112 811 = 659 838.

But what does that mean in words? This row total is the total number of births to mothers under 30 in the United Kingdom and the Netherlands taken together, which was given before as 659 838. So our numbers add up correctly!

The remaining number in the table is the 966 264 in the bottom right-hand corner. This is just the grand total number of live births to all mothers living in the United Kingdom and the Netherlands in 1989. (So you can probably see that the two row totals should add up to this grand total, and that the two column totals should also add up to it.)

Armed with all these data, it is now possible to come up with an answer to the original question. It is clearly not true that *every* British mother is younger than *every* Dutch mother. But do British mothers *tend to be* younger than their Dutch counterparts? Can this question be answered on the basis of Table 6.2? The table tells us that, for example, 112 811 live births took place to Dutch mothers under 30. But this figure is not much help on its own; it must be compared with the *total* number of births to Dutch mothers. It is informative to say that: 'Out of

188 979 live births to Dutch mothers in 1989, 112 811 were to mothers aged under 30'. Or, even more usefully, we can use the numbers to work out the *proportion* of Dutch mothers who were under 30, and it is common to express this as a **percentage**. In other words, we want to express 112 811 as a percentage of 188 979. This is done by *dividing* 112 811 by 188 979 and multiplying the result by 100:

$$\frac{112\,811}{188\,979} \times 100 \text{ per cent} = 59.7 \text{ per cent}$$

Thus 112 811 is 59.7 per cent of 188 979. So, 'Out of 188 979 live births to Dutch mothers in 1989, 59.7 per cent, that is 59.7 in every 100, were to mothers aged under 30.'

☐ Fill in the blank in this sentence: 'Out of 777 285 live births to United Kingdom mothers in 1989, ... per cent were to mothers aged 30 or over.'

■ The required percentage is:

$$\frac{230\,258}{777\,285} \times 100,$$

which comes to 29.6 per cent.

Table 6.2 is an example of a **contingency table**, which is the technical term for a table of *counts*. Each of the numbers in the table is obtained by *counting* how many mothers fall into a certain category. (Tables like this are sometimes called *cross-tabulations*.) But to answer our question, it is probably more useful to present a *table of percentages*, like Table 6.3.

Table 6.3 Percentages of live births in 1989 in the United Kingdom and in the Netherlands, classified by the mother's age

Mother's age when child was born/years	Mother's country of residence	
	United Kingdom %	Netherlands %
under 30	70.4	59.7
30 and over	29.6	40.3
total numbers (= 100%)	777 285	188 979

(Calculated from data in Table 6.2)

The two percentages just calculated appear in this table: check that you understand why they appear where they do. The figures in the row marked 'total numbers (= 100 %)' are the column totals from Table 6.2; they give the number of births to mothers from the United Kingdom and mothers from the Netherlands respectively. (It is a common practice, and a good one, to include these actual numbers from which percentages are calculated, as they usually provide useful information. Here, for instance, they show clearly that there are, overall, many more births in the United Kingdom than in the Netherlands.)

☐ Express in words what the 70.4 at the top left of Table 6.3 means.

■ 'Out of the 777 285 live births to United Kingdom mothers in 1989, 70.4 per cent were to mothers aged under 30.'

☐ On the basis of these 1989 data, did United Kingdom mothers tend to be younger than Dutch mothers in that year?

■ It would appear so. Whereas the majority of mothers in both these countries was under 30, a considerably greater percentage of United Kingdom mothers (70.4 per cent) was under 30 than the corresponding percentage (59.7 per cent) of Dutch mothers.

The data in Table 6.3 can be represented in a diagrammatic form using **pie charts** (Figure 6.3). The two 'pies' are divided up into a slice for mothers under 30 and a much smaller slice for older mothers. The size of each slice represents the percentage of births in the corresponding group. The United Kingdom pie is much larger than the Dutch to show there were, in total, many more

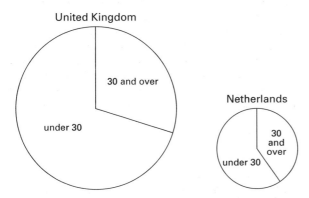

Figure 6.3 *Live births in 1989, grouped according to the mother's age and country of residence. (Data from Tables 6.2 and 6.3)*

births in the United Kingdom—in fact, the area of each pie has been made proportional to the number of births in the corresponding country. Again, it can be seen that a greater percentage of United Kingdom than of Dutch mothers was under 30 in 1989.

Does this answer the original question? One major problem is that we have looked only at 1989 data. Other years may be different. Perhaps the 1989 age difference was just a chance fluctuation in the usual state of things. Another problem is that the age classification used was fairly rough and ready. Although a greater proportion of the United Kingdom mothers was aged under 30, it might be the case that most of these were *just* under 30, whereas the Dutch mothers aged under 30 may have been much younger still. This possibility can be investigated by splitting up the total number of births into a larger number of mother's age categories (Table 6.4).

Table 6.4 Number of live births in 1989 in the United Kingdom and in the Netherlands, classified by the mother's age

Mother's age when child was born/years	Mother's country of residence	
	United Kingdom	Netherlands
under 20	63 173	4 243
20–24	208 972	30 359
25–29	274 882	78 209
30–34	164 215	58 300
35–39	55 537	15 601
40 and over	10 506	2 267
column totals	777 285	188 979

Data from United Nations (1992) *1990 Demographic Yearbook*, United Nations, New York, Table 10.

The column totals are the same as those in Table 6.2 because both tables refer to the same births. The row totals have been omitted because we are not going to use them here. Again, a table of percentages (Table 6.5) can be calculated from this contingency table.

Table 6.5 Percentages of live births in 1989 in the United Kingdom and in the Netherlands, classified by the mother's age

Mother's age when child was born/years	Mother's country of residence	
	United Kingdom %	Netherlands %
under 20	8.1	2.2
20–24	26.9	16.1
25–29	35.4	41.3
30–34	21.1	30.8
35–39	7.1	8.3
40 and over	1.4	1.2
total numbers (= 100 %)	777 285	188 979

(Calculated from data in Table 6.4. Because of slight inaccuracies introduced by rounding the percentages to one decimal place, the Netherlands percentages add up to 99.9 instead of 100. This is nothing to worry about.)

□ Does this table support the tentative conclusion that United Kingdom mothers tend to be younger than their Dutch counterparts?

■ Yes, it does. Consider the two youngest age groups. The percentage of United Kingdom mothers aged below 20 was 8.1, compared with only 2.2 per cent of Dutch, and again a higher proportion of United Kingdom mothers were aged between 20 and 24. A higher proportion of Dutch mothers fell into all the older age groups, apart from the '40 and over' group where in any case the numbers are very small.

This process of calculating a table of percentages from a contingency table can be extremely useful in investigating patterns in the data in the table. In our examples, the percentages calculated have been percentages of the *column* totals; in other circumstances it may be more useful to calculate percentages of the *row* totals. Often you will find that the work of calculating percentages has been done for you in published statistics. But when this has been done, be sure you know whether percentages of row totals or of column totals have been calculated. There is no logical or arithmetical difference between the process of calculating these two percentages—which one is calculated in a particular context depends on what the rows and columns represent *in that context.*

But even after a table of percentages has been calculated, as in Table 6.5, it can still be tricky to see the pattern in the data. The fact that United Kingdom mothers tend to be younger does not exactly leap out at you from the table. Often the pattern can be clearer if a diagram is

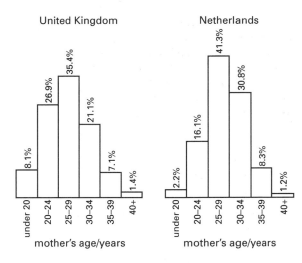

Figure 6.4 *Histograms of mother's age at the time of birth for live births in 1989 in the United Kingdom and in the Netherlands. (Data from Table 6.4)*

drawn. Figure 6.4 shows the same information as Table 6.5, in the form of two **histograms** (also known as *bar charts*). Look at the United Kingdom histogram first. It has six bars of equal width, each corresponding to one of the rows representing an age group in Table 6.5. The *area* of each bar represents the percentage of all live births to United Kingdom mothers in 1989 in which the mother's age fell within the appropriate range.[2] (The percentages have been marked above the bars in this example.)

It is clear from the histograms that in both populations most births occurred to mothers in their twenties. Fewer United Kingdom babies born in 1989 had mothers in their thirties, and even fewer had mothers under 20 or over 40. The histogram for births to Dutch mothers generally shows the same sort of pattern, though the areas of the 'under 20', '20 to 24' and '40 and over' bars are greater and the other bars smaller than for the United Kingdom. This reflects the finding that, in 1989 at any rate, United Kingdom mothers tended to have their babies at rather younger ages than Dutch mothers. The diagram makes it very clear that a greater proportion of Dutch than British mothers give birth in their 30s. But

[2]In this case, since all the bars have the same width, we could just as well have said that that the *height* of each bar represents the percentage. This is true for the great majority of histograms you will meet. But there are some histograms (Figure 6.13 for example) where the bars do not all have the same width, and here it is the area rather than the height which is important.

again it is worth emphasising that we have only looked at data for 1989. To see if it represented a *general* pattern, we should need to look at what happened in other years as well.

Now let us look at further ways of representing data in diagrams.

Graphs and relationships: place of birth

In 1960 in England and Wales, only about 65 per cent of births took place in a hospital or maternity home; almost all the rest occurred at the mother's home. In 1990, nearly 99 per cent of English and Welsh babies were born in hospital. This is a massive change in the pattern of place of birth. The reasons for the change are not simple; but an important part of the pressure for change undoubtedly came from certain parts of the medical profession, who claimed among other things that hospital birth is generally safer. Let us examine some data related to this claim.

Figure 6.5 shows the percentage of maternities in different places in England and Wales in each year between 1969 and 1990. (For the purposes of these data, a *maternity* is an occasion of giving birth, including stillbirths; thus when twins are born the official statistics count two births but only one maternity.) The three categories of place of birth shown are the standard ones used in official statistics in England and Wales, and distinguish between 'NHS hospitals A' where all mothers are cared for under the supervision of their general practitioner (GP) (usually small maternity units), and 'NHS hospitals B' where maternity care is supervised by consultant obstetricians (doctors who specialise in maternity)—though these may include some beds where GP care is available. (The graph excludes the small numbers of maternities in non-NHS hospitals, and maternities neither at home nor in a hospital, such as births in taxis on the way to hospital.)

Look at Figure 6.5. Remember to check where the scales begin. In this instance the vertical scale starts at zero, whereas the horizontal scale of years does not.

☐ Describe the general patterns of change over time as shown in Figure 6.5. To describe data like these, you need to look at whether the lines on the graph are sloping up (showing an increase) or down (showing a decrease) from left to right. You might also want to describe the *manner* in which the lines are rising or falling (e.g. 'smoothly' or 'erratically'). Then it is often useful to make a rough estimate of *how much* change has taken place over the period in question. You could express this in absolute numbers (e.g. 'up from about 2 000 to about 3 000' or 'up by about 10 000') or as a fraction (e.g. 'up by about half').

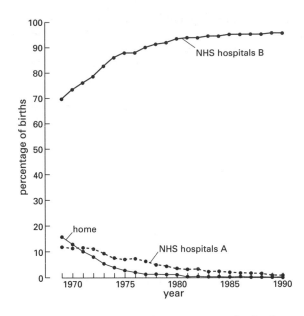

Figure 6.5 *The percentages of maternities in England and Wales taking place in different types of establishment, 1969–1990. 'NHS hospitals A' are hospitals and homes under the National Health Service (NHS) where maternity care is supervised by GPs (and not by consultant obstetricians). 'NHS hospitals B' are the remainder of hospitals and homes under the NHS (in general those where at least some of the maternity care is provided by consultant obstetricians). 'Home' refers to the usual place of residence of the mother. (Data from annual Office of Population Censuses and Surveys (OPCS) reports)*

■ Throughout the period, most maternities took place in NHS hospitals B, and the proportion of births in this category rose substantially, from about 70 per cent to well over 90 per cent. Most of this rise occurred during the 1970s, though it did continue more slowly in the 1980s. The proportions of maternities in NHS hospitals A and at home both fell during the period. During the 1970s home births fell more rapidly, to around 1 per cent of all maternities in 1981, but the proportion remained fairly steady at this level during the 1980s. Births in NHS hospitals A fell more slowly but continued to fall during the 1980s as well as the 1970s.

So, not only are fewer births taking place at home, but the births in hospital are increasingly being concentrated in (usually large) hospitals with (predominantly) consultant obstetric care rather than in (generally smaller) hospitals and maternity homes whose maternity care is supervised by GPs.[3]

These trends are reasonably easy to see in Figure 6.5; but more detailed information can also be obtained from such graphs.

☐ What percentage of births in England and Wales took place in NHS hospitals A in 1974?

■ About 8 per cent. This can be read off the graph.

☐ In which year did the proportion of births in NHS hospitals A first exceed the proportion of births at home?

■ 1971. The NHS hospital A and home lines on the graph cross between 1970 and 1971.

☐ Did the proportion of births in NHS hospitals B rise more quickly between 1970 and 1980, or between 1980 and 1990?

■ Between 1970 and 1980. In this period, the NHS hospital B line on the graph rises more steeply than it does in the period 1980–90.

The question of whether these changes in the pattern of place of birth are desirable is difficult and has been contested; but as we have mentioned, one claim that has been made is that birth in hospital, and in large centralised hospitals in particular, is 'safer'. In other words, the claim is that there is a relationship between the place of birth and the safety of birth. Later in this section, and in the next two chapters, you will learn about ways of investigating relationships of this kind. But, in order to use numerical methods to do so, we need to *measure* or *operationalise* safety; and safety is not an easy thing to measure. (This question of operationalising concepts, such as safety or health, was discussed in Chapter 5.)

For the present, we shall use the number of *perinatal deaths* to measure the safety of maternity services. A **perinatal death** is officially defined as a death occurring between the twenty-eighth week of pregnancy and one week after birth, that is including stillbirths where the child is born dead (having survived at least 28 weeks of pregnancy). The fewer the perinatal deaths, the safer we

shall take the maternity services to be; though, as you will see, there are important difficulties in using perinatal deaths as an *indicator* for the *concept* of safety.

As you probably know, England is (at the time of writing) divided into 14 health regions for administrative purposes. Each of these regions has a Regional Health Authority, responsible for strategic planning and some aspects of management of the NHS services in its region.[4] In 1990, there were 299 perinatal deaths of babies whose mothers lived in the Oxford health region (which consists of the counties of Berkshire, Buckinghamshire, Oxfordshire and Northamptonshire). The corresponding figure for the North West Thames health region (northwest London together with Bedfordshire and Hertfordshire) was 378.

☐ Does this mean that the maternity provision in the Oxford region was safer than that in the North West Thames region?

■ Not necessarily, for many reasons. One very important reason is that the *total number of births* to mothers living in the two regions has not been considered.

There were 51 010 births (live and stillborn) to mothers in the North West Thames region in 1990, and 36 605 to mothers living in the Oxford region. So, all other things being equal, one would expect there to be more perinatal deaths in North West Thames. In comparing the *numbers* of perinatal deaths, one must ask the question: 'Is the *proportion* of all births that lead to perinatal deaths higher in Oxford or in North West Thames?'

To answer this kind of question, we must work out, for example, how great the number of 299 perinatal deaths in the Oxford region is as a proportion of the 36 605 births that took place in that region. You could work this out as a percentage. It comes to:

$$\frac{299}{36\,605} \times 100 = 0.82 \text{ per cent}$$

That is, 0.82 per cent (somewhat less than 1 in every 100), of the 36 605 births to Oxford region mothers in 1990 resulted in a perinatal death. In fact, this proportion is usually not expressed as a percentage, that is so many per hundred. It is conventional to express it as so many per thousand, to make the numbers easier to handle. Because 0.82 births per hundred resulted in a perinatal death in the Oxford region, one can say that 8.2 births per

---

[3]This is partly because fewer births were supervised by GPs and partly because GP maternity care has largely been centralised in hospitals that have consultant obstetricians too. We discuss the underlying reasons for these trends and the impact on the health of mothers and babies in another book in this series, *Birth to Old Age: Health in Transition* (Open University Press, 1985 and revised edition 1995).

[4]As we go to press at the end of 1993, the Secretary of State for Health has announced that the Regional tier of health service administration is to be abolished.

thousand resulted in perinatal death. This figure of 8.2 per thousand births is the **perinatal mortality rate (PNMR)** for births to Oxford region mothers in 1990. The perinatal mortality rate (per thousand births) can therefore be worked out using the formula:

PNMR (per thousand births) =

$$\frac{\text{number of perinatal deaths}}{\text{total number of live and still births}} \times 1\,000$$

(If you are not happy with how this formula works, check that it really gives 8.2 as the perinatal mortality rate for the Oxford region.)

☐ What was the PNMR for births to North West Thames region mothers in 1990? Remember there were 51 010 births and 378 perinatal deaths.

■ The PNMR was:

$$\frac{378}{51\,010} \times 1\,000$$

which comes to 7.4 per thousand births.

So, although there was a greater *number* of perinatal deaths in North West Thames than in the Oxford region in 1990, when the total number of *births* is taken into account, North West Thames turns out to have a *lower* rate of perinatal mortality than the Oxford region. That is, a smaller *proportion* of the births in North West Thames resulted in a perinatal death.

☐ Does this mean that maternity provision in the North West Thames region was more effective in bringing about safer births than that in the Oxford region in 1990?

■ The answer is again 'not necessarily', for many reasons. Among these are the following. First, a perinatal death is a relatively rare event (in this country at any rate). A birth can be unsafe in many ways without resulting in a stillbirth or a baby that dies before it is a week old. For instance, the baby may be seriously ill at birth but may still survive. Even if unsafe practices were being carried out at birth, most babies would survive.

Second, it might be true that the higher perinatal mortality rate in the Oxford region has nothing at all to do with maternity facilities. A baby may die for reasons unconnected with the care its mother receives; for instance, it may be born with very severe congenital defects (i.e. defects that were present before birth). The Oxford region might give *safer* maternity care than North West Thames, but still end up with a higher perinatal mortality rate.

So perinatal mortality is far from being a complete measure of the safety of maternity services. One can take into account the number of births by using a *rate* (e.g. 8.2 per thousand births) rather than just the *number* of perinatal deaths, and this idea of using rates rather than numbers is of great importance in medical statistics. But this does not avoid all the problems of interpreting these data. There are other ways of measuring (operationalising) safety in obstetrics, but each has its difficulties. In the meantime, let us go ahead and use perinatal mortality rates, despite all their faults.

One way of investigating whether giving birth in large hospitals has any relationship with safety might be to look at data on place of birth and PNMR for different health regions. Table 6.6 presents some data for the English health regions and for Wales.

Table 6.6 Percentages of births taking place in NHS hospitals B and PNMR, for mothers residing in each English health region and in Wales, 1990

Region	Percentage of all births taking place in NHS hospitals B	PNMR (per 1 000 births)
Wales	97.0	7.4
Northern	96.5	7.8
Yorkshire	96.4	7.9
Trent	97.3	8.4
East Anglian	93.6	5.9
North West Thames	95.9	7.4
North East Thames	95.4	8.5
South East Thames	97.8	8.2
South West Thames	93.9	7.0
Wessex	91.1	7.0
Oxford	95.7	8.2
South Western	94.9	7.0
West Midlands	97.5	10.1
Mersey	99.4	7.7
North Western	98.3	8.9

Data from OPCS (1992a) *Birth Statistics 1990, England and Wales*, Series FM1, no. 19, HMSO, London and OPCS (1992b) *Mortality Statistics, Perinatal and Infant, Social and Biological Factors: England and Wales 1990*, Series DH3, no. 24, HMSO, London.

What do these figures mean, if anything? It is not easy to say just by looking at the table. Apart from anything else, it is very hard to *see* whether there is any pattern in the data.

Things are made easier if a diagram is drawn, and the appropriate kind of diagram for data such as these, in which there are *two* figures for each region, is a **scatter diagram**, or **scattergram** (Figure 6.6). A scattergram starts off with two scales or *axes* (singular: axis) at right angles, like a graph. Points (small dots or crosses) are then plotted on the diagram, one for each region. We have labelled the one for Wales as an example. Notice that the scales on both axes do not start at zero. (If they did, most of the diagram would consist of blank paper!) Even on the scattergram the data do not show a really clear pattern; but there is a clear tendency for the points on the left-hand side of the diagram to be somewhat lower than points on the right-hand side.

Other scattergrams can show this tendency more clearly. In Figure 6.7 each point corresponds to the height and weight of one of 30 eleven-year-old schoolgirls in Bradford. There is a clear tendency for the points to be lower on the left-hand side of the diagram than on the right. But girls corresponding to points on the left are girls who are relatively short, and girls whose points are low are girls who are relatively light, so the pattern in the points merely reflects the fact that short girls tend to weigh less than tall girls. That is, the height and weight of girls are *related*; there is said to be a **relationship** between these quantities. If you know a girl's height, you can make a better guess about her *weight* than you would if you knew nothing about how tall she is. Now this relationship between weight and height is not perfect. You can see from Figure 6.7 that *some* tall girls are lighter in weight than some short girls. Nevertheless, the relationship is fairly strong; there is a clear pattern in the points, going up from left to right.

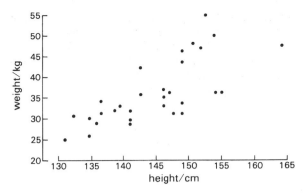

Figure 6.7 *A scattergram of height and weight for 30 eleven-year-old girls. (Data from Heaton Middle School Bradford, in The Open University, 1983, MDST 242 Statistics in Society, Unit C3 Is My Child Normal?, The Open University, Milton Keynes, Figure 3.12.)*

☐ Refer back to Figure 6.6. Is there a relationship between the data on place of birth and the PNMR data in this diagram?

■ As there is some tendency for the points in the figure to be lower on the left and higher on the right, there is a relationship between the percentage of births in NHS hospitals B in a health region and its PNMR. However, the relationship is perhaps not as strong as that in Figure 6.7 because the pattern of points is not quite as clear.

☐ Describe what this rather weak relationship means.

■ Regions with a lower percentage of births in hospitals with consultant obstetric beds tend to have a lower PNMR. Regions with a higher percentage of births in these hospitals tend to have a higher PNMR.

☐ Does this mean that hospitals with consultant obstetric beds are more dangerous places to give birth than GP maternity units or the mother's home?

■ No. The data certainly do not *disprove* this, but they do not prove it either. There are many other possible explanations of the data.

What are these alternative explanations? First, the scattergram does not show a very strong relationship. If some of the points on it were moved a short distance, the relationship would disappear. It might be that there is no real relationship to explain. Second, perinatal mortality varies from one year to another anyway—perhaps the pattern in Figure 6.6 would not be there in another year. But even if the pattern is not merely the result of a variation from year

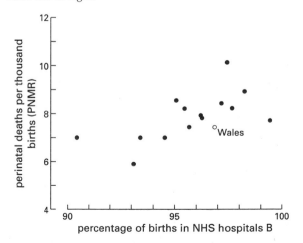

Figure 6.6 *A scattergram of the percentage of births in NHS hospitals B plotted against the PNMR for English health regions and for Wales in 1990. (Data from Table 6.6)*

to year, there are still other explanations. Perhaps some regions have a high PNMR because they have a lot of mothers who are very young, or very old, or at high risk in some other way. Perhaps these high-risk regions have increased the proportion of hospital births to try to *reduce* the PNMR—so in these regions the PNMR is high, but not as high as it might have been with fewer hospital births. On the other hand, it may be that consultant obstetric beds do increase the PNMR. The point is that *you cannot tell from these data alone.*

Whenever a relationship between two quantities is found in data, great care must be taken in interpreting it. You *cannot* infer that the relationship is **causal**, that changes in one of the quantities cause changes in the other. (At least, you cannot make this inference from the data alone; other things must be taken into account. We shall return to this point in Chapter 8.) In this example, the *data* do not tell us whether (a) changing the percentage of births in consultant beds will cause the PNMR to change, or (b) changing the PNMR will cause the percentage of births in consultant beds to change, or (c) neither of these is true and there is some other explanation for the relationship. In the terms introduced in Chapter 5, the *causal direction* is not clear, and there may be some *spurious* association involved.

So the data in Table 6.6 and Figure 6.6 did not tell us the whole story. There was only a weak relationship between the PNMR and the place of birth, and even if it had been strong it would not have meant that hospital consultant care necessarily raised the PNMR—or lowered it for that matter. But before leaving this subject, it is worth looking at a few more data. The data in Table 6.6 were **cross-sectional**; that is, the table gave figures for a lot of different places at one point in time. Another possibility is to look at **longitudinal** data—data for *one* place at *many* points in time. There are several ways to do this. In Figure 6.8 each point corresponds to the percentage of births in 'NHS hospitals B' and the PNMR for the *same* place—actually the whole of England and Wales, but for eleven *different* years, 1970 to 1980. Each point has a label showing which year it corresponds to.

This scattergram shows a much clearer pattern, but the points go the opposite way to those in Figure 6.6. In Figure 6.8 the points are high up on the left and low down on the right; they slope down from left to right. If the scattergram looks like this, the two quantities or variables involved are said to have a *negative relationship* (i.e. *high* values of one of the quantities are associated with *low* values of the other). In Figures 6.6 and 6.7 the points tended to slope upwards from left to right. When this

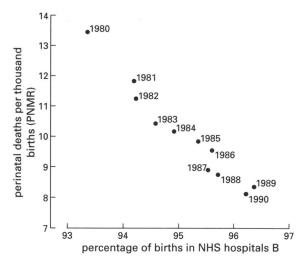

Figure 6.8 *A scattergram of the percentage of births in NHS hospitals B plotted against the PNMR, for England and Wales, 1980–1990. (Data from annual OPCS reports)*

happens the two quantities or variables are said to have a *positive relationship* (i.e. *high* values of one of the quantities are associated with *high* values of the other). (Note that here the words 'positive' and 'negative' are being used in a purely mathematical sense—they have no evaluative connotations.) You should be aware that some relationships are neither positive nor negative, as in Figure 6.9.

The negative relationship in Figure 6.8 says that, between 1980 and 1990, the greater the proportion of births in consultant obstetric units was, the lower the PNMR generally became. This tendency has been observed for a much longer period than is shown in Figure 6.8, and it has been used in the past to support the argument that obstetric units are safer.

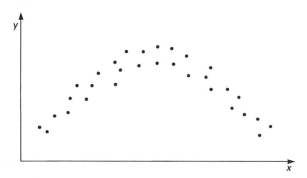

Figure 6.9 *A scattergram showing a relationship that is neither negative nor positive.*

□ Does the existence of the negative relationship *prove* that consultant obstetric units are safer?

■ No. The pattern in the data over more than a decade is rather too strong to admit the possibility that it is simply the result of random variation (i.e. of the 'luck of the draw'). But, apart from all the problems of whether the PNMR is a good measure of safety, there is nothing in these data to show that increasing the proportion of births in NHS hospital B *caused* the PNMR to fall. This might be so, but it might also be that some other factor caused the PNMR to fall coincidentally with the rise in obstetric unit births.

PNMR has been falling in England and Wales, as in other industrialised countries, for many decades (Figure 6.10). It might even be that the PNMR would have fallen *faster* if the rise in obstetric unit births had not occurred.

Perhaps the main thing to learn from Figures 6.6 and 6.8 is that there appears to be a positive relationship in the cross-sectional data (Figure 6.6) and a negative relationship in the longitudinal data (Figure 6.8). This does not always occur. In some circumstances the relationships in corresponding cross-sectional and longitudinal data could both be positive, or both be negative. The point here is that you *cannot tell* what a relationship in longitudinal data will be like by looking at cross-sectional data (and vice versa). To interpret a graph properly, you should always be clear whether the data involved are cross sectional or longitudinal.

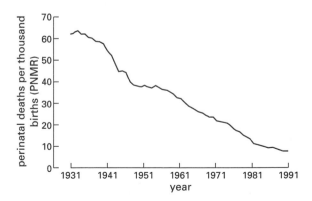

Figure 6.10 *The perinatal mortality rate in England and Wales, 1931 to 1990. (Data from annual OPCS reports)*

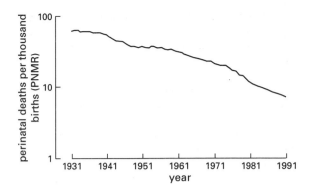

Figure 6.11 *The perinatal mortality rate in England and Wales, 1931 to 1990, drawn with a logarithmic scale on the vertical axis. (Data as in Figure 6.10)*

Figure 6.11 is an alternative way of presenting the decline in PNMR over time, which you saw in Figure 6.10. Look carefully at the scale on the vertical axis. The numbers are not equally spaced. The gap between 10 and 100—an interval of 90—is the same length as the interval of 9 between 1 and 10. This rescaling has an obvious visual effect of reducing the apparent rate of decline of PNMR in the early years of the period shown, compared to the impression given by the graph (Figure 6.10) with the evenly-spaced or **linear scale**. Figure 6.11 has what is known as a **logarithmic** or **log scale** on the vertical axis. There are very good reasons for using such a scale in some circumstances. Often a quantity may change *exponentially* over time, which means that it changes by the same *ratio* or *percentage* every year. It therefore doubles (or halves) in equal periods of time. In these circumstances, a graph of its change over time which uses a logarithmic scale will produce a straight line. This straight line can be easier to deal with for some purposes than the curved graph that would result if a linear scale were used. The slope of the line on the graph with the log scale depends on the halving (or doubling) rate, and it can be used to estimate this rate from a set of data.[5] For these reasons it is often appropriate to use a log scale for data showing how rates and ratios change over time, and when you come upon such graphs you should check carefully whether a log scale has been used.

[5]The mechanics of doing this estimation are beyond the scope of this book. If you are interested, essentially these methods work because, on the log scale, distance is proportional to the logarithm of the quantity being measured, rather than to the quantity itself.

Where have we got to? You should have learned something about dealing with and interpreting data in graphs and scattergrams. But what about the question we were investigating? Originally, this question was whether consultant obstetric units were safer places to be born in. But there are problems in measuring safety and, even ignoring these, the data we looked at were certainly not conclusive. In a sense they seemed to be contradictory, with a positive cross-sectional relationship and a negative longitudinal one between the percentage of births in consultant units and PNMR. So an answer to the original question is still a long way off. Yet the complications have arisen not because the *data* are difficult, or because the *methods of analysis* we have used are difficult, but because the *situation* itself is complicated. Perhaps you will be consoled by the observation that interesting questions hardly ever have easy answers; often, that is just what makes them interesting!

Averages and variability: gestation

So far you have seen several ways of making patterns in data clearer by drawing a diagram. Now we turn to ways of simplifying or summarising data by replacing many numbers with a single number. To see how this is done and why it is useful, we consider another example.

How long does human pregnancy last? Everyone must know that a figure of 9 months comes into the picture somewhere. You may well have learned that the average length of human pregnancy (or the length of *gestation*, to use the biological term) is about 40 weeks, measured from the start of the mother's last menstrual period. Some babies are born prematurely. Others are born late. What status does the 40 weeks figure have? It is an *average*, but what does that mean? To help you to learn more about what an average is, and what it can and cannot tell you, let us look at some data.

Ten pregnancies lasted the following numbers of weeks: 40, 43, 36, 43, 33, 30, 41, 35, 41, 40. Figure 6.12 is a histogram of these data. Only two of these pregnancies lasted 40 weeks. One was as short as 30 weeks, and two lasted 43 weeks. But it is difficult to see much pattern in so few data. If you had to choose a single number to represent these 10 numbers perhaps 40 would not be a bad choice. It is somewhere in the middle of the range. In fact, as many of the numbers are less than 40 as are greater than 40, and because of this 40 is called the **median** of this set of data.

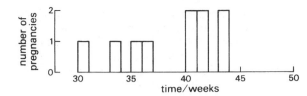

Figure 6.12   *The duration of ten pregnancies.*

Another very common way of finding a single number to represent a whole batch of numbers is to calculate their **mean**. This is done as follows.[6]

1   Add up all the numbers in the batch to give their total.

2   Count how many numbers there are in the batch; that is, find the size of the batch.

3   Then, the mean = $\dfrac{\text{total}}{\text{size}}$

The mean of the data on length of pregnancies can be found as follows:

1   Total = 40 + 43 + 36 + 43 + 33 + 30 + 41 + 35 + 41 + 40, which comes to 382.

2   Size = 10 because there are 10 numbers in the batch.

3   So, the mean = $\dfrac{\text{total}}{\text{size}} = \dfrac{382}{10} = 38.2$.

That is, the mean of the lengths of gestation for these 10 pregnancies is 38.2 weeks—rather less than 40 weeks.

But one cannot tell much from only 10 pregnancies. Figure 6.13 is a histogram of the length of gestation of almost 3 000 pregnancies, which occurred in Australia in 1965–7. In this histogram, the bars are not all of equal width. For example, a single bar represents all pregnancies lasting between 28 and 37 weeks (because the exact lengths of those pregnancies were not given in the original data). But its *area* still represents the number of pregnancies lasting between 28 and 37 weeks.

☐ How would you describe the pattern in Figure 6.13?

[6]Strictly speaking, this procedure gives you the *arithmetic mean*. This is what people are usually talking about when they refer to an average. There are other types of mean, but when we use the term it is the arithmetic mean to which we are referring.

■ Most of the pregnancies lasted somewhere round 40 weeks—and 40 weeks was in fact the most common length of gestation. But a few of the pregnancies lasted much longer or shorter times than this. Some lasted only 28 weeks; others lasted well over 40 weeks. One actually lasted 47 weeks.

The mean duration of gestation for the 2 803 pregnancies in Figure 6.13 was 39.6 weeks. Looking at the histogram, it seems that this figure represents the lengths of gestation pictured there as well as any single figure could. But finding the mean of this set of data is not the only way to find a single representative figure. Another way which has been mentioned briefly is to find the median. The median of a set of numbers is the middle value when the numbers are arranged in order. It turns out that the median duration of gestation of all the pregnancies in Figure 6.13 is 40 weeks.

You might be wondering why anyone bothers with the median as well as the mean—for the data in Figure 6.13 they both come out to be about the same. But this does not always happen. Look at Figure 6.14, which shows the gross weekly earnings of a sample of over 77 000 male employees in Britain for one week in April 1992.

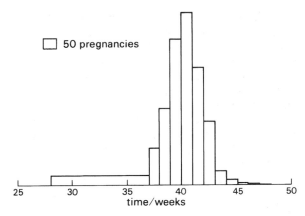

Figure 6.13 *The duration of pregnancies of 2 803 women at the Royal Women's Hospital, Melbourne, 1965–67. (The area of the small box labelled '50 pregnancies' can be compared to the area of the bars to gauge how many births each bar corresponds to.) (Data from Beischer, N. A., Evans, J. H. and Townsend, L., 1979, Studies of prolonged pregnancy. I The incidence of prolonged pregnancy, American Journal of Obstetrics and Gynecology, **103**, pp. 479 and 481)*

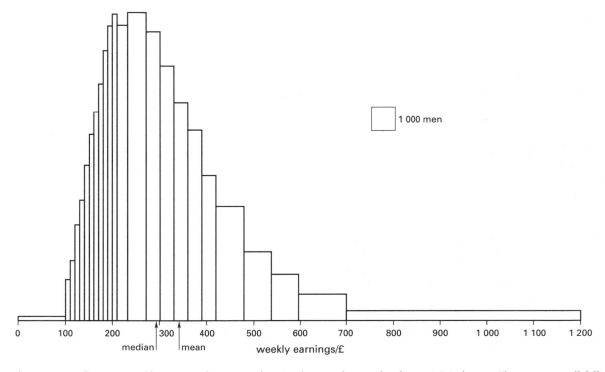

Figure 6.14 *The gross weekly earnings for one week in April 1992 of a sample of 77 709 British men. The men were all full-time employees on adult rates of pay, whose earnings were not affected by absence from work. (Data from Department of Employment, 1992, New Earnings Survey 1992, Part A, HMSO, London, Table 19.)*

The mean and the median are marked on Figure 6.14, and they differ quite considerably. The median is £295.90 because exactly half of the men in question earned less than £295.90, and half earned more. So £295.90 is a representative figure for the level of earnings of these men. The mean, however, is rather larger than this at £340.10. Over 60 per cent of these men earned less than the mean.

□ Can you explain why the mean is greater than the median in this case? (Think about the way the mean is calculated, and about the general shape of the histogram in Figure 6.14.)

■ Looking at Figure 6.14, you can see that the histogram is spread out much more thinly on the right-hand side than on the left. This reflects the fact that there are a few men (to the far right of the histogram) who earn far more than the general level of earnings. The mean is calculated by adding up the gross earnings of the 77 709 men, and dividing this total by 77 709. So it is the amount each man would get if they lumped all their earnings together and divided the total up equally. The large amounts earned by a few have the consequence that far more of the men would receive higher earnings than would receive smaller earnings if this sharing were done. The median is much less affected by these few people with atypically high incomes.

So the median and mean both represent the general level of earnings, but they do so in different ways. Which is most appropriate depends on the question being considered. In other circumstances, the mean can be less than the median. Both are types of average, in that each is a single figure that represents the general level of a set of figures. But one figure very rarely tells the whole story.

Figure 6.15 is a histogram of the length of gestation of 819 pregnancies in cows. The mean length of gestation here is 40.5 weeks, very close to the mean length of human gestation. Yet the pattern in Figure 6.15 is very different from the one you saw earlier, in Figure 6.13.

□ What is the main difference?

■ The *spread* of the lengths of gestation in Figure 6.15 is much less than that in Figure 6.13.

You may be able to think of reasons why this should be so. But whether there is a reason for the difference or not, Figures 6.13 and 6.15 demonstrate that there is more to a set of figures than just their mean.

In the short-term planning of maternity services, the length of (human) gestation must be taken into account. If a maternity unit knows well in advance when mothers are going to give birth, it can plan its services efficiently, and anticipate peaks in demand for maternity beds. Yet

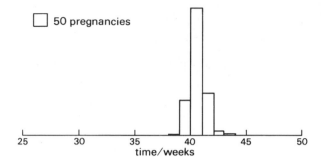

Figure 6.15 *The duration of pregnancies of 819 cows. (Data from the Milk Marketing Board.)*

Figure 6.13 shows that this planning can never be perfect. Babies can arrive unexpectedly early or late. The hospital must plan on the basis that whereas most pregnancies will last about 40 weeks, a substantial proportion will be two or three weeks longer or shorter, and a few will be longer or shorter still. Maternity unit administrators might look longingly at Figure 6.15—if they were providing a service for cows, things would be simpler. Again, not all bovine pregnancies last exactly 40 weeks, but the vast majority in this sample lasted between 39 and 41 weeks.

So the **spread** of a batch of data can have great importance. You may have met various ways of measuring the spread numerically (the *standard deviation*, the *variance* and the *interquartile range* are perhaps the most common). We shall not explain further exactly what these terms mean; but you should be aware that the more widely spread out the data are, the larger these measures of spread will be. The idea of spread plays an important part in formal statistical methods of making decisions. This will be discussed again in Chapter 8, but the general idea is as follows. Suppose one were interested in whether a particular group of women tended to have longer pregnancies than average. One would probably look at the length of gestation of pregnancies of women in the group to see whether they were unusually long. But what does 'unusually long' mean? A human pregnancy lasting 42 weeks is not really unusually long—but a cow's pregnancy lasting 42 weeks is probably unusual, on the evidence of Figure 6.15. What is unusual in this context depends on the spread, and so any decision on whether this particular group of women was unusual must depend on the spread of the length of pregnancy in women in general.

In this chapter you have encountered some of the ways that numerical data are summarised and presented. The next two chapters are concerned with further study methods in health and disease that involve the production and use of numerical data; you will be able to practise your skills in interpreting graphs and tables, and to develop them further.

OBJECTIVES FOR CHAPTER 6

When you have studied this chapter, you should be able to:

6.1 Describe the patterns in data presented in contingency tables, and calculate row and column percentages where appropriate.

6.2 Describe the basic pattern of data presented in a histogram, a graph, a pie chart or a scatter diagram.

6.3 Define perinatal mortality rate.

6.4 Say what is meant by a relationship between two quantities, and distinguish between positive and negative relationships.

6.5 Distinguish between longitudinal and cross-sectional data.

6.6 Describe what is meant by the mean and the median and, in general terms, by the spread of a batch of data.

QUESTIONS FOR CHAPTER 6

Question 1 (*Objective 6.1*)

Table 6.7 is derived from the 1991 Census, and gives the usually resident population of two neighbouring districts of Buckinghamshire, broken down according to age.

Table 6.7 Resident populations of two Buckinghamshire districts in 1991, classified by age

| District | Age group/years | | | | |
	0–19	20–39	40–64	65 and over	Row total
Milton Keynes	53 941	59 894	44 850	17 645	176 330
Aylesbury Vale	39 427	45 436	43 130	17 938	145 931

Data from OPCS (1992c) *1991 Census, County Report for Buckinghamshire*, Part 1, HMSO, London.

(a) Calculate the row percentages for this table, i.e. the percentage of the population of each district that falls into each age group.

(b) Describe the general pattern in the data shown by these percentages.

Question 2 (*Objectives 6.2 and 6.3*)

This question uses some data on social class, using the Registrar-General's definition of social classes. In this system, people are assigned to a social class according to their job. Broadly, there are six classes: I (professional), II (intermediate), IIIN (other non-manual), IIIM (skilled manual) IV (partly skilled manual) and V (unskilled). In the data here, the social class of a baby is defined by its father's occupation and only births within marriage are included.

(a) In 1990, there were 63 995 births (live and still) of babies whose fathers were in social class IV. Of these, 607 resulted in perinatal deaths. What is the perinatal mortality rate per thousand births for the babies of fathers in social class IV?

(b) Figure 6.16 shows the corresponding PNMR for 1990 for all six social classes. Describe the pattern in these data.

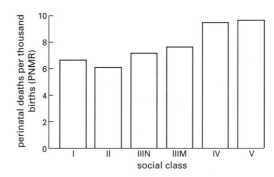

Figure 6.16 *The variation in the PNMR for babies born within marriage in 1990, according to the father's social class. (Data from OPCS, 1992b,* Mortality Statistics, Perinatal and Infant, Social and Biological Factors: England and Wales 1990, *Series DH3, no. 24, HMSO, London)*

Question 3 (*Objectives 6.4 and 6.5*)

In this scatter diagram (Figure 6.17) each of the 69 dots corresponds to a particular group of occupations, such as 'farmers, horticulturalists, farm managers' or 'textile workers'. The quantity on the horizontal axis is a measure of the average death rate from lung cancer by men aged 20–64 years in the occupational group in 1979–83; the greater this number, the greater the importance of lung cancer as a cause of death for that group of men. (The calculation of these standardised mortality ratio figures, or SMRs, is described in Chapter 7.) The quantity on the vertical axis is the same measure of lung cancer mortality, but calculated for married women aged 20–59 whose *husbands* were in each of the occupational groups. The data were gathered with the aim of investigating the extent to which lung cancer is caused by specific occupational hazards.

(a) These two quantities are related. Is the relationship positive or negative?

(b) How would you describe the relationship in words?

(c) Does the relationship show that lung cancer in married women is caused to some extent by lung cancer in their husbands?

(d) Are these data longitudinal or cross-sectional? Why should you be cautious when interpreting such data?

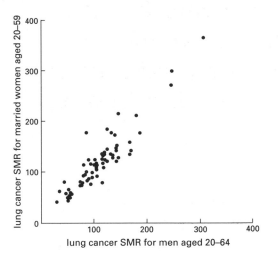

Figure 6.17 *The relationship between lung cancer mortality in men and married women from various occupational groups (defined by* husband's *occupation for the women). (Data from OPCS, 1986, Occupational Mortality: the Registrar-General's Decennnial Supplement for Great Britain, 1979–80, 1982–83, Series DS, no. 6, part 1, HMSO, London, Table 6.9)*

Question 4 (*Objective 6.6*)

The following data are the heart rates (in beats per minute) of seven patients after receiving a certain drug: 90, 82, 95, 80, 88, 75, 83. What are the mean and median heart rates of these patients?

7

Some basic ideas of demography and epidemiology

This chapter lays the groundwork for much of the numerical data to be presented in the rest of this series of books. The chapter does not aim to turn you into a demographer or epidemiologist; the important thing is to understand the basic principles rather than the details of the calculations. If you have done little numerical work recently, you may find the section on birth and death rates heavy going. If so, we suggest you read through it quickly to get the general picture, and then work through it in detail. On the other hand, if you are familiar with this kind of material, a quick read through may be all you need to achieve the objectives. Again you will find an electronic calculator handy.

What are demography and epidemiology?

When you visit your doctor with a health problem, you expect him or her to be interested in you and in your problem. You would not expect your GP to be more interested in how many people in your town or your country had the same problem, where they lived and what they ate. You would probably be even more surprised if your doctor made comments about people who did *not* have your health problem. Clinical medicine is traditionally centred round the patient, and other people are considered only in so far as they affect the patient. Other approaches take a broader view; they take large groups of people as the basis for study, and look at patterns of disease in whole communities, whole societies, or even the whole world.

Often, research of this nature begins with clinical observation. For instance, by observing a number of individuals with the same condition—a *case series*—an alert clinician may notice some factor common to all of them. In the 1950s it was noted that several people suffering from nasopharyngeal cancer (cancer at the back of the nasal cavity) had been employed as woodworkers. Yet it took further research to establish that the cancer was *caused* by materials to which the woodworkers were exposed. This research involved investigating not only woodworkers with cancer, but also people in other occupations with the same type of cancer, and indeed people who did *not* have this cancer. By the end of Chapter 8, you should be able to see why this was necessary.

Approaches to studying health and disease as they occur in large groups of people may seem at first to be too depersonalised, almost inhuman somehow. Surely it is individuals who get diseases? But people do not exist in isolation from one another; we live in societies, large and small. In this chapter you will encounter some of the basic ideas and terms used in discussing health and disease at the level of substantial groups of people. These ideas come from fields of study known as demography and epidemiology.

Demography is the study of whole populations of people, with particular reference to the *numbers* of people involved. Demographers are interested in such matters as how many people live in a particular area, how old they are, how many are female and how many male, how many are born, marry or die each year. They study how quickly these numbers change, whether they are increasing or decreasing, and forecast how they may change in the future. The basic data of demography come from censuses, registrations of births, deaths and marriages, and similar sources. The methods used by demographers have links with geography, mathematics and statistics. Demography itself is not usually seen as a branch of health studies, but its relevance to health and disease is considerable. Demographers are interested in birth and death; so are doctors. Health service planners need to know *how many* people need maternity beds or dental services. Epidemiologists use demographic information as a basis for their work.

Epidemiology sounds as if it ought to mean the study of epidemics. It does include this, but the term is much wider. It describes the study of the distribution and determinants of disease and disability in human populations. The field of study of epidemiology can be divided into two main areas, in the context of this book. They could be summarised rather crudely as: 'Who gets ill?' and 'Why do they get ill?'. Yet epidemiologists do not normally study these questions just for their own interest. A driving force behind the need to find out who gets ill and why is the aim to do something about the illness. Thus epidemiologists along with other health workers are interested in a third question, 'What should the response be?', and some of the ways of answering that question involve epidemiological ideas and methods.

The first area ('Who gets ill?') consists of the description of patterns of disease in populations, and involves the measurement of mortality, morbidity (illness) and disability. It is in this area that epidemiology and demography have most in common. You have already seen a brief example of this kind of work in the discussion of PNMR in the last chapter; in the rest of this chapter we shall concentrate on the methods used to study this area of epidemiology.[1]

The second area of epidemiology we shall consider ('Why do they get ill?') is properly referred to as the *aetiology* of disease; that is, the study of what causes disease. A famous example of an epidemiological study in this area was John Snow's work on cholera. Snow (1813–58) was interested in the role of drinking water in the spread of cholera. In studying the 1848 London cholera epidemic he found that people who had drunk water provided by a particular water company were much more likely to contract the disease than those who had not. The company in question drew its water from the Thames near a point where vast quantities of sewage were discharged. This supported the hypothesis that the disease was transmitted by something carried in drinking water, as opposed to hypotheses involving either direct transmission between individuals, or miasma ('bad air'), which were current at the time. (Snow was working before the theory of infection by germs or microbes had been established.) In 1854 there was another major

cholera outbreak in London. Snow noted the location of all the cholera cases in Soho, and later plotted them on a map (see Figure 7.1). He found that all these people had drunk water from a pump in Broad Street (now called Broadwick Street). People using nearby wells had escaped the disease. Snow managed to get the handle of the Broad Street pump removed, and the outbreak stopped (though, to spoil the story rather, it has been claimed that the outbreak was coming to a halt anyway).

Although Snow was *concerned* about the individuals in Soho, his study did not concentrate on them *as individuals.* He was interested in the patterns of where the victims lived and where they got their water, and of where the people who escaped the disease got *their* water. Yet his study led directly to a better understanding of the disease at the individual level, and ultimately contributed to the control of the disease in industrialised countries.

Snow's work brings out two important points about epidemiology. First, epidemiology is a science. It aims to describe and explain things in the natural world. It is a science that operates at the level of populations. But its findings can be applied to individuals. Second, because epidemiology works at the population level, it cannot directly provide explanations in terms of what happens *within* the individual. Snow found that drinking certain water caused cholera. The link between drinking water contaminated by sewage and cholera was established long before it was known exactly what it was about the contaminated water that caused cholera, or how it acted in the sufferer's body to produce symptoms of the disease. To study such causes, biological methods such as those introduced in Chapter 9 are needed. Yet this biological understanding was not necessary to produce an effective intervention; it was not essential for Snow to understand the underlying biology to see that removing polluted water would halt the spread of cholera.

The third area discussed in this book is the study of what happens after a person has a disease. Speaking narrowly, this is not part of epidemiology; but epidemiological methods can be used (alongside other methods) to investigate the effectiveness of a treatment for a disease, and of the health service that provides the treatment. How many people does it cure? Is a new treatment better than an existing one? Is prevention better than cure? How should the health service be organised to help people with a certain disease?

How do the rest of this chapter and the next fit in with these three areas? This chapter continues with a look at demographic methods, and then we turn to methods and concepts used by epidemiologists to quantify the impact

---

[1] *World Health and Disease* is also largely concerned with this area of study.

Figure 7.1 *A (redrawn) portion of Snow's map of the spread of cholera in Soho. Bars represent the number of fatal cases in each house. The position of the Broad Street pump from which all the victims had obtained water is also marked.*

of specific diseases. These methods and concepts are largely the province of the 'Who gets ill?' area of epidemiology. In the next chapter we turn to the other areas, and discuss first some of the methods used by epidemiologists to investigate the causes of diseases. Ways of evaluating treatments are discussed later in the next chapter.

It is worth emphasising that the purpose of the material on epidemiology in this chapter and the next is to make you familiar with the *methods* used by epidemiologists rather than the *results* of their work. Epidemiological methods are used in a much greater range of contexts

than those that we have space for in this book. Other books in the series cover other contexts.[2]

[2]For example, *World Health and Disease* illustrates epidemiological methods in use to compare the health status of different countries, and of different groups within the United Kingdom, and another book in this series, *Dilemmas in Health Care* (Open University Press, 1993) contains material on the use of epidemiological methods and concepts in evaluating and planning health-care systems.

Counting and comparing births

How do demographers count births (and deaths)? And how do they compare numbers of births (and deaths) at different places and at different times? In 1990, 706 140 births occurred to mothers resident in England and Wales and, as described in Chapter 6, this figure was calculated on the basis of registration returns. (A national system of registration of births and deaths (and marriages) has been in operation in England and Wales since 1837, though the practice of registering christenings, burials and weddings in parish registers had been going on since the sixteenth century, as was discussed in Chapter 4.)

☐ In 1930, there were 648 811 births to English and Welsh mothers. Does this mean that the English and Welsh population was more fertile in 1990 than in 1930?

■ It depends on what is meant by 'more fertile'. In one sense, the 1990 population was more fertile because it produced more babies. But you probably know that there were more people living in England and Wales in 1990 than in 1930 so that, other things being equal, you would expect there to be more births in 1990.

In 1990 there were an estimated 50 718 800 people living in England and Wales, compared with only about 39 800 000 in 1930.[3] So, just as we did for perinatal deaths, if we are to compare like with like, in comparing the births in 1990 and 1930, we must look at *birth rates*.

Crude birth rates

In 1990, a total of 706 140 babies were born from a population of 50 718 800. The birth rate (per cent) is the number of births expressed as a percentage of the population; that is the number of births *divided by* the total in the population, *multiplied* by 100 per cent:

$$\frac{706\ 140}{50\ 718\ 800} \times 100 \text{ per cent}$$

which comes to 1.39 per cent. Thus, for every hundred people in the population of England and Wales in 1990, 1.39 babies were born. As with the perinatal mortality rate (PNMR), it is more usual to express birth rates per thousand rather than per cent (per hundred). The birth

rate per thousand people in the population is then ten times the birth rate per cent, that is, 13.9 births per thousand. The birth rate per thousand population can be found directly using this formula:

crude birth rate per thousand population in a particular year

$$= \frac{\text{number of births that year}}{\text{total population that year}} \times 1\ 000$$

(This rate is called the *crude* birth rate in comparison with other types of rate you will meet later. It is based on the *total* number of people in the population.)

For 1930, the crude birth rate per thousand population was:

$$\frac{648\ 811}{39\ 800\ 000} \times 1\ 000$$

which comes to 16.3 per thousand. You could interpret this by saying, 'For every thousand people living in England and Wales in 1930, 16.3 babies were born'.

But you have just read that, in 1990, 13.9 babies were born per thousand people living in England and Wales. So although *more* babies in total were born in 1990 than in 1930, it seems reasonable to say that the population was *less* fertile in 1990 than in 1930 because the crude birth rate was lower.

Birth rates, death rates, and various other kinds of rates, are widely used in demography and epidemiology. They enable comparisons to be made between numbers of births, for example, at different times and places, taking account of the size of the population involved. Using a birth rate, one can check whether an increase in *numbers* of births is merely caused by an increase in the size of the population. But this can be done only if more information is available. Births are actually counted as they occur, by the Registrars' Offices. However, to calculate birth *rates*, the size of the population is needed as well, but the population is counted only once every ten years, at the census. So birth rates for years between censuses have to be based on *estimates* of the population size, and because of that they may be less accurate than figures for total numbers of births. This inaccuracy will probably be negligible when birth rates for the whole country are calculated, but can be more of a problem in birth rates for smaller areas. (In Third World countries, where birth registration may be patchy or non-existent and censuses rare and inaccurate, it is much more difficult to estimate the birth rate.)

☐ In Chapter 6 you saw that in the Oxford health region, there were 36 605 births in 1990. The total population of the region was estimated to be

2 563 900 in 1990. What was the crude birth rate, and how does it compare with the rate for England and Wales as a whole?

■ The rate was:

$$\frac{36\,605}{2\,563\,900} \times 1\,000$$

which comes to 14.3 per thousand population— slightly above the crude birth rate in England and Wales of 13.9 per thousand for that year.

Specific birth rates

Although it is very useful to compare numbers of births with the total population, by calculating a crude birth rate, it is not always the most useful way to proceed.

□ Can you think of some problems that might arise when the *crude* birth rate is used? (Think about who actually gives birth to the babies!)

■ There are several problems, but perhaps the most important is that the *total* population includes a large number of people who cannot give birth: men, young girls and women over childbearing age. This might distort the picture given by the crude birth rate.

One area might have a low crude birth rate, not because its women are not very fertile, but because there is an unusually large proportion of men in its population. The number of births per thousand people would be low, therefore, only because most of every thousand people were men. To avoid presenting a misleading picture, it might be necessary to compare the number of births with the number of women in the population capable of giving birth. To do this, one would need to know how many such women there were—not an easy thing to estimate. But what *can* be done is to use an estimate of the number of women of childbearing age, and this is very often taken as being the number of women aged 15 to 44 years inclusive. This figure is used to calculate what is known as the **general fertility rate**:

general fertility rate (per thousand women of childbearing age) =

$$\frac{\text{number of births}}{\text{number of women aged 15–44}} \times 1\,000$$

In England and Wales in 1990, there were estimated to be 10 984 300 women aged 15–44, so the general fertility rate was:

$$\frac{706\,140}{10\,984\,300} \times 1\,000 = 64.3 \text{ (per thousand women of childbearing age)}$$

That is, for every thousand women of childbearing age, about 64 gave birth that year.[4]

□ Thus, in 1990 for England and Wales the crude birth rate was 13.9 per thousand (total population) and the general fertility rate was 64.3 per thousand (women of childbearing age). In 1932, the crude birth rate was higher, at 15.3 per thousand, but the general fertility rate was lower at 62.6 per thousand. Can you think of any reasons why this might be so? (Think about the number of old people in the population in 1932, compared with the number of young women, and how this might have changed by 1990.)

■ It was because women of childbearing age made up a greater *proportion* of the total population in 1932 than in 1990. Since the 1930s, people are living longer and having fewer children on average, so that a greater proportion of the population consists of older people. The crude birth rate was lower in 1990 than in 1932, largely because the population included a lower proportion of young women (and many more old people).

In 1932, in fact, women aged 15–44 years accounted for about 25 per cent of the total population: the corresponding figure for 1990 was around 22 per cent.

Population structure

In order to understand fertility within a population, it may be necessary to look beyond the total size of the population and to consider the **population structure**, that is the age and sex of the people. But for this, more information is needed. (Age and sex are recorded at the census, but for years between censuses, detailed estimates have to be made.)

One method of picturing the way a population is broken up into groups according to age and sex is the **population pyramid**.[5] Figure 7.2 (*overleaf*) shows population pyramids for the populations of England and Wales at the censuses of 1931 and 1991.

---

[4]Many writers on birth rates would refer to this rate simply as '64.3 per thousand', without making it explicit that it is a rate per thousand women of childbearing age. In working with data on birth and death rates, it is important to check the basis of calculation of the rates.

[5]Population pyramids and their interpretation are discussed further in *World Health and Disease*, Chapter 2.

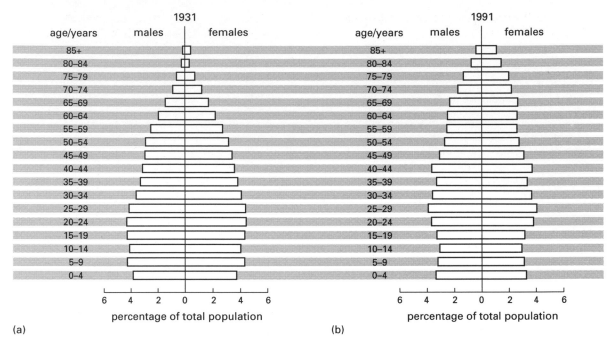

Figure 7.2 *Population pyramids for England and Wales in 1931 and 1991. (Data from official reports on the Great Britain Census of Population)*

The length of each bar in Figure 7.2 represents the proportion of the total population that is in that particular age–sex group. Thus the bottom left-hand bar on the 1931 pyramid indicates that, at the 1931 census, 3.8 per cent of the total population consisted of males aged 0–4 years.

☐ What are the most obvious differences between the age and sex structures of the populations in England and Wales in 1931 and 1991? (Look at the differences in shape between the two pyramids in Figure 7.2, and work out what they mean in terms of the populations.)

■ Perhaps the most noticeable feature is that the 1991 diagram is wider at the top, which means that a greater proportion of people were old, as we have mentioned. The bars corresponding to women aged 15–44 are longer in the 1931 pyramid than in the 1991 pyramid, again confirming what has been said before. Two other notable features in the 1991 pyramid are the two 'bulges', showing that there were relatively many people aged between about 20 and 34 and between 40 and 44 in that year, and the fact that there were far more women than men in the oldest age groups.

☐ In what years were the people aged 20–34 in 1991 born?

■ They must have been born between 1957 and 1971.

The reason there were relatively many people aged 20–34 in 1991 is that, during the late 1950s and the 1960s, birth rates were higher than they were in the early and mid-1950s, and again after 1971. The other, narrower, bulge at age 40–44 on the 1991 pyramid relates to people born during the post-World War II 'baby boom'.

But the explanation for the preponderance of older women over older men cannot be explained in terms of births, so let us leave births for the time being, and turn our attention to the other end of the lifespan.

Measuring mortality

Deaths interest demographers just as much as births, and they can be studied using similar techniques. In industrialised countries, numbers of deaths are collected through the registration process. They can be used to calculate the **crude death rate**, using the formula:

crude death rate (per thousand total population) in a particular year

$$= \frac{\text{number of deaths that year}}{\text{total population that year}} \times 1\,000$$

So for England and Wales in 1990, there were 564 846 deaths out of a population of 50 718 800, giving a crude death rate of:

$$\frac{564\,846}{50\,718\,800} \times 1\,000$$

which comes to 11.1 per thousand population. That is, out of every thousand people in England and Wales in 1990, 11.1 of them died (on average).

Comparing death rates

However, as with the crude birth rate, there can be difficulties in using the crude death rate. For the whole of the United Kingdom in 1989, the crude death rate was 11.5 per thousand. The corresponding death rate for Chile in the same year was only 5.8. Does this surprise you? Surely Chile is a rather poor country, with health services less developed than those in England and Wales?

☐ Can you think of an explanation for this apparent paradox?

■ The discussion of the birth rate may have led you to suspect that differences in the age and sex structures of the two populations are involved. They are!

With birth rates, it made sense to calculate the general fertility rate, which ignores men, and women outside the childbearing years. Now, everyone can die, but not everyone has the same chance of dying in a given year. An 82-year-old man is more likely to die in the year than, say, a 26-year-old woman. Figure 7.3 shows the population pyramid for Chile in 1989. The United Kingdom population pyramid for 1989 is not shown, but it would be very similar to the pyramid for England and Wales 1991, given in Figure 7.2.

☐ How do the Chile 1989 and England and Wales 1991 populations differ?

■ The Chile pyramid is a completely different shape from that for England and Wales. It looks much more like a *real* pyramid, with a vast preponderance of children and young people aged under 30. (This is largely because until recently the total size of the population of Chile was growing rapidly.)

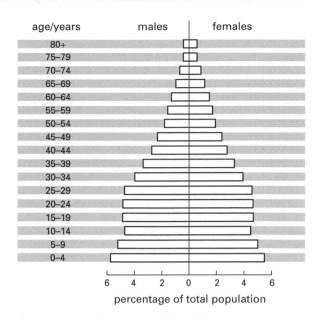

Figure 7.3 *Population pyramid for Chile in 1989. (Data from United Nations, 1991, 1989 Demographic Yearbook, United Nations, New York)*

So there must have been similar, major, differences between the age structures of the populations of Chile and the United Kingdom in 1989.

☐ How does this difference in the age structures of the populations explain the difference in crude death rates between Chile and the United Kingdom in 1989?

■ A far greater proportion of the Chilean population consists of young people, who, relatively speaking, are less likely to die in a given year than old people are. So the crude death rate in Chile will be lower than it would be if Chile had the same population age structure as the United Kingdom.

Another way of seeing this is to imagine what would happen if the United Kingdom age structure were suddenly made like the Chile age structure by magically introducing millions more young people into the United Kingdom. The *number of deaths* in the United Kingdom would not change much, because it is mainly old people that die. But the total size of the population would have gone up a lot. Therefore the number of deaths *per thousand people in the population* would go *down*, to a level similar to the Chilean level.

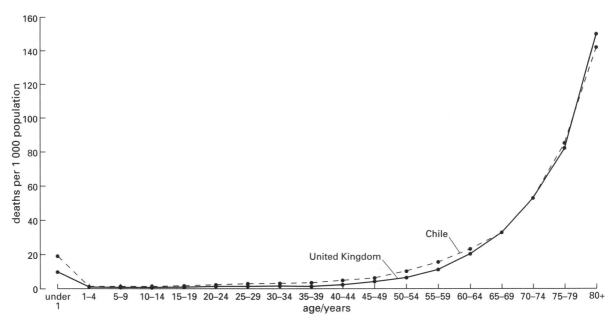

Figure 7.4 *Age-specific death rates for men in Chile and the United Kingdom in 1989. (Data from United Nations, 1992,* 1990 Demographic Yearbook, *United Nations, New York)*

Age-specific death rates

How can the death rates in countries with different population age structures be compared? There are several approaches. One is to calculate death rates for different age groups separately. Because the chance of dying depends on sex as well, these **age-specific death rates** are generally calculated separately for the two sexes. (This, of course, means that the *age* of people who die must be recorded—not always an easy thing to achieve, particularly in many parts of the Third World where it is not part of the culture for people to know their age.) For example, in the United Kingdom in 1989 there were an estimated 1 600 600 women aged 65–69, and in that year 29 297 women aged 65–69 died. So the age-specific death rate (per thousand) for females of age 65–69 was:

$$\frac{29\,297}{1\,600\,600} \times 1\,000$$

which comes to 18.3 per thousand women in that age-group. That is, for every 1 000 women aged 65–69 in the

United Kingdom in 1989, on average 18.3 of them died during the year. Figures 7.4 and 7.5 show the age-specific death rates for males and for females in Chile and the United Kingdom in 1989. The general shape of all four lines on the two graphs is the same. For both sexes and in both countries the age-specific death rate is relatively high for very young children under 1 year of age, falls to a very low level during the rest of childhood, and then gradually rises with age, in what is sometimes known as a 'bathtub' shape. Age-specific death rates for all countries have this characteristic shape, though the slopes of the different parts of the 'bathtub' differ greatly between countries. Comparing the corresponding lines in Figures 7.4 and 7.5, it is possible (though not easy) to see that at all ages, in both Chile and the United Kingdom, the age-specific death rates for males are above the rates for females of the same age. This is true for *most* countries, though in some Third World countries the difference between the sexes is much smaller, and in a very few the age-specific death rates for women may even exceed those for men.[6]

[6]These features of age-specific death rates are considered further, with more examples, in *World Health and Disease*, Chapter 2.

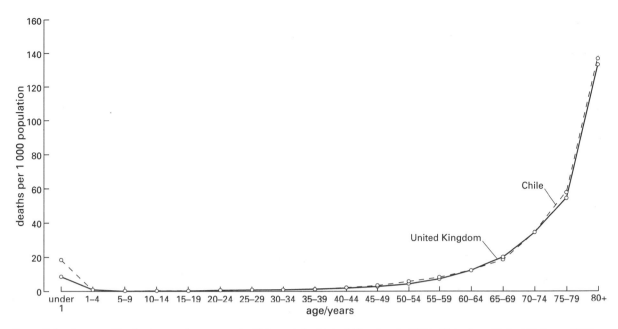

Figure 7.5 *Age-specific death rates for women in Chile and the United Kingdom in 1989. (Data from United Nations, 1992,* 1990 Demographic Yearbook, *United Nations, New York)*

But, most importantly for our story, at all ages below 60 the Chilean death rates are slightly above those for the same sex in the United Kingdom. (Above the age of 60, the difference between the two countries is smaller, though some of the United Kingdom rates are rather higher than the Chilean rates.) This pattern tends to confirm that the lower *crude* death rate in Chile is due to the very different age structure of the population there. At any given age during childhood or middle age, a Chilean person is *more* likely to die than a British person of the same sex, but the difference in age structure disguises this when we look at the crude death rate.

Life expectancy

Although the age-specific death rates provide a fairly complete picture of the mortality in an area, they have the disadvantage that they provide thirty-odd figures to work with rather than only one. (Figures 7.4 and 7.5 show 18 different points for each sex and each country, so there are 36 age- and sex-specific death rates for each country.) So various ways have been used to compare death rates *allowing* for differences in age structure, while still using only one number or rate, or frequently two (one for each sex). We shall consider two such methods in this book. One method involves calculating what is known as the *standardised mortality ratio* or *SMR*. This process is

described later in this chapter, mainly in the context of deaths caused by a particular disease, though as you will see it can be used more generally. First, though, let us look at the other method, which involves calculating what is called the **expectation of life** or **life expectancy**.

Life expectancy is, roughly speaking, a measure of average length of life. The basic idea behind it is that, in places with high mortality, *on average* people do not live very long. However, life expectancy is not just the average length of life of an *actual* group of people. The problem is that people live through time, and any kind of average length of life will be affected by death rates in many different years.

Life expectancy, therefore, is calculated from the average lifetime of a *hypothetical* group of people. Suppose we assume that the age-specific death rates that occurred in Chile in 1989 were to continue *unchanged* in all following years, until all the people born in Chile in 1989 had died.[7] Then the hypothetical average (mean) lifetime of the people born in 1989 could be calculated,

---

[7]To be technically precise, the calculations are actually made on the basis that the *chance* of dying at any particular age remains constant. If the calculations were done on the basis of constant age-specific death rates, the result would differ, though only slightly.

and this is taken to be the *expectation of life at birth* for Chile for 1989. This is not the *actual* average lifetime of the real people born in 1989, because age-specific death rates do change over time. But this hypothetical lifetime *can* be calculated from the 1989 age-specific death rates, rather than waiting a hundred years or more until everyone born in 1989 had died. This use of a hypothetical group of people allows length of life (a fundamentally *longitudinal* concept) to be used to measure the *cross-sectional* idea of mortality in any *single* year, without allowing age structure to confuse the picture.

In Chile in 1989 the expectation of life at birth was about 68 years for men and about 75 for women. The corresponding figures for the United Kingdom were 72.2 years for men and 77.9 for women. These reflect the earlier findings from the age-specific death rates: in both countries male mortality is higher than female, but in Chile mortality is higher (during youth and middle age) than in the United Kingdom.

The concept of expectation of life at birth can be extended to expectation of life at other ages. For instance, the 1989 United Kingdom figure for male expectation of life at birth is the mean length of life of the group of males born in 1989, assuming that age-specific death rates do not change. But consider the group of males born in, say, 1944, who are aged 45 in 1989. What impact would the 1989 age-specific death rates have on them, assuming again that these rates do not change? The rates can be used to calculate the expectation of life at age 45 for the United Kingdom in 1989, which is the mean number of *extra* years which men aged 45 in 1989 would live if age-specific death rates did not change. In fact, this figure turned out to be 29.6 years.

   □ Given that this group is aged 45, that seems to imply that their average age at death is 45 + 29.6 or 74.6 years. But the male expectation of life at birth in the same year in the same country was only 72.2 years. Can you explain this discrepancy? (Think about people who die before they are 45.)

   ■ The expectation of life at birth is the average lifetime of the *whole* of a (hypothetical) group of people born in a particular year, including those who die before the age of 45. The expectation of life at age 45 is the mean number of *extra* years lived by those who have actually reached 45—the calculation *excludes* those who died before 45. So the average age of this 'part-group' will be greater than the average lifetime of the whole group.

Recording the cause of death

In this discussion of mortality, we started by merely counting all deaths, and went on to look at age structure—which involved knowing the age at which people died. What other aspects of death are important to demographers and epidemiologists? Epidemiologists are often concerned with investigating the impact of a specific disease on the health of a population, as Snow was with cholera. How can mortality data be used in this context?

In birth registration in the United Kingdom, the only information recorded about the baby itself is its name, sex, date and place of birth. (The other information refers to the baby's parents.) In death registration, more information is gathered. The age and occupation of the dead person, and where they lived are recorded. But a key piece of information recorded is the **cause of death**. For most deaths, this information comes from a death certificate completed by a doctor who attended the deceased during his or her last illness. Figure 7.6 shows part of the certificate used in England and Wales.

The doctor fills in the 'cause of death' box in the middle of the form, which is eventually sent to the Office of Population Censuses and Surveys (OPCS) in London. There, trained coders convert the information in the box into a number, which refers to one of the causes on a list called the International Classification of Diseases, Injuries and Causes of Death. These are generally known as **ICD numbers**. (As an example of the kind of cause given on the ICD list, 'cancer of the trachea, bronchus and lung' is ICD number 162 on the ninth revision of the International Classification, the version in use from 1979 until 1992.[8] The trachea is the 'windpipe' that carries air past the larynx (voice box) into the chest cavity, and the bronchi are the smaller tubes carrying air from the trachea into the lungs.)

[8]The tenth revision of the ICD is coming into use at the time of writing, 1993. In the tenth revision, causes of death are coded with a letter followed by numbers rather than one number. Also, the list has changed its name to the International Statistical Classification of Diseases and Related Health Problems, though it is still abbreviated to ICD. Most or all of the ICD-coded data in this series of books uses the ninth revision of the ICD (or an earlier revision), since it dates from before 1993.

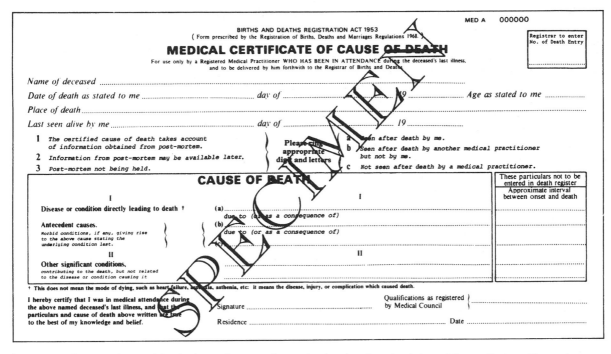

Figure 7.6 *The central part of the death certificate used in England and Wales. The design of the medical certificate of cause of death is Crown copyright and is reproduced with the permission of the Controller of HMSO. (Source: OPCS)*

Knowing what people died of is clearly going to be of more use to most health researchers than merely knowing how many people died of all causes put together. But as usual, the extra information comes at a cost of potential inaccuracy. If you were guillotined by the State, the cause of your death would be easy to determine and classify. (In fact, like all deaths involving accident or violence, it would come under two ICD codes: 806 fracture of vertebral column with spinal cord lesion and E978 legal execution, in the ninth revision.) But think about an old man, who has problems with many of his bodily systems. When he dies, his doctor must judge which of the diseases he suffered from caused his death, and which were merely subsidiary. This judgement is not straightforward. Several studies, both in the United Kingdom and the USA, have shown that the cause given on the death certificate is often different from that derived from the person's hospital case notes or the findings of a post-mortem. There may be discrepancies in as many as 30–50 per cent of cases. Once the cause or causes of death have been recorded on the death certificate, the OPCS coder has to convert what might be a considerable amount of information on the certificate into a single ICD number. Studies conducted by the World Health Organisation indicate that, although coders within a single country are pretty consistent in the way they assign these codes, there can be severe inconsistencies between coders from different countries. So the recording and coding of the cause of death is by no means an entirely objective process.

Standardised mortality ratios

Despite the many problems associated with recording the cause of death, it is possible to calculate and use meaningful death rates from a particular cause, provided these problems are borne in mind when interpreting the resulting data. In 1990, a total of 34 287 people in England and Wales were recorded as dying of lung cancer (including tracheal and bronchial cancers, ICD 162). So the crude death rate *from this cause* per thousand people in 1990 was:

$$\frac{\text{number of deaths from lung cancer}}{\text{total population}} \times 1\,000$$

$$= \frac{34\,287}{50\,718\,800} \times 1\,000 = 0.676 \text{ per thousand people.}$$

Rather than dealing with small numbers like this, it is customary to calculate death rates from specific causes per hundred thousand (or per million) instead of per thousand.

The crude death rate from lung cancer per hundred thousand people in England and Wales in 1990 was:

$$\frac{34\,287}{50\,718\,800} \times 100\,000 = 67.6$$

With many causes of death, it is valuable to look at the two sexes separately. For men, the crude death rate from lung cancer in England and Wales in 1990 was 95.6 (per hundred thousand men). The corresponding rate for women was 40.9 per hundred thousand women, a much lower figure.

To illustrate further the kinds of question that arise in dealing with deaths from specific diseases, let us consider data for two English counties.

□ In 1990, there were an estimated 1 009 800 males living in the metropolitan county of West Yorkshire in the north of England. There were 961 male lung cancer deaths. What was the lung cancer death rate for males living in West Yorkshire?

■ It was:

$$\frac{961}{1\,009\,800} \times 100\,000$$

or 95.2 per hundred thousand males in West Yorkshire (slightly below the *national* rate of 95.6 per hundred thousand males in England and Wales).

□ The corresponding lung cancer death rate for males living in Dorset (on the English south coast) was 103.8 per hundred thousand. Does this mean lung cancer was a more severe problem in Dorset than in West Yorkshire? (Think about what you know of the age of the people that live in the metropolitan areas of the north of England and on the south coast.)

■ At first sight, lung cancer does appear to be more of a problem in Dorset. But people who die as a result of lung cancer tend to be middle-aged or older. You may know that the population of areas like Dorset contains more than its 'fair share' of older people, many of whom have moved to the coast on retirement. People in counties such as West Yorkshire tend to be younger. Perhaps the high lung cancer death rate in Dorset merely reflects the fact that its population is older, and does not indicate that lung cancer is more prevalent there.

So, as with the example of Chile and the United Kingdom, the age structure of the populations of the two counties must be considered. This can be done in various ways; for example, we could calculate age-specific death rates for lung cancer for both counties and compare them, as we did for the age-specific death rates (for all deaths) in the

United Kingdom and Chile. But suppose we want just *one* figure for each sex. Although variations on the idea of life expectancy can be used, they are more difficult to interpret when considering deaths from a particular cause rather than all deaths combined. An alternative is to use what is known as **age standardisation**. To do this one needs to choose a **standard population** for reference. When one is looking at death rates in parts of a country, the population of the whole country is often a useful standard population to choose: for example, England and Wales would be an appropriate standard population to choose if you are interested in comparing West Yorkshire and Dorset.

The main method of age standardisation you will meet here involves calculating the **standardised mortality ratio** (**SMR**). To arrive at the SMR one uses age-specific death rates for the standard population. So to work out the SMR for male deaths from lung cancer in West Yorkshire, using England and Wales as the standard, the first step would be to find out the age-specific death rates for lung cancer for men in England and Wales. These can be used to work out how many men *would have* died of lung cancer in West Yorkshire if the impact of the disease on men of any given age there was the *same* as it was nationally.

Let us see how this works out in practice. Calculations of this sort typically use age-specific death rates for a large number of age groups, but to keep things simple here, only four age groups are used: 0–44, 45–64, 65–74, 75 years and over. For men aged 45–64, nationally in England and Wales, the 1990 age-specific death rate for lung cancer was 105.1 per hundred thousand men in that age group. In West Yorkshire in 1990, the estimated number of men aged 45–64 was 217 100. Another way of expressing this number is to convert it to a decimal, and write it as 2.171 hundred thousand. If the national age-specific death rates had applied in West Yorkshire in 1990, the number of men aged 45–64 dying of lung cancer would have been 228. This is calculated as follows:

105.1 (deaths per hundred thousand men aged 45–64 nationally) × 2.171 (hundred thousand men aged 45–64 in West Yorkshire) = 228 deaths.

□ In 1990, the national age-specific mortality rate from lung cancer for men aged 65–74 was 454.0 per hundred thousand. The estimated number of men in this age group living in West Yorkshire was 78 000. If national lung cancer death rates had applied in West Yorkshire, how many men aged 65–74 would have died of lung cancer in West Yorkshire in 1990?

■ 454.0 × 0.78, or 354 deaths.

Table 7.1 Expected numbers of male deaths from lung cancer in West Yorkshire in 1990

Age group/years	Age-specific mortality rate for males dying from lung cancer, England and Wales 1990, per 100 000	Estimated male population, county of West Yorkshire	Expected number of male deaths from lung cancer in West Yorkshire, based on national mortality rates
0–44	1.5	668 900	10
45–64	105.1	217 100	228
65–74	454.0	78 000	354
75 and over	706.5	45 800	324
Total		1 009 800	916

Data derived from OPCS (1991) *Key Population and Vital Statistics, Local and Health Authority Areas,* Series VS no. 17, PP1 no.13, HMSO, London and OPCS (1992d) *Mortality Statistics, Area, 1990,* Series DH5 no. 17, HMSO, London.

The calculations for the remaining two age groups are shown in Table 7.1. Taking all ages into account, if national lung cancer death rates had applied in West Yorkshire in 1990, a total of 916 men would have died of lung cancer.

In fact, as previously stated, the *actual* number of men dying from lung cancer in West Yorkshire in 1990 was 961. The *standardised mortality ratio* for male deaths from lung cancer is found by expressing the actual number of deaths, 961, as a percentage of the expected number of deaths, 916. Thus the SMR is:

$$\frac{961}{916} \times 100 = 105$$

This is over 100, which means that, on the whole, more men (5 per cent more) died of lung cancer in West Yorkshire than might have been expected from the figures for England and Wales, allowing for differences in age structure.

Now let us see how the SMR allows us to compare West Yorkshire with Dorset in terms of lung cancer mortality. If we repeated the whole process as described above for Dorset instead of West Yorkshire, we would find that the SMR for lung cancer for males in Dorset in 1990 was only 82. This is considerably less than 100, so fewer men (18 per cent fewer) died of lung cancer in Dorset than might have been expected from the national figures. Therefore lung cancer seems to be a more important cause of death in West Yorkshire than in Dorset—the opposite of the conclusion you might draw from the crude death rates.

It is perhaps still not quite obvious to you exactly how the process of finding the SMR allows for differences in age structure.[9] But it is important to remember that it *does,* and that the bigger the SMR, the more deaths there are in the area being studied compared with the number you would expect from death rates in the standard population.

Standardised mortality ratios can be used in many circumstances other than the one that has been described. It is possible to calculate an SMR that takes into account both sexes at once, by using both male and female death rates and population estimates to calculate the expected number of deaths, and then comparing this with the total number of deaths for both sexes.

As well as using SMRs to compare mortality from a *single* cause, they can be used with age-specific death rates from *all causes* to calculate an SMR relating to all causes of death. Figure 7.7 (*overleaf*) shows a map of England and Wales which indicates the SMR for each of the counties, again using the total population of England and Wales as the standard population.

[9]Calculating the SMR is not the only possible way of doing age standardisation. It is an example of what is known as *indirect* standardisation. There is a technique called direct standardisation as well, which is rather less used in the context of death rates. Each method has its advantages and its drawbacks; but a discussion of these matters is beyond the scope of this book.

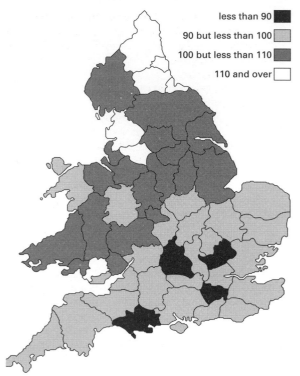

less than 90

90 but less than 100

100 but less than 110

110 and over

Figure 7.7 *Map showing standardised mortality ratios (both sexes, all causes of death) for English and Welsh counties in 1990. (Source: OPCS, 1991,* Key Population and Vital Statistics, Local and Health Authority Areas, *Series VS no. 17, PP1 no.13, HMSO, London, p. 5)*

SMRs can be used in a similar way to compare mortality in different countries, as we did for Chile and the United Kingdom, using age-specific death rates and life expectancy. Often, in international SMR calculations like this, the USA in some appropriate year is used as the standard population, because it is a large industrialised country for which data are easily available. Using the USA in 1989 as the standard population, the SMR for Chile, for all causes of death and both sexes taken together, was 120—rather higher than the corresponding SMR of 111 for the United Kingdom. Again, this confirms what was found earlier; in 1989 Chile had a worse experience in terms of overall mortality than did the United Kingdom.

All the previous examples have involved comparisons of mortality in different places at the same time, but the same techniques can be used to compare mortality in the same place at different times. In this instance, the standard population used for standardisation is generally the population at some time in the middle of the period being studied. Thus, the changing impact of a particular cause of death can be studied.

There can be difficulties in using SMRs, but the fact that they can correct for differences in population age structures makes them very useful—and widely used. (Similar techniques can be used to standardise for other differences in structure, for instance, differences in social class or occupation.) But again, the gain in usefulness has cost something in terms of the time and cost of collecting those data, and in potential accuracy. As well as knowing the number of deaths and the size of the population, one must know or estimate the age structure of the population being studied *and* of the standard population, and one must know the age at death of the people who died in the standard population. These things are not always easy to measure or estimate. In demography, as with most other things, there is no such thing as a free lunch.

Sources of mortality data

In an industrialised country like the United Kingdom a lot of the work required for demographic analysis is done routinely by government bodies. The OPCS publishes a wide range of mortality data, largely derived from the registration of deaths. These data include analyses by cause of death, age and sex; by cause of death and area of residence; and, every ten years in connection with the Census, by cause of death and the occupation of the deceased. Regular publication of such data allows for the study of changes over time.

But OPCS data are not to be treated uncritically. Some of the problems of assigning and recording a cause of death have already been mentioned. Other problems arise with data on occupation. The next-of-kin reports the deceased person's last occupation; but this might not be what the person had worked at for most of their life, and what may have contributed to the cause of death. Indeed, the next-of-kin may not know, or remember, exactly what the dead person did at work. A related problem is that, for many of the published statistics on women, the recorded occupation for a married women is that of her husband; while this may possibly have been appropriate once, it is becoming problematic at a time when increasing numbers of women are in employment, often in very different occupations from their husbands.

The World Health Organisation and the United Nations produce weighty volumes annually, containing digests of demographic and mortality data from as many countries as possible. Routine mortality statistics are produced in most industrialised and many Third World countries, but their accuracy and completeness varies considerably from one country to the next. Apart from questions of accuracy, there can be differences in the definitions used. For example, in most countries, for statistical purposes, if a fetus dies before 28 completed weeks of pregnancy, a miscarriage is recorded, and if it dies after that a stillbirth (or late fetal death) is recorded; however, in France, the distinction between the two types of event occurs at 26 weeks.

Measuring disease

Epidemiologists study health and disease in populations, and we have just been discussing ways of measuring mortality in populations. But, luckily for the human race, not every illness kills. The great majority of episodes of illness end in recovery rather than death. So how can disease be measured in populations? Does it make any difference what the disease is?

First of all, there are three important differences between counting instances of disease and counting deaths.

1   It is, relatively speaking, easy to define when a person is dead; it is much less easy to define when a person is ill. When is a cold a cold, and when is it just a sniffle? Does a person count as having lung cancer when he or she feels ill, but has not yet had the disease diagnosed? Doctors' definitions of disease are known to differ considerably from patients' views of their illness, and the majority of symptoms that trouble people are never taken to the doctor anyway.[10]

2   Deaths are (almost) all registered officially, in developed countries at any rate. Some diseases have to be officially *notified* in Britain (the attending doctor sends a form to a central disease registry)—mainly certain infectious diseases such as measles, though in practice very many of these illnesses are not reported.[11] In addition, there are voluntary schemes for notifying other diseases—notably cancers, where notification is thought to be around 70–80 per cent complete. But most episodes of disease are recorded only in the doctor's notes and hospital records—if the person gets as far as consulting a doctor.

3   Death occurs at a certain point in time, so it makes sense to talk about the time of death. A person suffers from a disease over a *period* of time—days, weeks, years.

[10]These matters of definition of illness and disease are dealt with further in *Medical Knowledge: Doubt and Certainty*.

[11]The notification system for TB is described in *Medical Knowledge: Doubt and Certainty*, Chapter 4.

The final point means that there can be two completely different counts of how common a disease is. First, one could count how many people *began* to suffer from the disease in a given period of time. This is the *incidence* of the disease. Second, one could count how many people actually had the disease at a given time. This is known as the *prevalence* of the disease.

Incidence and prevalence

As with births and deaths, to compare how common a given disease is in different places or at different times, it is necessary to compare the number of cases of the disease with the size of the population involved or, to be more precise, with the population at risk of having the disease. And as usual, this is done by calculating rates.

The **incidence rate** of a disease over a *period* of time is:

$$\frac{\text{number of new cases over the period}}{\text{population at risk}}$$

(Very often, the period of time involved is a particular *year*.)

The **prevalence rate** of a disease at a *point* in time is:

$$\frac{\text{total number of cases of the disease at that time}}{\text{population at risk}}$$

Both these rates are generally expressed as percentages, or as rates per thousand or per hundred thousand people in the population. As an example, suppose that in a certain (imaginary) town the following data were recorded.

1   Number of *new* cases of diabetes in the year 1987 was 289.

2   Total number of people who had diabetes on 30 June 1987 was 3 492.

3   Population of the town in 1987 was 176 000.

So the incidence rate for this disease per 100 000 townspeople in 1987 was:

$$\frac{289}{176\,000} \times 100\,000 = 164.2$$

The prevalence rate per 100 000 townspeople on 30 June 1987 was:

$$\frac{3\,492}{176\,000} \times 100\,000 = 1\,984.1$$

Note that the incidence rate refers to the whole year 1987, while the prevalence rate refers to a particular time point in 1987. (To confuse matters rather, you may well see published prevalence rates which refer simply to 'the 1987 prevalence rate' or something of the sort, perhaps to compare it with 'the 1977 prevalence rate'. In these cases, what is usually meant is the prevalence rate on a particular date in each year.)

☐ In the imaginary town (population 176 000) there were 4 500 new cases of influenza in 1987, and the total number of people with this disease on 30 June 1987 was 60. What were the corresponding incidence and prevalence rates per 100 000 townspeople?

■ The incidence rate for 1987 was:

$$\frac{4\,500}{176\,000} \times 100\,000 = 2\,556.8 \text{ per } 100\,000$$

The prevalence rate on 30 June 1987 was:

$$\frac{60}{176\,000} \times 100\,000 = 34.1 \text{ per } 100\,000.$$

☐ For diabetes, the prevalence rate is considerably greater than the incidence rate. For influenza it is the other way round. Can you explain this?

■ Diabetes is a *chronic disease;* that is people usually suffer from it for many years. So the number of new cases in any year is small compared with the number of existing cases, and the incidence rate is smaller than the prevalence rate. Influenza is an *acute disease* and lasts a much shorter time (normally just a few days), so many more people catch it in a year than actually suffer from it at a given time, and the incidence rate is greater than the prevalence rate.

Sources of morbidity data

Perhaps the main difficulty in using incidence and prevalence rates to measure disease is actually finding the data necessary to calculate them. In Britain, statistics on illness, so-called **morbidity statistics**, come from several sources. In the past, they were based mainly on the use of National Health Service facilities. For example, from 1952 to 1985 the Hospital In-patient Enquiry (HIPE) was in operation. This system recorded various characteristics of one in every ten hospital in-patients. Other systems were established in the 1970s to record demographic data on the patient (age, sex, residence, marital status), clinical data (diagnoses, operations) and administrative data for each episode of in-patient care. These systems were all revised in the late 1980s, following the recommendations of the Korner Report (the Report of the Steering Group on Health Service Information Requirements), and the amount of information routinely published from these sources has been reduced. Summary data are given in volumes entitled *Health and*

Personal Social Services Statistics, published separately (and on rather different bases) for England, Scotland, Wales and Northern Ireland. A limitation of these systems is that their statistics relate to *episodes of care* rather than to individual patients. If a person returns to hospital several times with the same illness, this will have the same impact on the statistics as if several people were admitted once each. If the consultant caring for a patient changes while he or she is in hospital, a new episode of care is reported. This can clearly distort calculations of incidence and prevalence.

A disadvantage of all these methods is that they cannot measure illness and disability that do not involve the health services. There are, however, sources of data that do not have this disadvantage. In particular, information on morbidity is sometimes derived from surveys of the population. Such surveys may be concerned with all types of illness, or they may concentrate on a particular disease or type of disability. They involve taking a representative sample of individuals from a particular population, using the methods described in Chapter 5, and the incidence or prevalence of the illness (or illnesses) concerned can be measured in, essentially, two different ways. Either the people in the sample can be asked about their health—**self-assessment surveys** or **health interview surveys**—or biomedical tests can be carried out on them by health professionals or other trained staff to indicate their state of health—**health examination surveys**. Some health surveys include elements of both self-assessment and professional examination.

☐ Consider Mildred Blaxter's survey on health and lifestyles, which you read about in Chapter 5. Was this a self-assessment survey, a health examination survey, or did it include both aspects?

■ It included both aspects. Fitness was assessed on the basis of physiological measurements made during an examination. Other aspects of health, disease and illness were based on the respondents' own reports.

The annual General Household Survey (GHS) conducted by OPCS is an important British example of a self-assessment survey. The resulting data are published (together with data on many other topics) in the annual GHS reports.

An important example of a Government-run health examination survey in England is the annual Health Survey for England, which was first conducted (by OPCS) in 1991. Initially this survey concentrated on heart and circulatory diseases, and on factors thought to affect the risk of such diseases. The survey involves an interview, which includes self-assessment of general health as well as questions about lifestyle; the examination element involves measurement of blood pressure and body size (height, weight, waist and hip), and a blood sample is taken for analysis.

An example of one problem that arises with health examination surveys is provided by a survey carried out in Bedford in the 1960s to investigate the prevalence of diabetes. A randomly chosen sample was taken of people of all ages, well or ill, living in the town. These people were given a standard test used to diagnose diabetes, which involved the measurement of the amount of sugar in the blood some time after they had eaten a measured amount of sugar. Straightforward, you might think. But in fact there is no general agreement on exactly where the line should be drawn between 'normal' blood sugar levels and the 'abnormally high' levels that indicate diabetes. Certainly, all diabetics do not have one blood sugar level and everyone else another. In the Bedford study, the number counted as having diabetes ranged between 7 per cent and 32 per cent of the sample, depending on where the line was drawn. Certainly it was not true that 32 per cent, or even 7 per cent, of the people in the sample *knew* they had diabetes.

Other aspects of the difficulty of operationalising the concepts of health and illness have been raised in Chapter 5. Apart from such problems of defining and diagnosing who has a particular illness, surveys that use a sample of the population involve all the aspects of questionnaire design and sampling that were covered in Chapter 5. Particular care needs to be taken with non-response in health examination surveys. People are generally less likely to agree to give a blood sample than they would be to answer a few questions. For example, in the 1991 Health Survey for England, 81 per cent of people included in the sample for the survey agreed to answer the questionnaire part of the survey, while the number who agreed to provide a blood sample was much less, 61 per cent.

In summary, surveys can provide very useful information about illness in a population, but as always, care must be taken in interpreting this information.

In this chapter, you have learned about ways of measuring some of the demographic characteristics of a population, as well as about measuring the impact of different diseases and causes of death. In the next chapter, we shall introduce some of the methods used by epidemiologists and clinicians to establish the causes of disease, and to evaluate methods of treatment and prevention.

OBJECTIVES FOR CHAPTER 7

When you have studied this chapter, you should be able to:

7.1 Broadly define the fields of study of demography and epidemiology, and outline the basic methods of inquiry of demography.

7.2 Define the terms: crude birth rate, general fertility rate, crude death rate, incidence and prevalence rates, and calculate them from given data.

7.3 Describe the process of registering births and deaths, and the production of fertility, mortality, and morbidity statistics in the United Kingdom, and outline the limitations of these statistics.

7.4 Give examples of the need to consider the age and sex structure of populations when investigating fertility and mortality.

7.5 Define, in general terms, the following: age-specific death rate, expectation of life, standardised mortality ratio; and interpret statements that use these concepts.

QUESTIONS FOR CHAPTER 7

Question 1 (*Objective 7.1*)

In which of the following would epidemiologists be particularly interested?

(i)   the number of deaths in Scotland in 1993;

(ii)   the number of deaths from burns in Scotland in 1993;

(iii)   the fact that Mr Lawson of Edinburgh had diabetes diagnosed in 1993;

(iv)   the data on lung cancer, presented in the previous chapter, in Figure 6.17.

Question 2 (*Objective 7.2*)

In Scotland in 1990, there were 65 973 live births and 61 527 deaths in an estimated population of 5 102 400. The number of women aged 15–44 years was estimated as 1 121 469. (These data come from Registrar-General for Scotland (1991).) Calculate, for Scotland in 1990:
(a) the crude birth rate;
(b) the crude death rate; and
(c) the general fertility rate.

Question 3 (*Objectives 7.1 and 7.3*)

Mrs Wells was a retired teacher who lived in Lancashire. She was elderly and ill. Her doctors diagnosed stomach cancer, and when she died, they considered that the cancer had been the main cause of her death. Describe how this information eventually gets into the published mortality statistics.

Question 4 (*Objectives 7.4 and 7.5*)

The data on lung cancer in occupational groups, which you met in Question 3 for Chapter 6 (Figure 6.17), gave the SMR for lung cancer for each occupational group. The standard population was that for the whole of England and Wales.

(a) Why is it preferable to use the SMR rather than the crude lung cancer death rate for each group?

(b) In these data, male welders had an SMR for lung cancer of 146, whereas male office managers had an SMR of 55. Express these data in words, referring to the standard population in an appropriate way.

Question 5 (*Objective 7.5*)

The expectation of life of 35-year-old females in England and Wales in 1987 was 44.3 years. A woman aged 35 in 1987 was born in 1952, when the expectation of life at birth for females was 71.5 years. Give *two* reasons why this figure is less than 35 + 44.3.

Question 6 (*Objective 7.2*)

In a certain town, the population was 56 300 in 1992. There were 119 people with multiple sclerosis on 30 June that year. During the year, 5 new cases of the disease were diagnosed. What are
(a) the incidence rate, and
(b) the prevalence rate
for multiple sclerosis in that town for 1992? (Take 30 June as the time point for calculating the prevalence rate.)

8

Investigating causes and evaluating treatments

Observational studies in epidemiology

Epidemiology uses many methods to investigate why people suffer from disease. At the beginning of Chapter 7 you met Snow's work on cholera; he used the simple, but often powerful, technique of plotting the location of cases of a disease on a map. Then there were several examples of data from officially published statistics—epidemiologists often use these in their work. Now we shall look at some of the types of epidemiological study that investigate causes of disease.

You have probably heard of spina bifida. It is a disorder that arises during the development of the human fetus in the mother's womb, in which the backbone, and the spinal cord it contains, do not develop properly. Babies born with this condition *may* be relatively unaffected, but many of them are severely handicapped. In biological terms, spina bifida can occur when something goes wrong in part of the developing fetus called the neural tube: for this reason, spina bifida and other related disorders are collectively known as *neural-tube defects (NTDs)*.

It has been estimated that in the United Kingdom in the late 1980s, an NTD was present in somewhat less than 200 births per year (Laurence, 1989).

Many different explanations of NTDs have been put forward. These defects are much more common in some geographical areas than others—over twice as common in Northern Ireland as in London, for example. In some areas (though not all), NTDs are considerably rarer among wealthier families than in those that are less well off. These observations could provide the basis for an explanation of the causes of NTDs.

□ Can you think of any characteristic of people, or of what they do, that varies from place to place, and from one social class to another within the same area, that might possibly lead to NTDs?

■ There are numerous possibilities. One is smoking—there are more smokers in some parts of the country than in others, and manual workers and their families are more likely to smoke than white-collar workers. Could something in the smoke affect the developing neural tube of the fetus? (In fact, there is no evidence that this is so: the babies of mothers who smoke do not seem to be particularly prone to NTDs, although many other adverse effects *have* been attributed to smoking during pregnancy.) Another possible cause, which several investigators have looked at, is diet. Again, this varies from place to place and across social classes, and it is plausible that what a mother eats, or does not eat during pregnancy, could affect her baby.

How might one investigate the theory that NTDs have something to do with the mother's diet during pregnancy? One way to start would be to look at the diets of mothers who have given birth to babies with NTDs. Suppose this research were undertaken and it was found that 60 per cent of the mothers studied had eaten no broccoli.

□ Can you conclude from this that failure to eat broccoli during pregnancy increases the risk of this condition?

■ No. There are many reasons why not, but the most important of these is the lack of other babies for *comparison.* You would also need to know what the mothers of perfectly healthy babies had been eating during pregnancy. It may be that 60 per cent of them also never ate broccoli. If so, the answer seems unlikely to lie in this particular aspect of diet. On the other hand, if over 90 per cent of the mothers of healthy babies say they *did* eat broccoli, then you may be onto something important.

Such comparative studies are known as **case–control studies**. In a case–control study, a group of **cases**—or individuals with the disease in question—is identified. Another group of **controls**, or people who do not have the disease, is then found. The idea is to find a group of controls who are similar to the cases, apart from the fact that they do not have the disease being studied. (A case–control study is rather different from a controlled *experiment* of the sort you were introduced to in Chapter 2, as will be made clear later in this chapter.) Most case–control studies are **retrospective**. A study is said to be retrospective if it looks back into the personal history of the people being studied and investigates things that happened before they were under study.

Much research on the causes of NTDs has been carried out by K. M. Laurence (a paediatrician and geneticist) and his colleagues, based in Cardiff. One of their studies (Laurence *et al.,* 1980) used just such a case–control method; the cases were babies born with an NTD

in South Wales, and the controls were babies who had been born to the same mothers but did not have NTDs. The mothers were asked about their diet during the 'case' and the 'control' pregnancies; these diets were classified as being 'good', 'fair' or 'poor'. ('Good' diets were varied, balanced, and considered to provide an ample supply of important nutrients.) It turned out that the mothers' diets during 'case' pregnancies were on average, rather worse than their diets during 'control' pregnancies.

□ Does this *prove* that a poor diet (as defined in this study) increases a mother's chance of having a child affected by an NTD? (Think about how you might react if you had one child that was affected and one that was not, and a doctor who was studying NTDs asked you about your diet in the two pregnancies.)

■ The result certainly lends support to the hypothesis of a dietary cause, but it does not prove it. One important difficulty is that the mother may *think* about her diets in the two pregnancies differently, even if they were identical, just because the pregnancies had different outcomes. For example, if the mother suspected that diet affects the chance of having a baby with an NTD, she might be more likely to report that her diet was worse during the pregnancy that produced the affected child.

This kind of difficulty is very often present with data collected retrospectively. (It was raised in the context of social surveys in Chapter 5.) If it is already known who got the disease and who did not, there is always a chance that this knowledge can bias the investigations. Of course, this bias may not have been present in the Laurence study, but it is *possible* that it was, and this has to be borne in mind when the results are interpreted.

A later study by the Cardiff group (James *et al.,* 1980) demonstrates another difficulty in interpreting retrospective case–control studies, though this time the difficulty stems from the case–control part, not from the retrospective nature of the study. (In fact, strictly speaking, the study was not retrospective at all, as you will see.) This time the cases were mothers who had had babies with NTDs in South Wales, and the controls were the *sisters* of these mothers, who had not had affected babies. The women were asked about their *present* diet rather than about their diet during pregnancy. (This reduces, though it does not remove, the problem of bias in what the mothers recall about their past diet; but it introduces a new problem, that a mother's diet may have changed since the pregnancy.) Table 8.1 summarises some of the data from this study.

Table 8.1 Quality of mother's diet in a case–control study of NTDs in South Wales

Group of women	Quality of diet (no. of women)			Row total
	Good	Fair	Poor	
cases	34	110	100	244
controls (sisters)	43	48	32	123

Data from Laurence, K. M., Campbell, H. and James, N. (1983) The role of improvement in the maternal diet and preconceptual folic acid supplementation in the prevention of neural tube defects, in Dobbing, J. (ed.) *Prevention of Spina Bifida and Other Neural Tube Defects*, Academic Press, London, p. 91.

☐ Summarise in words what this table shows.

■ The cases tend to have worse diets than the controls.

If this is not obvious, it is worth working out the row percentages (Table 8.2). This makes it easier to see that, for example, far more of the controls (35.0 per cent) had a good diet than did the cases (13.9 per cent).

Table 8.2 Quality of mother's diet in a case–control study of NTDs in South Wales (row percentages)

Group of women	Quality of diet (percentage of women)			Total number
	Good	Fair	Poor	(= 100%)
cases	13.9	45.1	41.0	244
controls (sisters)	35.0	39.0	26.0	123

(Calculated from data in Table 8.1)

☐ Does *this* prove that a poor diet during pregnancy tends to cause NTDs? (Think about other ways in which the cases might differ from the controls.)

■ Again the data tend to support this conclusion, but perhaps the cases and controls differed in some way *other* than diet, and it may be this other difference that causes NTDs in the cases. So there is room for doubt.

Such doubt arises from the nature of case–control studies, which depend for their validity on the cases and controls being comparable in *all* respects, apart from the presence of the disease (in the cases) and the factor which causes the disease (which would be more common in cases than controls). However the process of checking for *all* possible differences between cases and controls is impossible. In practice this checking is restricted to factors that the investigators believe *may* affect the disease being studied. Although such a restriction is clearly essential on practical grounds, it does mean that a case–control study can never on its own *prove* or *disprove* a causal hypothesis, but can only demonstrate a statistical *association* between the presence of the disease and the presence of the possible cause. In other words, a case–control study might show that people who are subject to the possible cause happen to be more likely to get the disease (statistical association), but it cannot show that they get the disease *because* they are subject to the possible cause (causal hypothesis).

Case–control studies all suffer from the fact that any difference observed between the cases and the controls *may* be due to the way the controls were chosen, rather than having anything to do with the disease in question.

Case–control studies are examples of what are known as **observational studies**, so-called because the researchers *observe* people and record their behaviour and state of health, rather than intervening to change behaviour or health directly. There is a different kind of observational study that avoids some of the problems of case–control studies. For example, a researcher might select a group of mothers-to-be before the start of their pregnancy, record their eating habits around the time of conception and during pregnancy, and eventually record whether their babies had NTDs. This avoids problems of matching cases and controls, *and* the fact that the outcome of the pregnancy may influence the way in which diet is reported. This is a **prospective cohort study**. In such a study, a group of people is chosen *before* any have the disease being studied. They are then followed up into the future, and their exposure to potential causes of the disease is recorded. Eventually, some of them will contract the disease, and the chance of contracting it can be compared for different levels of exposure to the possible causes. It is called a *prospective* study because instead of looking back at personal history that has already occurred, the study follows people forward through time. It is a *cohort* study because those being studied form a *cohort;* that is, they share a common experience—in this instance being pregnant at about the same time and in the same area.

It is possible to carry out other types of study, such as a retrospective cohort study.

□ How would you go about setting up a retrospective cohort study?

■ A *cohort* of people would be chosen on the basis of their *previous* exposure to, or experience of, the factor under study, regardless of whether or not they had the disease in question. One would then record whether they did have the disease, and go back into their personal histories to look for potential causes.

Retrospective cohort studies have been used, for example, to investigate the possible risks to health of working in plants dealing with nuclear fuel. Cohorts of people who worked in such plants in the past have been compared with people who worked elsewhere, to measure the extent to which the ex-nuclear workers were more likely to have developed diseases such as cancer.

The main disadvantages of a prospective study compared with a retrospective one are that it usually takes longer to carry out and may cost much more. In the study of diet during pregnancy, the time factor may not be too important, as pregnancy lasts only nine months. But prospective studies of, for example, potential causes of cancer may run for decades, because the disease may not become apparent until long after the exposure to the factor suspected of making the disease more likely. A retrospective study can be done much more rapidly and cheaply.

The main problem in using a cohort study rather than a case–control study lies in the number of people one has to study. Cohort studies can require far more people, if the disease being studied is relatively uncommon.

For example, NTDs affect less than one pregnancy in 500 in the United Kingdom. (This figure includes the many affected pregnancies which do not continue to term because of a miscarriage or termination.) To end up with an adequate number of affected pregnancies to study, you would need to have a huge number of mothers-to-be in the cohort. Depending on the exact nature of the study, you would almost certainly need well over 100 affected pregnancies to have a reasonable chance of finding out what might lead to an increase in the risk of an NTD. To find 100 affected pregnancies, you would need over 50 000 pregnant women. In a case–control study, you would need to study only the 100 affected pregnancies and a relatively small number of controls to compare them with—perhaps another 100, though a study of this nature might well use more controls than this. Two per case, or 200 in all, might be used. Because of these problems, prospective cohort studies tend to be much more expensive in time and money than retrospective case–control or cohort studies—so the retrospective studies are much more common.

One way of reducing the number of people studied and the cost of cohort studies is to concentrate on a group of people known to be at high risk. Women who have already had a pregnancy affected by an NTD are more likely to have another. Several studies had shown that, in such women, on average something like 5 per cent of subsequent pregnancies were affected by an NTD. The Cardiff workers followed up their retrospective studies with prospective cohort studies that investigated the question: 'Does poor diet cause mothers who have already had an NTD pregnancy to be more likely to have another?'. Some of the results from the prospective part of the second study are given in Table 8.3.

Table 8.3 Mother's diet and the outcome of pregnancy in a prospective study of the recurrence of NTDs in South Wales. (All these mothers had had a previous pregnancy affected by an NTD.)

| Outcome of pregnancy | Diet during first three months of pregnancy (no. of mothers) | | | |
	Good	Fair	Poor	Row total
normal	68	76	27	171
NTD	0	0	5	5

Data from Laurence, K. M., Campbell, H. and James, N. (1983) The role of improvement in the maternal diet and preconceptual folic acid supplementation in the prevention of neural tube defects, in Dobbing, J. (ed.) *Prevention of Spina Bifida and Other Neural Tube Defects*, Academic Press, London, p. 91.

All these mothers had previously had affected babies, so they were all 'cases' in Tables 8.1 and 8.2. On average, their diet was better than that of the cases in Tables 8.1 and 8.2. (They had received counselling to improve their diet.)

□ What does Table 8.3 show?

■ All the recurrences of NTDs were to mothers whose diet had been poor in early pregnancy. This gives support to the view that a poor diet during pregnancy, particularly early pregnancy, is associated with NTDs.

However, there is another important point to take into account. One of the main reasons for studying diet and NTDs is to find a way of preventing such defects in the future. If you look at the 176 women in Table 8.3 in isolation, there is clearly a statistical association between poor diet and the recurrence of NTDs. But what would have happened if more women had been included in the study? Would the results have been the same? The 176 women in the study can be regarded as a sample from the population of women in South Wales who may be at risk of having a second child with an NTD, now, in the past, or in the future, and compared with the sample sizes in some of the social surveys you read about in Chapter 5, a total of 176 women does not make a particularly large sample. What do the results from this sample tell us about the population as a whole?

Dealing with chance

In terms of this population, there are two possible explanations of what the Cardiff team observed in their sample. First, perhaps there really is a statistical association between poor diet and the recurrence of NTDs that is reflected in the sample and requires further investigation (to establish whether it is causal, for instance). Second, perhaps there is no such association in the population, and the sample results look as they do by chance. It is necessary to investigate this possibility.

☐ Suppose that there were *no* association between poor diet and the recurrence of NTDs in the population as a whole. Do you think it would be *likely* that results like those in Table 8.3 could be obtained from a sample of 176 women from the population?

■ You probably thought that results as extreme as those in the table would be very unlikely, if the supposition of no association in the population were true.

☐ What would you therefore conclude about the supposition of no association?

■ It is unlikely to be true. That is, it seems that poor diet and the recurrence of NTDs *are* statistically associated in the population (though we still do not know whether the association is causal).

This line of reasoning is not entirely clear-cut, so it is worth looking at it again slightly differently. It can be thought of like this.

Supposition   Diet and the recurrence of NTDs are *not* associated in the population.

Observation   The data in Table 8.3 were collected.

Reasoning   The observation is not completely inconsistent with the supposition. A coincidence *might* have occurred. But it is very unlikely that an observation as

extreme as this would have been made, if the supposition were true. So major doubt is cast on the supposition.

Conclusion   The supposition is probably wrong. There probably *is* an association between diet and the recurrence of NTDs in the population.

This method of reaching conclusions about a population on the basis of data from a sample follows the general lines of a statistical **significance test**. The key step in the argument is the remark that, if the supposition of no association were true, then results as extreme as those obtained would be unlikely; and it is this step that is formalised in significance testing.

To carry out this formalisation, it is necessary to attach a numerical value to statements such as, 'It is very unlikely that an observation as extreme as this would have been made, if the supposition of no association is true.' Exactly *how* unlikely is it? The scale used is called **probability**. On this scale, an event that cannot occur at all—as unlikely as can be—is given a probability of 0. An event that is certain to occur is given a probability of 1. Anything between—which might or might not occur—has a probability between 0 and 1. The more likely it is to occur, the higher the probability. If you toss a coin, it is just as likely that a head will come up as a tail. That is, a head is as likely as not, so that the event 'head comes up' has a probability halfway along the scale from 0 to 1; its probability is 1/2 or 0.5. Thinking of this in another way, there is one chance in two (1/2) that a head will come up. Similarly, there is one chance in six of throwing a two on a dice—the probability is 1/6. Probabilities attached to more complicated events—for example, 'in a group of 176 pregnancies, *all* the NTDs occurred in children of women with poor diets'—are not so obvious, but they can be calculated.

Different significance tests are used in different situations,[2] but they follow the same general method:

1   Begin with a *supposition* that the effect or association you are looking for is *not there* in the population as a whole. That is, suppose that any association in your sample is there purely by chance or coincidence. (This supposition is usually called the **null hypothesis**—'null' because it assumes no association.)

2   Work out (or, more often, use a computer to calculate) the probability of getting results at least as extreme as those you actually *observed*, if the supposition of no association is true.

[2]It is beyond the scope of this book to show you how to *perform* significance tests, but this chapter should show you how to *interpret* conclusions from such testing.

3   If this probability is small enough, then the results obtained are unlikely under the supposition of no association. This casts doubt on the null hypothesis—so it is rejected, and the conclusion is that the effect or association you are looking for *does* exist in the population as a whole.

You will see later what happens if the probability calculated in step 2 is *not* small enough to reject the null hypothesis. But, first of all, let us return to the Cardiff study. Referring to the data in Table 8.3, the researchers reported that 'This distribution [of NTD recurrences] was unlikely to have occurred by chance ($P < 0.01$)'. (Laurence *et al.,* 1983, p. 91). That is, they had carried out an appropriate significance test, and had calculated that *if* diet and the recurrence of NTDs were *not* associated in the population, then the probability (P) of getting a result as extreme as theirs was less than ($<$) one in a hundred ($0.01 = 1/100$). Therefore, they rejected the null hypothesis of no association and concluded that poor diet and the recurrence of NTDs *were* associated in the population. (You should bear in mind that this argument is necessarily based on probabilities; so there is a small but unavoidable chance that the conclusion is wrong.)

Laurence and his colleagues took the view that a probability of less than one in a hundred of getting a result as extreme as theirs *if* NTDs were *not* associated with diet was sufficiently small to reject the explanation that their results were solely due to chance. Most people would agree with them—but what if their results had been less clear-cut and the probability had been larger? Generally in statistics there is a strong convention that a probability of less than 0.05 is small enough to reject the null hypothesis, whereas anything larger than 0.05 is not small enough. This corresponds to one chance in 20, because $1/20 = 0.05$. It is also referred to as a 5 per cent **significance level**—5 per cent because $0.05 = 5/100$—and a result that gives a probability of 0.05 or less is said to be (statistically) significant at the 5 per cent level. (This use of the word 'significant' in a statistical sense has nothing to do with medical or biological significance.) However, using a 5 per cent significance level is only a convention, and is not always sensible. For example, in a situation where more caution is called for, a smaller significance level—perhaps 1 per cent—may well be more appropriate.

What happens if the results are *not* (statistically) significant; that is, the calculated probability is *not* less than 0.05 (or whatever significance level is being used)?

□ Suppose the Cardiff researchers had obtained different data, and had calculated a probability of, say, 0.2 in their significance test. What should they have concluded?

■ On this result they could not have ruled out the null hypothesis, so it would have remained plausible that diet and the recurrence of NTDs were *not* associated. However, it would still be *possible* that there was such an association in the population, even though it could not be convincingly demonstrated in this sample of women.

Particularly when small samples are involved, it can be unwarranted to conclude that the null hypothesis *is* true just because it is not rejected. (It is usually possible to perform calculations of what is known as the *power* of a significance test, which throws light on this question.) So, usually, 'results not significant' means 'we have not ruled out the explanation that the observed results are purely due to chance'; it does not mean that this chance explanation is the *only* plausible one.

In this discussion we have concentrated on significance testing because it is the method of drawing conclusions from a sample most commonly used in biomedical and social research. But it is certainly not the only technique available. Rather than asking whether diet has *any* effect on the chance of recurrence of NTDs, it may well be more useful to ask *how large* an effect it has. This cannot be answered with a significance test. A wide range of techniques of *estimation* is available to deal with questions like this. For example, in the Cardiff study, 5 out of 27 mothers on a poor diet had a second child with an NTD. In other words, the rate of recurrence for mothers in the sample was 18.5 per cent ($5/27 \times 100 = 18.5$). But this does not mean that the rate of recurrence in the *population* of all mothers on a poor diet will be exactly 18.5 per cent. In fact, it can be calculated[3] that any value between 6 per cent and 38 per cent would be a reasonable rate of recurrence to expect in the population, on the basis of this sample. In other words, if the recurrence rate in the population were in reality anywhere between 6 per cent and 38 per cent, it would not be improbable to find a recurrence rate of 18.5 per cent in a sample of this size. (These calculations involve the notion of *sampling error* that you met in Chapter 5.)

This range of values (6 per cent to 38 per cent) is known as a *confidence interval* for the rate of recurrence of NTDs—because the sample is fairly small (27 mothers), the range of the confidence interval is wide. If

[3]The method of doing these calculations is not covered in this book. If you want to know how to do them, see the recommendations for further reading.

the Cardiff team had instead observed ten times as many women and found 50 recurrences in 270 mothers on a poor diet, the corresponding confidence interval would run from 14 per cent to 24 per cent. The interval is considerably narrower than it was with 5 recurrences out of 27. (To be precise, these confidence intervals are actually *95 per cent confidence intervals* because there is a probability of 0.95 that a confidence interval calculated this way from a *sample* does include the true rate for the population.) In recent years, confidence intervals have been used more frequently in analysing biomedical and epidemiological data.

Intervention trials

Let us return again to the data from the Cardiff study, given in Table 8.3. You have seen that we can be reasonably sure that their results were not simply due to chance; the statistical association between NTD recurrence and diet is very likely to exist in the population from which this sample of women was drawn.

□ Can we *now* conclude that a poor diet during pregnancy *causes* an increase in the chance of having a baby with an NTD?

■ No, because as mentioned before, the association may not be causal. Some other factor may be causing some mothers to eat poorly and, *independently*, causing the recurrence of NTDs.

A factor of this sort is called, in statistical jargon, a **confounding factor** because its effects are inevitably confused with, or *confounded* with, the effects of diet. A confounding factor may mean that the observed association is *spurious.*

□ Suppose the association between diet and NTDs *were* wholly or partly due to a confounding factor like this. Could the recurrence of NTDs be prevented or reduced by improving diet?

■ Not necessarily, because the confounding factor would not necessarily be changed by this improvement in diet.

□ In Chapter 5 you read about another difficulty in establishing causal explanations from statistical associations: the *direction* of cause is not always clear. Could that be a problem in this case? In other words, could these data have arisen because an NTD pregnancy causes diet to be poor?

■ This seems very unlikely, because diet was recorded right from the start of pregnancy and there is no way that the presence of a fetus affected by an NTD could work backwards in time to cause poor diet.

Because of the way they are conducted over time, prospective studies can usually rule out explanations involving reversed causal direction. However, they cannot rule out explanations involving confounding factors. So, it is important to consider whether a statistical association is causal before proposing an *intervention*—a method of preventing, curing or alleviating the disease in question. In the study of maternal diet, a non-causal association would mean that the groups of women who had different diets differed also in some other way—in terms of an unknown confounding factor. If it could be arranged that the groups of women differed *only* in their diet, then a confounding-factor explanation would be ruled out, and we could be more confident in concluding that poor diet caused the recurrence of NTDs. But it is extremely unlikely that two groups of women who happened to have different standards of diet would *not* differ in any other way. In any study that relies solely on observing mothers' diets (as did the case–control and cohort studies you met earlier in the chapter) such confounding-factor explanations cannot be ruled out. This difficulty is inherent in the nature of observational studies.

In theory, however, you could get out of this problem. You could take a group of pregnant women that was as homogeneous as possible. You could split it into two groups and feed one group on a good diet and one on a poor diet, and see what happened. This time, if the group with a poor diet produced more children with NTDs, you would be fairly safe in concluding that poor diet had caused the defects. But such an action would not be ethically acceptable in our society. What are the alternatives? It *might* be considered ethically acceptable to carry out an experiment like this on animals; but a deeper biological understanding of what is involved would be needed in order to decide whether the results could be applied to humans. (These matters are discussed in Chapter 9.) But ethical problems do not rule out *all* experiments with humans.

Studies such as those in South Wales, research with animals and some consideration of the biological processes involved in the development of the neural tube, led several researchers to consider it possible that it was not poor diet *in general* that increased the chance of an NTD, but that the defect was caused by a deficiency of a particular vitamin, folic acid. They thought that women who did not take in sufficient folic acid in their food before conception and during early pregnancy might be more likely to have an affected baby.

☐ If this hypothesis were true, what implications would it have for preventing NTDs?

■ If pregnant women were given extra folic acid, either by improving their diet or by giving them folic acid pills, then there would be fewer NTDs.

The problem is to decide whether such an intervention really does work. Again, most of the studies conducted so far have been concerned with the effect of this sort of intervention on the *recurrence* of children with NTDs to mothers who have already had one affected child.

☐ Suppose you gave extra folic acid to such a mother, and her next baby was not affected. What does this tell you?

■ Not much. The chances are that the baby would not have been affected anyway.

☐ What if you gave folic acid to a thousand such mothers, and only ten had an affected child?

■ This would give you some fairly solid information, but it would not tell you whether your intervention *improves* things; you still do not know how many of them would have had babies with NTDs *without* the folic acid.

What is needed is a *control* group—a group of mothers who do not receive the extra folic acid, but are otherwise as similar as possible to the first group. Then, if fewer of the mothers in the group receiving extra folic acid had affected babies, and if the difference was large enough to be statistically significant, one could conclude that the intervention did have a useful outcome. This is an example of an **intervention trial**. It is an *experiment*—because the researcher intervenes and changes what would otherwise happen, rather than merely observing. (Recall the discussion of experiments in Chapter 2.)

You might wonder why folic acid is not given to all pregnant women anyway. The reason is that it is not impossible, in the light of biological knowledge, that large doses of it may be harmful in some way, even though it is a vitamin. In addition, from the point of view of society, it would be wasteful to spend money on folic acid supplementation if it is ineffective.

In the intervention trial we have just outlined, one group of women would receive folic acid and the others nothing, so the comparison is between folic acid treatment and no treatment. In other trials, a different comparison may be made. Suppose, for example, a new drug to treat high blood pressure were developed. Reasonably effective drugs for this condition already exist.

☐ Would it make sense to run an intervention trial in which some patients with high blood pressure got the new drug and the others got no treatment at all?

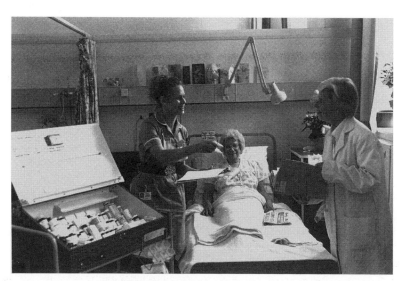

New drug treatments are routinely evaluated using intervention trials. (Photo: Mike Levers)

■ No, for two reasons. First, the patients who received no treatment would be worse off than if they were not in the trial—when they would receive an already existing treatment rather than nothing at all. This would not be considered ethically acceptable. Second, a researcher is much more likely to be interested in comparing the new drug with existing treatments, rather than with no treatment. The question asked will probably be, 'Is this drug any better than what is currently used?' rather than, 'Is this drug better than nothing?'

Most intervention trials, therefore, proceed by giving the treatment or intervention being studied to one group of people—the **experimental group** (or *test* group)—and giving either an established treatment, or nothing at all, to another group—the **control group**.[4]

Planning an intervention trial

In a trial of this kind, if the results *are* to be used to investigate causal explanations rather than merely associations, the two groups must be as similar and homogeneous as possible in every way, other than receiving different treatments. This requirement imposes several limitations on the way an intervention trial is designed and run. Three things need to be specified precisely: the type of person to be studied, the treatment, and how the outcome will be measured.

First, it is important to specify exactly what type of person will be eligible for inclusion in the trial. In a trial of folic acid to prevent the recurrence of NTDs, for example, only mothers who had previously had an affected baby would be included. Also the study might be limited further, say, to mothers in a particular age group. There is a balance to be struck between the homogeneity achieved by such *selection criteria* and the fact that such limitations also limit the applicability of the results. If all the mothers in the trial were aged between 20 and 25 years, then the conclusions of the trial could, strictly speaking, be applied only to mothers in this rather narrow age range. Some people will be included or excluded on practical grounds; there would be no point in including a mother who refused to take any pills, for example, and current ethical criteria generally support the rights of individuals to refuse to take part in intervention trials. The criteria used for inclusion or exclusion should be made clear in reports on the trial, so that readers can decide for themselves exactly how the results can be used.

[4]This type of trial is said to be *group-comparative* because it compares two separate groups of individuals. There are other kinds of trial that are organised differently.

Second, it is important to specify exactly what treatment will be given to the people in the two groups. It would be no good reading a report that said merely, 'One group had extra folic acid, and the other did not'. How much folic acid? When was it taken? There is another important point about treatments. Suppose the mothers in one group take a folic acid pill each day, and the others do not.

□ Apart from the folic acid content of the pills, how do the groups differ?

■ The control group of mothers have not taken a pill.

This is not as silly as it sounds. Often, taking a pill without any active ingredients at all can have an effect on a person. Some illnesses can even be cured by such apparently inert pills, which are called **placebos**. This **placebo effect** is by no means confined to particularly credulous or suggestible people. So it is common practice, in trials where the experimental group receives a drug in pill or injection form and the control group gets no active treatment, to give the control group an inert placebo pill or injection. (Similar ideas have even been used in some trials of surgical procedures—the controls had a 'sham' treatment such as a brief general anaesthetic and even a shallow incision in their bodies—though some people would question whether this is ethically acceptable.) If a trial is designed so that the patients are unaware of which treatment they are receiving, because for example placebos are being used, the trial is said to be *blind*.

Third, it is important that the way the outcome of the trial is to be measured is clearly defined. For instance, in a study of NTDs, one must specify exactly which deformities will count as NTDs. This specification is very important. Most trials are carried out by more than one investigator, and it is essential that they are all measuring exactly the same things. Users of the trial results may also need to know exactly what was measured to understand what is going on. (This does not mean that nothing else is ever recorded. For example, if a new drug produces severe adverse effects in some patients, this would also be recorded.)

Consider another feature of intervention trial design. Suppose a new drug for treating depression is being tested in a trial, against an old drug. A doctor is asked to report on how patients respond to the drugs. Suppose the doctor knows which patients had which drug. Consciously or unconsciously, this could affect his or her assessment of the patients' condition, so that any observed difference might again be partly or entirely caused by differences in what is *reported* rather than real differences between the treatments. To guard against this, the investigators who measure the outcome of the treatment are often kept in the dark about exactly which treatment each patient has received, until *after* all the results have been collected. If the patients are also unaware which treatment they are receiving, because for example the control group are taking placebos, or new and old drugs are packaged identically, the trial is **double-blind**. Double-blind trials are sound practice because they help to ensure that experimental and control groups are treated alike. But they are not always possible. For instance, in the follow-up to a surgical operation it may be obvious to the observer whether or not a particular procedure has been performed.

The final method of ensuring that experimental and control groups are as similar as possible is in some ways the most important. Suppose you were running a trial of folic acid to prevent the recurrence of NTDs, and had found a reasonable number of eligible women willing to take part. The control group is to be given placebos.

□ How would you decide who gets the folic acid and who does not? (Remember that the aim is to make the experimental and control groups as alike as possible.)

■ Perhaps the first thing you would think of doing is to make sure that the age distribution, social class distribution, and so on, are similar in both groups. But the difficulty is the 'and so on'. If you tried to match up the groups like this, there would always be the possibility that you would fail to match them on some important characteristic which you did not even know to be relevant. Instead, the answer would be to allocate the women to the two groups *at random*. For instance, you could toss a coin for each woman. If the result was a head, she would get folic acid, if a tail, the placebo.

In practice, this **randomisation** is not usually done by tossing a coin; there are more sophisticated methods, but the principle is the same.

It may seem paradoxical to use a random method, involving chance, to achieve two comparable groups. But a random allocation will tend to achieve roughly the same distribution of age, social class, and anything else you might *or might not* have thought of, in both groups. Much the same reasoning lies behind the use of random samples in surveys. However hard you *try* to make your sample representative of the population, if random

methods are not used the sample might end up being unrepresentative in some way you have not even thought of.

In the folic acid trial, then, if the groups are chosen at random, and if they are sufficiently large, it is unlikely that they will differ systematically except that one gets folic acid and the other does not. This makes it much more plausible that any observed difference in the number of NTDs between the two groups is caused by the folic acid rather than anything else. Randomisation is perhaps the most important feature of a properly run intervention trial; it is the randomisation that enables causal conclusions to be drawn from the results.

However much effort is put into ensuring that the different individuals in the trial are treated in the same way, different people will respond differently to the same treatment. Because individuals vary, and therefore the results of interventions vary from one person to another, statistical techniques such as significance tests and confidence intervals are used widely in intervention trials to determine what conclusions can be drawn from the trial results about the general effectiveness of the interventions being studied. So, significance tests and confidence intervals are important in this context. Yet these statistical methods can play an important role even before a trial has started, in helping to determine how many people should be studied.

Obviously, the more individuals that are studied in a trial, the clearer will be the picture given by the results. But there are limitations on the number of people that can be involved. In practical terms, suitable individuals may be hard to find, and resources of time, money and people to conduct the trial are limited. In ethical terms, it is unsatisfactory to conduct a trial after one treatment has been clearly shown to be better, because this would not be in the best interests of the people receiving the inferior treatment. So, ideally, a trial should include as many individuals as is necessary to judge whether the interventions being studied do really differ to an extent that is medically important, but it should not include *more* people than this. Statistical calculations based on the ideas of significance testing can give a firm indication before the trial starts of how many people need to be included to satisfy these objectives, and indeed to determine if a particular trial is worth doing at all. Deciding on the number of people to include in a trial is, or should be, one of the most important parts of its design. A trial that is too small to produce usable results is a waste of resources—and yet such trials have been conducted all too often.

Intervention trials in NTD prevention

Let us return to the question of providing extra vitamins to women to prevent the recurrence of NTDs. In the Reader[5] there are reports of three different trials that investigated the effectiveness of such interventions around the time of conception. The first of these trials is described in Smithells *et al.* (1980) 'Possible prevention of NTDs by periconceptional vitamin supplementation'. Read the article and the accompanying correspondence from the *Lancet,* and then work through the questions and answers here.[6]

☐ The trial reported by Smithells *et al.* used a group-comparative design. Were women allocated to the groups at random?

■ No. The controls were women who were already pregnant when they entered the study, or who refused the vitamin supplement. In a sense, they mostly chose themselves.

☐ Was the study double-blind?

■ No. The women knew whether or not they were taking vitamins, and so did the investigators.

☐ Briefly summarise the results.

■ NTDs recurred much less often when mothers had received the vitamin supplement. The difference was statistically significant.

☐ How do the authors interpret this?

■ In the 'Discussion' they put forward four possible interpretations. One is that the vitamin supplementation tends to prevent NTDs, although they noted that this might be a placebo effect. The other explanations are essentially that, for some reason, the groups differed in some way that had nothing to do with the vitamin supplements.

You might have wondered why Professor Smithells and his colleagues did not carry out a double-blind trial using random allocation and placebos. The correspondence shows that they wanted to, but they were not allowed to by some of the ethics committees involved. Research on human subjects in hospitals in the United Kingdom has to be approved by such committees, whose function is essentially to make ethical judgements on proposals for research.

A double-blind, randomised trial of folic acid supplementation to prevent the recurrence of NTDs *was* carried out in Britain in the 1970s, by Laurence and his co-workers in South Wales. Now read the article, 'Double-blind randomised controlled trial of folate treatment before conception to prevent recurrence of NTDs'[7] by Laurence *et al.* (1981) in the Reader, and then return to the questions here.

☐ In the study by Professor Laurence and his co-workers, out of the 60 pregnancies in women given folate tablets to provide folic acid, 2 resulted in NTDs. Out of the 51 pregnancies in women given placebos, 4 resulted in NTDs. This difference is not statistically significant. On what basis do Laurence *et al.* argue that folic acid supplementation does work?

■ Essentially, they divided the folic acid group into 'compliers' who had taken the tablets and 'non-compliers' who had not. They did this on the basis of the amount of folate in the bloodstream (in fact, their basis for deciding who complied has been criticised). They then counted the non-compliers in with those who had been given no folic acid to begin with, and there *was* a statistically significant difference ($P = 0.04$) in the recurrence of NTDs between this group and the compliers.

The division of the experimental group into compliers and non-compliers was not done at random; these subgroups were self-selected. But still it could be argued that this study suggested that *folic acid* was effective in reducing the chance of recurrence of NTDs, but that the *intervention* of giving folic acid tablets was not necessarily effective, because the difference between the group given tablets and the group given placebos was not significant.

☐ Does this last result mean that giving folic acid tablets has *no* effect on NTDs?

■ No. Remember that 'difference not significant' means 'chance not ruled out'—and *that* could be

---

[5] *Health and Disease: A Reader* (The first two trial reports are in both the 1984 edition and the revised edition, 1994; the third one is only in the 1994 edition).

[6] Smithells *et al.* refer to 'amniotic-fluid AFP level' in their report. NTDs can be diagnosed during a pregnancy by a procedure called *amniocentesis* which involves drawing off a sample of the *amniotic fluid* which surrounds the developing fetus in the womb. If the fetus is affected by an NTD, the level of a substance called alpha-fetoprotein (AFP) in the amniotic fluid is likely to be higher than normal.

[7] Laurence *et al.* generally use the term 'folate' for what we have referred to as 'folic acid'.

because insufficient evidence was collected. On balance, it may be more likely that the number of individuals in the trial was not large enough to detect a true difference than that the difference really does not exist. But the trial itself is inconclusive on this question.

These two studies, other studies by the same workers and, in particular, the proposal in 1982 to run a further large intervention trial under the auspices of the Medical Research Council (MRC), raised a considerable furore, which spilled out of medical circles into the general press. Questions of ethics in intervention trials became, briefly, a matter of public debate. Some of the ethical controversy is represented by the rest of the material reprinted under the heading, 'Ethical dilemmas in evaluation' in the Reader. You might like to look at this now if you have time. The MRC trial was eventually performed, beginning in 1983. An extract from the report of this trial is given in the Reader,[8] and you will be asked to read it later in this chapter. However, some of its key results are presented in terms of a measure known as *relative risk*, and we now turn to the definition of that measure.

Risk and its measurement

In both the Smithells and the Laurence study, and in every other study on the recurrence of NTDs, the great majority of mothers who did *not* receive the active treatment still gave birth to babies without NTDs. It is extremely unlikely that vitamin supplementation could change *every* pregnancy in these mothers from one affected by an NTD to one unaffected. Its aim must be to *reduce the risk* of an NTD. Most medical interventions are of this kind; they do not offer a certain cure in an otherwise hopeless situation, but instead they aim to reduce the risk of disease, disability or death. Another way to think of this is that they aim to improve matters *on average*. Similarly, most causes or possible causes of ill-health do not act in a completely clear-cut way. Cigarette smoking does not inevitably cause *all* smokers to contract lung cancer or heart disease; it produces a marked increase in a smoker's *risk* of contracting these diseases and others. Because so many aspects of health and disease involve increases or decreases in risk, it is important to have ways of quantifying changes in risk.

Table 8.4 reprints some data from the Smithells *et al.* study given in the Reader. It includes those pregnancies recorded only in terms of their amniotic AFP levels but omits those ending in a miscarriage in which it was not known whether an NTD was present. Of the 'control' pregnancies, where the mother did not take the vitamin

[8]*Health and Disease: A Reader* (revised edition, 1994, only).

Table 8.4 Outcome of pregnancy in terms of NTDs in mothers receiving full vitamin supplementation and control mothers

Outcome of pregnancy	Number of women given vitamin supplementation	
	Full	None
no NTD	177	247
NTD	1	13
total	178	260

Data from Smithells, R. W. *et al.* (1980) Possible prevention of NTDs by periconceptional vitamin supplementation, *Lancet*, **i**, p. 339.

supplements, 13/260 or 5.0 per cent resulted in an NTD. Another way of putting this result is that the *risk* of an NTD recurrence in babies of unsupplemented mothers was 5.0 per cent.

□ What was the risk of an NTD recurrence for mothers receiving full supplementation?

■ As a percentage, the risk was $1/178 \times 100$ or 0.6 per cent.

A reduction in risk of an NTD from 5.0 per cent to 0.6 per cent seems rather marked, though as you have seen it was controversial at the time to what extent the reduction was due to the vitamin supplementation. It is often useful to express a reduction or increase in risk as a single number; the most common way of doing this is to calculate the *ratio* of the two risks. Compared to the risk in unsupplemented pregnancies, the risk of recurrence in supplemented pregnancies was

$$\frac{0.6}{5.0} \text{ or } 0.12 \text{ times as large.}$$

(In other words, since 1/8 is about 0.12, the risk of recurrence in supplemented pregnancies was only about one-eighth of the risk in unsupplemented pregnancies.) This ratio of 0.12 is known as the **relative risk** in fully supplemented pregnancies compared to unsupplemented pregnancies. It is possible to calculate confidence intervals for relative risks, to obtain a range of plausible values for the relative risk in the population from which data like these are a sample. In this case, a 95 per cent confidence interval runs from 0.005 to 0.67. In other words, it is plausible on the basis of the data in Table 8.4 that the risk of recurrence in fully supplemented pregnancies is anything between 0.005 times and 0.67 times the risk in unsupplemented pregnancies. That is, the *reduction* in risk from supplementation might be very considerable (a

0.005 relative risk means that the risk in supplemented pregnancies is only one two-hundredth of the risk in unsupplemented pregnancies, since 1/200 = 0.005), or it might be rather small (a 0.67 relative risk means that the risk in supplemented pregnancies is two-thirds of the risk in unsupplemented pregnancies, since 2/3 = 0.67). Again, the confidence interval is quite wide because the sample size is not particularly large.

As well as their use in analysing and reporting the results of intervention trials, relative risks are very commonly used in observational epidemiological studies. For example, the Western Collaborative Group Study collected data on over 3 000 men aged 39 to 59 in California in the early 1960s, to investigate the relationship between several possible risk factors and the risk of coronary heart disease (CHD). Out of 1 652 men who did not smoke cigarettes, a total of 98 were recorded as having CHD. There were 292 men in the study who smoked 30 or more cigarettes per day, and of these, 39 had CHD (Selvin, 1991, p. 189).

☐ What was the relative risk of CHD for men smoking 30 or more cigarettes a day compared to men who did not smoke cigarettes?

■ The risk for non-smokers, as a percentage, was

$$\frac{98}{1\,652} \times 100 = 5.9 \text{ per cent}$$

(i.e. in every 100 non-smokers, almost 6 got lung cancer).

The risk for smokers of 30 or more cigarettes per day was

$$\frac{39}{292} \times 100 = 13.4 \text{ per cent}$$

(i.e. in every 100 heavy smokers, more than 13 got lung cancer).

Therefore the relative risk was

$$\frac{13.4}{5.9} = 2.3$$

In other words, in this study, heavy smokers of cigarettes were over twice as likely to have CHD as were non-smokers.

As with other measures that boil down the results of a complicated study to a single number, the interpretation of relative risk needs some care. In particular, it is important to take account of the *absolute* level of the risks involved. The importance of smoking as a risk factor for CHD arises not merely because the relative risk for heavy

smokers is over 2. In addition, it is because the risk of CHD for *non*-smokers is fairly high, so that the doubling of risk for heavy smokers leads to a very large number of additional CHD cases. But, for rare conditions, a doubling of the already low risk might be of little medical significance. A further important consideration is that, particularly in epidemiological studies, the rates involved in calculating the relative risk may need to be adjusted to allow for such things as difference in age structure between the groups of people involved.[9] Nevertheless, relative risk remains an extremely useful concept in epidemiology.

The Medical Research Council Vitamin Study

The MRC trial of vitamin supplementation for the prevention of recurrence of NTDs began in 1983, and involved researchers (and mothers) in seven different countries, though almost half the pregnancies studied took place in the United Kingdom. The plan was to obtain data from at least 2 000 pregnancies unless a sufficiently clear-cut result emerged before then; in the event, the trial was terminated in 1991 after data on about 1 200 pregnancies had been obtained. Most large-scale clinical trials (and many smaller ones) involve procedures whereby the data are monitored at regular intervals during the course of the trial, so that the trial can be cut short if the results become clear enough before its planned end. The trial had a rather more complicated design than those you have read about so far. There was a control group who received a placebo, but in addition there were three different groups receiving possibly active treatments. The treatments were folic acid alone, folic acid together with a mixture of seven other vitamins, and the seven other vitamins without folic acid.[10] You should now read the abstract (summary) from the trial report, together with an accompanying *Lancet* editorial, in the Reader.[11]

☐ What were the main conclusions from the trial?

■ Folic acid tablets reduced the rate of recurrence of NTDs. The reduction was significant, both statistically and medically. The estimated relative risk for

---

[9]The methods for doing these adjustments are beyond the scope of this book.

[10]Because the treatments were defined in terms of two *factors* (folic acid, and the other vitamins), this trial is said to have a *factorial* design.

[11]*Health and Disease: A Reader* (revised edition, 1994, only). (They can be found at the end of the collection entitled 'Ethical dilemmas in evaluation'.)

women taking folic acid compared to women not taking it was 0.28, with a 95 per cent confidence interval running from 0.12 to 0.71. (Note that, even with data from over 1 100 pregnancies, this interval is still quite wide.) The other vitamins showed no significant effect on recurrence rate.

□ Did the vitamin supplementation have any adverse effects?

■ The abstract states that 'there was no demonstrable harm from the folic acid supplementation'.

Naturally, some of the pregnancies involved abnormalities other than NTDs, and there were rather more of these in the groups receiving vitamins than in the controls. However, the researchers concluded on statistical grounds that this difference 'could readily have arisen by chance'. (MRC Vitamin Study Research Group (1991), p. 134).

□ Why do you think the trial took as long as eight years to complete?

■ NTDs are not common. To enter the trial, a woman had to have had a previous pregnancy affected by an NTD, to be planning another pregnancy, to be taking no vitamin supplements, and of course to be willing to take part. There are not very many women around satisfying these entry criteria. Therefore it took eight years to accumulate enough data.

□ Did the trial answer all the outstanding questions on vitamin supplementation for the prevention of NTDs?

■ Far from it, as the Lancet editorial makes clear. Among the important unanswered questions are the appropriate dose of folic acid and the timing of the supplementation relative to conception, and the extent to which vitamin supplementation would be appropriate for mothers who have not previously had an affected pregnancy.

The MRC Vitamin Study is an example of a **randomised controlled trial** or **RCT**, because the subjects were allocated to treatments using random methods, and because the trial design involved appropriate control groups. Intervention trials play a major part in medical research, and in the Western medical tradition RCTs are generally seen as providing by far the most reliable evidence of the efficacy of an intervention. But for various reasons they are more widely used in some areas of medicine than in others. For example, clinical trials are routinely used in drug therapy. (A **clinical trial** is an intervention trial in which the people being studied are patients.) Properly conducted clinical trials of some other types of intervention, such as surgery, are much less common.[12]

The intervention trials you have been reading about here have begun to take us out of the area of epidemiology, and into areas which operate at the level of individual people. Indeed, they have involved theories and measurements of what happens *inside* individuals' bodies. In order to unravel the biological mechanisms involved, it is necessary to use biomedical research methods, and these are the subject of the next chapter.

[12]These issues are discussed further in a television programme for OU students, 'Therapies on trial'.

OBJECTIVES FOR CHAPTER 8

When you have studied this chapter, you should be able to:

8.1 Define the major features of prospective, retrospective, case–control and cohort studies; distinguish between them, and interpret simple conclusions from such studies.

8.2 Give examples of the limitations of prospective, retrospective, case–control and cohort studies, and of such observational studies in general.

8.3 Describe the basic approach of statistical significance testing; interpret conclusions from such tests; and outline the basic limitations of significance testing. Define and use appropriately (without going into technical detail) the terms probability, null hypothesis, confidence interval.

8.4 Describe the basic methodology of intervention trials and their role in identifying causes. Describe and use appropriately in this context the terms control group, placebo, randomisation, double-blind.

8.5 Define and use appropriately the concept of relative risk, and calculate it in simple cases.

QUESTIONS FOR CHAPTER 8

Question 1 (*Objectives 8.1, 8.2 and 8.5*)

(a) In 1939, F. H. Müller reported the results of an investigation of lung cancer and smoking. He studied a group of people with lung cancer, and another matched group who did not have the disease. He found that the cancer patients had smoked much more than the people in the other group. Was this a retrospective or a prospective study? Was it a case–control or a cohort study?

(b) In 1956, Richard Doll and A. Bradford Hill published the first main report on their findings from a prospective cohort study in which they sent questionnaires to all male British doctors about their smoking habits, and recorded lung cancer deaths among the doctors as they occurred. They reported that the age-standardised death rate from lung cancer among doctors who were heavy smokers was 166 per hundred thousand, and that the rate was 7 per hundred thousand for non-smoking doctors. Could death rates such as these be calculated from the results of a case–control study?

(c) What was the relative risk of lung cancer for heavy smokers compared to non-smokers in the Doll and Hill study?

Question 2 (*Objectives 8.3 and 8.4*)

Multiple sclerosis is a chronic degenerative disease of the nervous system for which there is at present (1993) no known cure. Suppose you discover a drug which, on the basis of studies in animals and some preliminary tests on humans, seems as if it might have a beneficial effect on multiple sclerosis patients. The drug is taken in tablet form. You decide to carry out a group comparative trial of the new drug.

(a) One group will receive the new drug. What treatment will the other group receive?

(b) You have available a number of patients who satisfy the eligibility criteria for the trial and have consented to take part. How do you decide which patients receive the treatment, and why?

(c) After the patients have had the course of treatment, a doctor will assess their condition. Should he or she know which treatment each patient has been given?

(d) Suppose the doctor rates each patient's condition on a scale from 0 (no symptoms) to 4 (very severely ill). A statistical significance test is to be carried out to investigate whether your new drug has an effect. Write down (in words) what the null hypothesis would be.

(e) In carrying out the significance tests, it is calculated that $P = 0.25$. Does this mean that your drug has no effect? Explain your answer.

9 Biomedical research methods

This chapter builds on the discussion in Chapter 2 of this book of the scientific method and the philosophies of reductionism and holism in scientific research. In this chapter, we assume no more than 'common knowledge' of a few familiar biological terms such as 'cell' and 'gene'. A later book in this series, Human Biology and Health: An Evolutionary Approach, *greatly extends the discussion of human biology begun here.*

Biomedical research in context

The previous chapter made it clear that, although epidemiological research can identify factors that are strongly associated with the incidence of a disease, epidemiological data *alone* are rarely enough to prove beyond reasonable doubt that the relationship is causal. Similarly, epidemiological intervention trials can demonstrate that a particular treatment or preventive action can alter the subsequent incidence of a disease, but cannot explain how that intervention achieved its effect on the body. In order to get closer to convincing proof of 'cause and effect' in human health and disease, it is necessary to turn to **biomedical research**, that is the use of biological concepts and experimental methods to investigate phenomena of medical interest.

However, it is worth pointing out that biomedical research often begins as a response to epidemiological data. For example, in 1976, the epidemiologists Richard Doll and Richard Peto published the results of a 20-year prospective cohort study showing a very strong association between the incidence of lung cancer and tobacco smoking among 34 000 male British doctors. This triggered an upsurge in laboratory research into the biological effects of tars and nicotine on lung tissue. Direct proof of the *carcinogenicity* (cancer-causing properties) of tobacco products was obtained by micro-

scopic examination of human and other animal cells exposed to these products and comparing them with similar cells which had not been exposed (controls), confirming the association identified by epidemiological research. All research is costly, so it makes sense where possible to focus expensive laboratory investigations on areas that have already been exposed as potentially fruitful, for example by epidemiological research.

Research that takes the results of epidemiological studies into the biology laboratory for further investigation is one branch of what is generally called *applied* biomedical research. From the outset, applied biomedical research has a clear connection to human health and disease, which suggests the possibility of applying the results for some practical benefit in the future. This kind of research also occurs in the development and testing of medical innovations: for example, new drugs and vaccines, advanced medical instruments such as body scanners, and new surgical techniques, and it consumes millions of pounds annually.[1]

A smaller volume of what is generally called *pure* biomedical research also occurs. This is research into an area of human biology of intrinsic interest, which attracts funding even though it has (at the outset) no obvious practical applications. In the future, applications may arise, but these were not the prime concern of those engaged in the research when they began 'fishing' for new knowledge in their chosen area. One example is the work of the Brain and Behaviour Research Group at the Open University, which (among other programmes) investigates the chemical and electrical basis of memory formation. After many years of pure research, this group has begun to shed light on human memory formation which may help to explain and ultimately treat disruptions to memory patterns, for example in Alzheimer's disease.

[1]The development, testing and marketing of medical innovations is discussed in *Dilemmas in Health Care*, Chapter 7.

In practice, there is considerable intellectual and practical overlap and 'cross-fertilisation' between applied and pure research: they involve the same methods and techniques and both are pursued with as much rigour and objectivity as possible, within the constraints discussed in Chapter 2 of this book. The history of biology and the history of medicine have been firmly intertwined from antiquity to the present day, and medical interests have driven much biological research towards medical applications.

Indoor and outdoor biomedical research

Earlier in this series, we discussed the medical *paradigm* of laboratory medicine, that is a 'world view' of health and disease that emphasises laboratory research as the dominant mode of investigating and solving medical problems.[2] The majority of biomedical research goes on in the 'indoor' arena of the laboratory, where the physical structure, functions and interactions of the molecules, cells, tissues and organs that make up the bodies of living things can be most precisely studied.

□ Suggest two major advances in medical knowledge, already described in this series, which took place as a result of laboratory research.

■ Koch's isolation of the bacteria that cause tuberculosis, and Harvey's description of the movement of blood around the body.[3]

Most of this chapter will deal with laboratory science, but first a very brief look at the contribution that can be made to an understanding of human health and disease from a study of 'outdoor' biology.

Outdoor biology focuses on the structure and behaviour of whole organisms and their interactions with each other and with the physical environment. It may involve observing living organisms in natural interactions, examining the fossil remains of humans and other animals and plants long since dead, or analysing the biological significance of artefacts left by human settlements.

□ How might a study of artefacts such as cooking pots, weapons and rubbish pits from different periods of human evolution shed light on human health and disease?

■ What was cooked, hunted or thrown away gives insights into the features of human diets in the past, which in turn may shed light on the effect of diet on human lifespans, height and bone development in human skeletons of the same period.[4]

Outdoor research frequently leads back indoors, into the laboratory, for example in the microscopic examination of samples collected 'in the field' or in estimating the age of fossils by measuring the number of radioactive particles they emit.

A major branch of outdoor biomedical research concerns **pathogenic organisms**, that is infectious microorganisms (certain bacteria, viruses, fungi and single-celled animals) and larger parasites, which cause disease in humans and their food animals and plants. This may involve a study of the natural habitat and life cycle of the pathogenic organism to identify its dependence on geographical features such as altitude, climate and natural breeding sites, and to investigate those aspects of human habitation and culture that assist the proliferation and transmission of the pathogen. For example, the single-celled parasite that causes malaria is transmitted to humans by certain kinds of mosquito, which can breed only under particular conditions, including uncovered water storage tanks in certain climates.[5]

Information obtained by observation of pathogenic organisms in the natural world frequently leads back to the laboratory, in this example to synthesise and test chemical insecticides for mosquito control, anti-malarial drugs, and vaccines to prevent infection. The continual exchange of information between those engaged in biomedical and epidemiological research is illustrated when the research moves back 'outdoors' to commence epidemiological trials of insecticide sprays, drugs and vaccines which have passed their initial safety and efficacy tests in the biology laboratory.

Biomedical research in the laboratory can best be understood by taking as our starting point the hierarchy of

---

[2]See *Medical Knowledge: Doubt and Certainty* (revised edition 1994), principally Chapters 3, 4 and 5.

[3]See *Medical Knowledge: Doubt and Certainty* (revised edition 1994), Chapters 4 and 5.

[4]This topic is discussed in greater detail in *Human Biology and Health: An Evolutionary Approach*, Chapter 2.

[5]The biology of several important infectious diseases, including malaria, is discussed together with related social and economic features in *World Health and Disease*, Chapter 3, and in several chapters of *Human Biology and Health: An Evolutionary Approach*.

organisation of biological material, from the complex structures comprising the human body to the atoms and molecules of which cells are made.

Biological systems: an organised hierarchy

All scientific research (whether in the natural or the social sciences) begins with observation. The most sophisticated 'tools' that scientists possess for making observations are their own senses: principally the eyes and ears, which obtain complex information from the outside world, and the nervous system which interprets that information into meaningful relationships. Despite the limitations of the human senses as precise measuring instruments, they are capable of feats of observation and analysis which cannot be matched by machines, yet 'naked eye' observations are often considered (by non-scientists) to be inferior to those requiring artificial aids. This may be an expression of the power of *reductionism* in scientific thought (see Chapter 2), that is, the belief among many scientists that the explanation for complex natural phenomena can best be understood by analysing their smallest constituents, the atoms and molecules, which are well beyond the reach of observation by the naked eye.[6]

At the most complex level of biological organisation, the 'big picture' obtained by unaided observation is sometimes the most useful, but the further down the hierarchy of organisation you go—from whole organisms to cells and molecules—the more essential it becomes to use technical assistance. Progress in biomedical research has been given huge impetus in the twentieth century by the development of very powerful microscopes and other scanning devices. Figure 9.1 (which spreads over pages 115 and 116) illustrates seven levels in the hierarchy of biological organisation.

The most complex level of biological organisation occurs in the interactions of many different **species** of living things in their natural environments. A species is defined as consisting of the members of a population that, in their natural habitat, interbreed and produce fertile offspring, but which do not normally interbreed successfully with members of other species. Each species is given a unique Latinised name, consisting of two words written in italics (e.g. *Plasmodium vivax,* one of the species of malarial parasite) by which it is known to biologists worldwide. In the causation of malaria, several species interact: malarial parasites, mosquitoes and humans (see Figure 9.1a).

Other levels of complexity are encountered within the bodies of **multicellular animals**, that is animals (such as humans, Figure 9.1b) composed of billions of tiny cells of many different kinds, organised into distinctive tissues and organs—each with a specialised function, and containing fluids in which single cells 'float' and molecules are dissolved. **Organs** such as the brain and heart are specialised structures with distinct boundaries, engaged in particular functions within the body, and are generally composed of several different tissues (Figure 9.1c). **Tissues** are groups of cells with a shared structure and function, 'woven' together into a recognisable sheet, block, column or matrix (Figure 9.1d, p.116).

Cells are the lowest level of biological organisation capable of performing all the activities necessary to maintain life. Many different types of cell, each with a distinctive appearance and specialised functions, occur in the bodies of large animals (two are shown in Figure 9.1e). Each cell has a distinct boundary (the *cell membrane*) and contains sub-cellular structures collectively known as *organelles* (Figure 9.1f).[7] In humans, only the very largest cells are just visible with the naked eye: most are so small that the newborn baby's finger contains more cells (about 10 billion) than there are people in the world. Some cells lead independent lives and may interact with humans for their mutual benefit, or they may cause harm: single-celled organisms (known collectively to biologists as *protistans*) include many tiny parasites (such as the malarial parasite in Figure 9.1a); all bacteria (some of which live in the human gut and aid digestion) also consist of a single cell.

The smallest level of biological organisation is that of the chemical **elements** from which all the structures previously described are formed. Chemical elements consist of 'particles' known as *atoms*; all the atoms in a given element are identical and each element has characteristic atoms. The most abundant elements in living things are oxygen, carbon and hydrogen (they comprise over 90 per cent of human body weight) which, together with many other elements, are combined in assemblies known as **molecules.** Some biological molecules contain hundreds of thousands of atoms of several different elements and

[6]Philosophers use 'reductionism' in a more general sense to mean reducing phenomena to just one explanation, which *might* be 'everything can be explained in terms of atoms and molecules' but could equally be 'everything can be explained as God's work' or 'as luck' or 'as matter in motion'. See Chapter 2 of this book.

[7]The structures and functions of cells and their internal organelles are discussed in several chapters of *Human Biology and Health: An Evolutionary Approach.*

Figure 9.1   The hierarchy of organisation in biological systems, illustrated by examples drawn from human biology. The use of microscopes sensitive to light or to electrons (photographs d–g, *overleaf*) is explained later in this chapter.

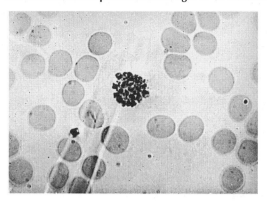

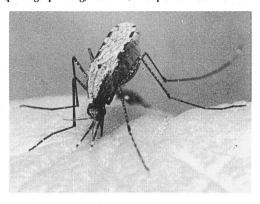

(a)   Interaction between members of different species: in this example, (left) Plasmodium vivax, *one species of the single-celled parasite that causes malaria, inside a human red blood cell (magnified 800 times); and* (right) Anopheles gambiae, *one species of mosquito that transmits malaria, taking a blood meal through the surface of human skin. (Photos: Wellcome Museum of Medical Science, and Wellcome Medical Foundation)*

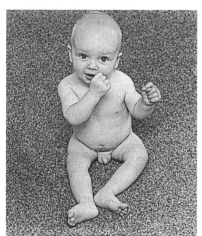

(b)   The whole organism: a human baby formed of organs, tissues, cells and fluids composed of molecules and atoms. (Photo: Mike Levers)

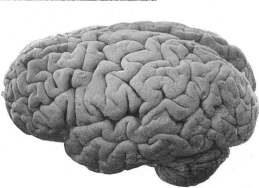

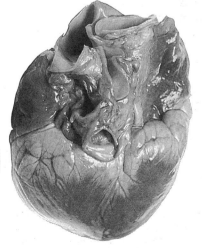

(c)   Organs are generally composed of several different tissues: in this example, (left) *the human brain, an organ weighing about 1.35 kilograms (3 lb) in an adult man, and* (right) *the human heart (Photos: Mike Levers)*

Figure 9.1 continued

(d)   Tissues are groups of cells with a shared structure and function: in this example, a sheet of skeletal muscle tissue (left) appears striped under the light microscope, whereas dense bone (right) has a 'whorled' appearance (magnified 500–750 times). (Photos: Open University Histology Laboratory)

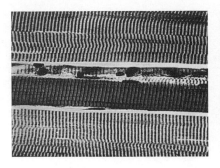

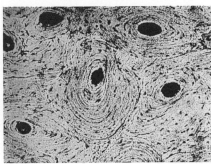

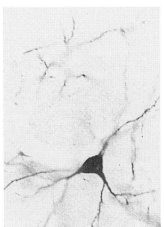

(e)   Cells of different types have characteristic appearances related to their specialised functions. Photographs taken through a light microscope, of (far left) a nerve cell (or neuron) with long branching filaments along which electrical messages are relayed (magnified 2 500 times); (left) an adipose cell acts as a store for fats (magnified 2 000 times). (Photos: Mike Stewart)

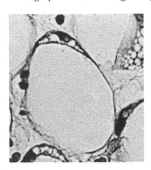

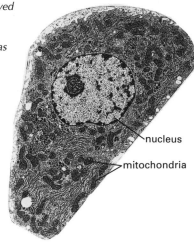

nucleus

mitochondria

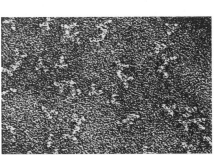

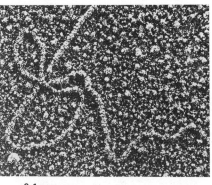

(f)   Sub-cellular structures (or organelles) include the nucleus, where genetic material is found, and the mitochondria which are sites of energy production in the cell: shown here (above) is a section through a liver cell, magnified 8 000 times by a transmission electron microscope (Photo: Open University Histology Laboratory)

(g)   Biological molecules can sometimes be so large that they are just visible with the most powerful electron microscopes: (top) the Y-shaped molecules are antibodies (specialised proteins used in defence against infection) and the tangled strand (below) is a molecule of DNA. (Photos: antibody courtesy of R. Dourmashkin and Gower Medical Publications; DNA courtesy of J. Griffith.)

0.1 μm

are large enough to be seen with the most powerful microscopes (Figure 9.1g). But others (like those of water, which has only two atoms of hydrogen and one of oxygen, H_2O) are very small—so small that a 'thought experiment' may be necessary to give a non-scientist some idea of their miniscule size. (This one was devised by the biologist Lewis Wolpert in his book *The Unnatural Nature of Science,* published in 1992.)

☐ Imagine that you had a glass of water in which each water molecule was in some way 'tagged' so that you could identify it again later. Suppose you poured all these tagged water molecules into the sea and waited long enough for them to disperse evenly throughout all the seas, rivers and lakes of the world. What do you think is the probability of catching one of the tagged molecules if you then filled the glass by dipping it in the sea?

■ The probability is extremely high, because water molecules are so tiny that an almost unimaginably huge number of them would occur in a single glass of water—a number far greater than the number of glasses of water that could be scooped from the sea. Thus, in each glass from the sea there is likely to be at least one (and probably several) of the original water molecules.

Biology is the most wide-ranging of the natural sciences, overlapping with the interests and methods of Earth scientists in the study of habitats, climatic factors and fossils at one end of the hierarchy shown in Figure 9.1, and requiring a knowledge of chemistry and physics at the other. At each of these levels of biological organisation, biologists are investigating structures and their functions. We will use this hierarchy later in the chapter to give some order to the principal laboratory (i.e. indoor) methods used in biomedical research, and the kinds of explanation that arise from investigating biological phenomena. But first we must define the main *aims* of biomedical research.

Diagnosis and intervention

Biomedical studies may be carried out in a routine manner, for example during the course of making a medical diagnosis, or they may be part of a research programme. In either case, two broad aims can be identified. The first is to describe and measure a pre-existing, naturally-occurring state in an organism during life or after death. This can be termed a **diagnostic study**, but it is not solely concerned with detecting pathology—indeed, one of its main functions is to define the limits of what is considered to be biologically 'normal'. In the context of human health and disease, the ranges of normal bodily functions

are defined by examining a large number of people who are not apparently ill, and comparing measurements taken from each person with the values obtained from all the others in the sample. The majority of measurements are found to cluster within a certain range. In this way, the normal range of (say) body temperature, or the number of heartbeats per minute, or the constituents of urine or blood can be determined in healthy individuals. Depending on the variable under consideration, the limits of the normal range may be quite large—for example, normal adult height in humans varies from about 1.4 to 2.0 metres (4 ft 7 in to 6 ft 6 in)—or it may be quite narrow, as in the case of blood sugar levels. We can use blood sugar to illustrate some general aspects of diagnostic studies.

The sugars we eat are mainly converted into a simple sugar, glucose, which is found dissolved in the liquid part of human blood (the *plasma*). Too much or too little glucose causes illness and can lead to death. Before breakfast the normal range of blood glucose is between 80 and 90 milligrams of glucose per 100 millilitres of blood.[8] After a meal, the glucose level normally rises to between 120 and 140 mg per 100 ml of blood for about an hour and then declines towards the fasting level. People whose blood glucose levels are substantially above this normal range generally feel unwell and are diagnosed as suffering from *diabetes mellitus* (usually referred to simply as diabetes). Diabetes is due to a deficiency (or diminished effectiveness) of the hormone *insulin*, a protein synthesised in an organ called the *pancreas*. Insulin is essential in regulating the amount of glucose dissolved in the blood.[9] In a person with severe, untreated diabetes the fasting level might be as high as 300 mg glucose per 100 ml of blood and after a meal it could rise to as much as 1 200 mg per 100 ml.

However, a word of caution is necessary about the use of diagnostic studies to define the limits of normal and abnormal biological function.

☐ Suppose that a person's fasting blood glucose was found to be 115 mg per 100 ml and after a meal it rose to 175 mg per 100 ml. Could you conclude from this that he or she is diabetic?

---

[8] 1 milligram (usually abbreviated to 1 mg) is one thousandth of a gram, and 1 millilitre (1 ml) is one thousandth of a litre (100 ml is about 5 tablespoons of liquid). In scientific notation, the normal fasting blood glucose level would be written as 80–90 mg $(100 \, ml)^{-1}$, but in this book we will use the rather more accessible form: 80–90 mg per 100 ml.

[9] Diabetes mellitus is discussed in more detail in *Human Biology and Health: An Evolutionary Approach*, Chapter 7.

■ Not for sure—the person *might* be mildly diabetic, but it is also possible that *their* normal blood glucose level is outside the range found in the majority of the non-diabetic population. You would need evidence of other characteristic signs and symptoms of diabetes before making a diagnosis.[10]

The diagnostic tests in routine use today have been accumulating since the nineteenth century, with new ones added to the list as innovations in technology or chemistry enable yet another 'marker' of bodily function to be measured. We will review some of the major ones later.

The second aim of biomedical research is to measure the outcome of intervening in a biological process, that is, by conducting **controlled biomedical experiments**. The outcome is determined by measuring one or more aspects of the *bodily state* of the subjects (be it a human or another animal) before and after the intervention. The measurements are usually compared with the normal range of values previously established from diagnostic studies. As Chapters 2 and 8 have illustrated, experiments usually involve at least two groups of subjects: the test (or experimental) group who receive the intervention and the control group who do not. There may be a placebo group who receive a substance that contains no active ingredient or who are given a 'sham' intervention which is indistinguishable (to the subject) from the 'real thing'.

□ How are subjects usually allocated to the various groups in a controlled biomedical experiment or an intervention trial? (Think back to Chapters 2 and 8).

■ Ideally, they are randomly assigned to different groups, or some attempt is made to match significant characteristics of individuals in one group with those in another.

There is no foolproof method of ensuring that the groups in an experiment are identical: living organisms are just too variable. In epidemiological research the subjects are always human, whereas in biomedical research other animals are frequently used as substitutes for humans—at least in the early stages of testing the outcomes of a new intervention.

[10]The techniques of medical diagnosis and the distinction between signs and symptoms are discussed in *Medical Knowledge: Doubt and Certainty*, Chapter 7.

The use of animals in biomedical research

Animals are sometimes kept in captivity so that their behaviour or their internal biology can more easily be observed and investigated; in such cases, the animal species is itself the subject of the research. We are not concerned here with this experimental use of animals, nor with the relatively small (and diminishing) use of animals for testing the safety of domestic products such as washing powders or cosmetics. Our focus is on biomedical research using whole animals as *substitutes* for humans in the development or testing of medical drugs and vaccines which are ultimately intended for human use, or in the investigation of human diseases and their causes. The over-riding ethical reason for using animals is that investigations or experiments that would be considered unacceptably risky or distressing for humans are sanctioned on certain animals by law and by the majority of members of most societies. Certain experiments may also be impractical to carry out on humans, for example, those that require very strict dietary control for long periods.

All experiments on animals in the United Kingdom are carried out under a Home Office licence, issued under the terms of the Animals (Scientific Procedures) Act of 1986, which limits the types of procedure that may be carried out and the number and species of animals used, sets standards for the conditions under which animals are kept and inspected, and requires proof of the competence of the researchers and the justification for using animals at all. The law in the United Kingdom is considered to be the strictest in the world, and yet in 1991, the number of procedures using animals (in all forms of research, including safety testing) was almost three and a quarter million.

Animal research raises a number of complex practical and ethical issues, as well having important consequences for the understanding and treatment of human health. The debate about the ethics of animal experimentation can be framed in terms of the relative value placed on human lives in comparison with the lives of other species. Members of animal rights organisations argue that experiments on captive animals—whether or not they suffer pain—are a violation of the animal's right to live naturally. This view is opposed by those who place the alleviation of human disease and disability as a 'greater good' than the absolute protection of other species, and believe that research on non-human animals can lead to progress in biomedicine.

We do not intend to take sides in the ethical debate here: our aim is to review the *practical* strengths and weaknesses of animal research and leave you to make up your own minds. Evaluation of the practical benefits and drawbacks of animal research primarily concerns the availability or non-availability of **animal models**, that is, animals that can act as biological substitutes for humans in experiments.

☐ Which species of animals would be the 'ideal' animal models in experiments to investigate an aspect of human health and disease, and why?

■ The species most closely related to humans are the apes (chimpanzees, gibbons, gorillas and orang-utans), which probably evolved from the same ancestral species as ourselves relatively recently in evolutionary time (about 30–40 million years ago).[11] Our internal biology is closer to theirs than to any other species, so they can be expected to respond to some kinds of threats to human health (such as stress or pollutants) and to potential drugs and vaccines in a similar way to humans.

However, apes are not humans and, no matter how close the biological relationship, it cannot be assumed that the responses of an ape (or any other species chosen as an animal model) are exactly the same as those of a human. Even though chimpanzees have 98 per cent of their genes in common with humans, there are still differences in their *anatomy* (the structure and form of the body), their *physiology* (the functions and interactions of complex organ systems) and their *biochemistry* (the chemical reactions in cells and body fluids).

☐ Aside from the ethical objections to experiments on apes, can you suggest any practical drawbacks to using apes as animal models for experiments to investigate human health and disease?

■ First there is the huge expense of trapping or breeding apes and keeping them in captivity, even where biomedical research is permitted by law. (In most parts of the world, only chimpanzees may be used and then only when no other species is suit-able.) Second, like humans, apes live a long time and produce few offspring, so experiments involving (say) degenerative diseases or effects on develop-ment in the embryo either take decades to complete or are restricted by having very few 'subjects' to investigate. Third, the captive existence of an ape is

[11]The evolution of humans and apes is discussed in *Human Biology and Health: An Evolutionary Approach*, Chapter 2.

so unlike its natural habitat and behaviour that con-finement alone may distort its response to any exper-imental procedure.

Similar practical problems apply to the use of monkeys as animal models for humans in biomedical research. These problems, coupled with a widespread reluctance by humans to experiment on our closest non-human rela-tives, explains why experiments on apes and monkeys are relatively rare. The great majority of research animals are small mammals, more than 80 per cent of which are rodents (usually rats and mice), bred in captivity for the sole purpose of biomedical research. They have the prac-tical advantages of being reasonably close to humans in biological terms (all *mammals* are warm-blooded and give birth to live young which are suckled by the mother), they are naturally short-lived and fecund (they produce large numbers of offspring in a short time), and are rela-tively cheap to breed and maintain in captivity in con-ditions that bear at least some resemblance to 'wild' habitats. Thus, experiments using rodents can involve sufficient numbers of individuals to ensure that the results are statistically valid, can be repeated relatively quickly and reproduced in other laboratories.

Laboratory rodents have been carefully selected for breeding for so many generations that many different *inbred strains* have been developed. The members of each inbred strain are virtually identical to one another (that is, they have almost identical genes), and in this sense they are like a huge population of identical 'twins' (see Figure 9.2).

Figure 9.2 *Inbred strains of rodents have been developed in laboratories by selective breeding. These mice have almost identical genes and would accept a transplant from any member of the same strain. (Photo: Mike Levers)*

□ Suggest one practical advantage and one disadvantage of using these inbred strains of rodents in an experiment to test the safety of a new drug, compared with testing on humans who are not genetically identical to each other.

■ One practical advantage of using inbred rodents is that the members of the test group and the control group would be exactly matched because each animal is nearly identical to all the others; thus, any difference between the two groups at the end of the trial can be reliably attributed to the drug. One disadvantage is that human populations vary in their genetic make-up (only identical twins have identical genes), so there is likely to be a whole range of responses to the drug among humans, whereas the inbred rodents will all have the same response; unwanted effects among *some* humans may not be predicted by the animal trial.

A further problem in the selection of animals as models for humans is that a great many human diseases and disabilities have no equivalents in animals.

□ Can you suggest a major category of human diseases for which there is no obvious animal equivalent?

■ Psychiatric disorders such as schizophrenia and depression are impossible to demonstrate in animals because diagnosis relies on subjective reporting of symptoms.

Some infectious diseases are also difficult to study in animals because the causative organisms only infect humans or some rare animal species (for example, HIV, the human immunodeficiency virus, multiplies and leads to AIDS, acquired immune deficiency syndrome, only in humans; the bacteria that cause leprosy grow only in humans and nine-banded armadillos). You may also have thought of inherited human diseases for which there are no animal equivalents, such as cystic fibrosis, haemophilia or sickle-cell disease, which involve defects in human genes.

Some diseases that do not occur naturally in animals (or occur too rarely to be useful in biomedical research) may be induced by experimental means, for example, by exposing animals to carcinogens (chemicals that promote the development of cancers). However, such treatment is not always a good model for the situation in humans, where cancers develop following exposure to a series of stimuli occurring over many years.[12] The shortage of naturally-occurring animal models for human disease has been partly overcome by the selective breeding of a number of inbred strains of laboratory rats and mice, each of which has a high incidence of a certain disease of medical interest (for example, one strain of mouse has been bred to develop diabetes, another strain has a high incidence of breast cancer). In the 1990s, it has also become possible to insert a very restricted number of human genes into laboratory rodents (so-called *transgenic* rats and mice), which results in the animal developing a disease that closely resembles its human equivalent. This procedure will, in the next decade, greatly increase the potential of animal research into human diseases.

In concluding this discussion, we reiterate that it is not our intention either to advocate or denounce animal experiments 'across the board', but to point to the factors that must be considered in any decision about whether or not to perform a particular biomedical experiment on animals. Some of these are ethical concerns, others are practical ones arising from the biology of different species.

Investigating the human body

In reviewing the principal methods of investigating the human body in health and disease, we will refer back to the hierarchy of organisation of biological systems (summarised in Figure 9.1) and the discussion of diagnostic studies, controlled biomedical experiments and animal models.

Studies of the whole organism

Experiments and investigations of living organisms are referred to as **in vivo** studies (*in vivo* means 'in life'). Methods of biomedical investigation of the whole organism can be roughly classified into four groups:

- *invasive* methods such as dissection and surgery;

- *scanning* methods such as X-rays (see Figure 9.3) and ultrasonic scans;

- *function measurement* such as recording breathlessness after exercise; and

- *sampling* methods such as biochemical analysis of blood.

[12]The biological aspects of cancer development are discussed in *Human Biology and Health: An Evolutionary Approach*, Chapter 8.

Figure 9.3 Four different ways of scanning the human head, which are routinely used in medical investigations.

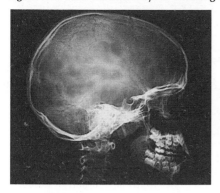

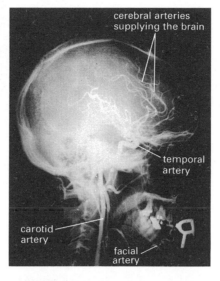

(a) **A conventional X-ray**. *Dense bone prevents the X-rays from passing right through the head and reaching a photographic plate, so bones appear white (unexposed) when the plate is developed. Soft tissues transmit X-rays easily and so are very difficult to visualise on a conventional X-ray plate because the exposed areas of film turn black. (Photo: Milton Keynes General Hospital)*

(b) **An angiogram**. *A substance that prevents the transmission of X-rays is injected into the bloodstream before taking a conventional X-ray of the head. This allows the network of blood vessels that cover the skull and penetrate the brain to be visualised. (Photo: Dr Marjorie England)*

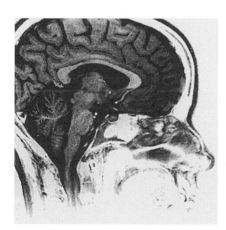

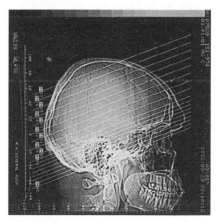

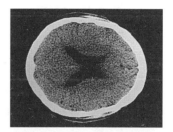

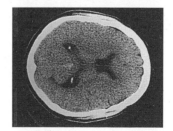

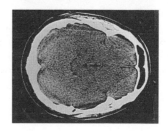

(c) **An MRI scan** *(MRI stands for magnetic resonance imaging). Parts of the body are exposed to a magnetic field inside a scanning machine and the image is produced by a computer which records information about the degree to which the atoms in different tissues 'resonate' (emit radio signals) in that magnetic field. Soft tissues such as the brain show up distinctly even when surrounded by bone. Unlike X-rays, MRI scans do not involve potentially harmful ionising radiation. (Photo: Siemens plc)*

(d) **A CT scan** *(CT stands for computed tomography). A narrow beam of X-rays is directed through the head from multiple positions around the patient (as indicated, above). The radiation transmitted through the patient at each of these positions is measured and a computer combines the data from each 'slice' (three different 'slices' are shown, right) to build up a more detailed picture of soft tissues than a conventional X-ray could achieve, but bone is still the dominant feature. (Photos: Milton Keynes General Hospital)*

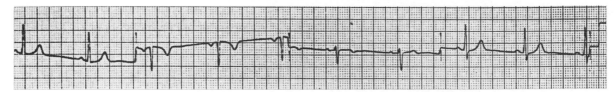

Figure 9.4 *Electrocardiogram trace obtained by recording the electrical activity in the muscles of a normal heart during a series of heartbeats (Source: National Medical Slide Bank)*

These investigations may be carried out on healthy human volunteers to establish 'normal' baselines, or they may be compared with measurements obtained from humans who are experiencing various states of pathology, or to evaluate the results of a controlled experiment. Alternatively, the investigation may occur in animals selected for their suitability as models for human biology.

Invasive methods have a long ancestry in postmortem dissection and experimental surgery, expanded in recent years to include new medical technologies such as laser 'scalpels' and ultrasonic beams to shatter kidney stones.[13] **Scanning methods** are techniques for looking into the living body; these have also made enormous progress (see Figure 9.3) since the first diagnostic X-ray photograph was taken in the USA in 1896. Note that some scanning techniques (such as X-rays) could also be classified as 'invasive' because they have the potential (albeit small) to cause damage inside the body.

Function measurement and **sampling of body fluids** include some tests that (at least in their general principles) have been in use for centuries, for example the measurement of body temperature, listening to the sounds made by the heart as it contracts, and detecting sugar in the urine as a sign of diabetes. In the twentieth century, these techniques have been greatly expanded by a number of developments in physics and chemistry, as well as in biology, for example the ability to record electrical signals from the brain and from the heart (see Figure 9.4), and the huge number of biochemical tests which enable the substances dissolved in body fluids to be identified and measured. These substances include *hormones* and *neurotransmitters* (molecules that act as chemical

'messengers' altering the output of specific parts of the body), *enzymes* (molecules that regulate chemical reactions), and *antibodies* (molecules involved in the defence against infection, see Figure 9.1g).[14]

The rationale behind all these tests derives from an essentially *holistic* philosophy, which maintains that the whole organism is an interconnecting web of biological activity, such that something can be learned about the function or dysfunction of the whole from an analysis of samples or parts. Thus, too much sugar in the blood or urine tells the physician something about the state of the subject's pancreas (the organ that produces the hormone insulin) and gives a strong indication of where else to look in the body for the damage to fine blood vessels that frequently occurs in untreated diabetes.

Research on living animals has produced a great deal of information about the ways in which the human body functions, which in turn has had important consequences for human health. To give just one example, in the 1920s, the Canadians Frederick Banting and Charles Best collected the juices secreted by the pancreas of dogs and demonstrated that they could keep diabetic dogs alive by injecting this juice into their bloodstream. This opened the way to insulin treatment for human diabetes, which was formerly a condition with a very high death rate.

Studying tissues and cells

Despite the emphasis so far on *in vivo* studies, a great deal of biomedical investigation is carried out on samples of tissue or cells removed from the whole organism and studied in the laboratory. Such methods are termed ***in vitro* studies**, from the Latin meaning 'in glass', that is, investigations occurring in laboratory flasks, dishes and test-tubes, or on thin sheets of glass (slides) for examination under the microscope. If thin sections of tissue are removed from a living animal (including

[13]Historical examples of experimental surgery and postmortem dissection occur in *Medical Knowledge: Doubt and Certainty* (revised edition, 1994), Chapters 3-6; modern surgical innovations such as quick-recovery anaesthetics, laser technology and arterial grafting are discussed in *Dilemmas in Health Care*, Chapters 7 and 10. Chapter 7 of that book also focuses on two scanning techniques: CT (computed tomography) and MRI (magnetic resonance imaging) scans.

[14]The functions of hormones, neurotransmitters, enzymes and antibodies are discussed and illustrated in *Human Biology and Health: An Evolutionary Approach.*

humans) and transferred rapidly to a nutrient fluid at the correct temperature, the cells of which it is composed often continue to function for hours, perhaps days, in many respects as they were doing in the whole organism. If the temperature is carefully reduced to just above freezing, whole organs may be kept alive long enough to be transported across country for transplantation.

If the cells from which a tissue is composed can be separated—for example by rubbing the tissue gently through a sieve, or using chemicals to break down the 'cement' that holds cells together—they can sometimes be induced to grow and multiply for many days or even weeks in a *tissue culture*. If a single cell is isolated and induced to multiply repeatedly by cell division, a *clone* of cells can be grown, i.e. a colony of identical cells (since all are derived from a single cell). However, relatively few types of cells derived from humans and other mammals survive longer than a day or two in cultures, placing limits on the scope of possible research on tissue or cell cultures as alternatives to using whole animals. Single-celled organisms of medical interest (such as certain bacteria, yeasts and fungi) may be grown more easily in flasks of nutrient fluid or on plates of nutrient jelly, but others—including many parasites and viruses—will only multiply in whole animals.

Cells in ultra-thin sections or single cells can be flattened onto glass slides in the path of a light beam and viewed through a *light microscope*, but even with special lenses it is difficult to make out the details of the transparent internal structure of living cells. They can be stained with special dyes, or with substances that emit fluorescent light or radioactive particles, to make their internal structures visible. (Look back at Figure 9.1 d and e; the tissues and cells were stained with dyes before the photographs were taken.) However, these processes usually kill the cells. The most powerful light microscopes can magnify the specimen about 1 500 times its actual size, but *electron microscopes*—which use a beam of electrons (electrically-charged particles within atoms) instead of light—can achieve magnifications as great as one and a half million times actual size. The electrons may be beamed *through* a cell (*transmission* electron microscopy, or TEM, as in Figure 9.1f), or scanned across the *surface* of a cell (*scanning* electron microscopy, or SEM).

The structures inside cells (the organelles) can also be investigated by breaking open the cell membrane and separating the solid contents into structures of different sizes and densities. Different organelles can be separated by passing the cell contents through a series of filters with microscopic holes of different sizes. Or the cell contents can be rotated at very high velocity in a machine called a *centrifuge*, which generates forces of up to a million times that experienced from gravity on the surface of the earth; in such a force field, organelles of different densities separate because they 'settle' at different rates. Such separation enables the researcher to investigate the functions of different organelles, such as the nucleus or the mitochondria, in relatively pure samples of each organelle.

Studying molecules and atoms

This progressively *reductionist* approach to biomedical research continues down to the level of the molecules and atoms from which the cells and fluids of the body are made. The molecule that has been the subject of the most intense research is **DNA**, *deoxyribonucleic acid* (Figure 9.1g), the genetic material in the cells of almost all living things. (A few kinds of viruses, including HIV, use a similar molecule called ribonucleic acid or RNA instead.)

The details of the structure of DNA and the manner in which it stores genetic information as a 'code' are beyond the scope of this chapter,[15] but from the viewpoint of biomedical research it is worth mentioning that the code is actually rather simple. It has only *four* units (known as *bases*), which can be combined in an almost infinite number of different sequences. In a human cell, there are about 3 billion (3 thousand million) copies of these four coding bases, but only about 5 per cent of them seem to be involved in the structure of *genes*. You can think of a gene as a 'meaningful' message or instruction to the rest of the cell, which contributes to the normal functioning of that cell.

Intense research has been in progress since the mid-1980s to determine the location of these meaningful messages, or genes, hidden in the molecules of DNA that the nucleus of each human cell contains. The most ambitious research venture is known as the Human Genome Project, which aims to 'map' the whole sequence of human genes; the size of the task means that the work is being shared out between laboratories around the world. The hard part is finding each gene: by 1993, only about 3 000 different human genes out of an estimated total of over 100 000 genes had been located. Once a gene has been found, the sequence of bases or coding elements within the gene can be chemically analysed—not in itself a difficult task since there are only four different bases. It is likely to be into the next century before all human genes have been located and analysed.

[15]The structure of DNA and the genetic code are described in *Human Biology and Health: An Evolutionary Approach*, Chapters 3 and 4.

The intention of the Human Genome Project is to be able to determine the function of each of these genes in humans, partly for its own sake (that is, pure research) and partly for its potential biomedical applications. It may enable scientists to determine the extent to which there is a genetic component in thousands of different diseases, to detect many diseases much earlier than at present and perhaps allow preventive or therapeutic action to be taken in time to change the course of a disease. This may involve what has come to be known as *gene therapy*. Experiments are already under way to introduce new genes into individuals who are suffering from diseases caused by a defective gene in their own DNA. It has already proved possible to introduce human genes into bacteria growing in vast culture vessels, effectively turning them into 'factories' manufacturing molecules of medical or economic importance. (For example, human insulin can now be manufactured in this way.) This is known as *genetic engineering*.

Research into gene therapy and genetic engineering raises profound ethical and practical questions, which are discussed elsewhere in this series.[16] Here we simply reflect on their potential to reinforce the pervasive view of science in general and biomedical research in particular as 'tinkering with nature' (Chapter 2). In the minds of some non-scientists, the pursuit of reductionist science has taken biomedical research into forbidden territory where the very fabric of what makes a human being can be extracted, or even manufactured, and 'spliced' into the cells of other species. They foresee danger ahead. Enthusiasts for gene therapy and genetic engineering foresee huge benefits for human populations in the next century—perhaps even the eradication of many important diseases or causes of disability. What these two apparently opposed views have in common is their *reductionist* focus—both see the 'gene' as the basic unit of human life, the determining feature of our humanity. In the words of Liz Evans, the director of the European Office of HUGO (the organisation that co-ordinates the Human Genome Project):

> It is also arguably the most important biological research project ever to be carried out, for it will lead to a complete description of the locations and structures of all the human genes. Such a 'handbook of human life' will be an invaluable reference source for biological and medical science. (Evans, 1993, p. 2)

[16]Genetic engineering and gene therapy are discussed in *Human Biology and Health: An Evolutionary Approach*, Chapter 9.

You may wish to ponder the consequences of such blatant *biological determinism* (discussed in Chapter 2) while looking back at Figure 9.1b and wondering whether the map of the human genome will supply us with a 'handbook of human life' that explains beauty, truth, creativity and love (and their opposites) half as well as it explains why some eyes are brown and others blue.

Levels of explanation

We conclude this chapter with a brief review of different types of *explanation* for complex phenomena in the biological sciences. They are not mutually exclusive, but tend to dominate different sorts of research programme.

Consider the question 'What causes lung cancer?' This question can be investigated by research methods that focus on a *single* level in the hierarchy of biological organisation we sketched in earlier. For example, research at the level of *organs* or at the level of *tissues* might explain the disease in terms of the damage to lung function caused by tumours obstructing the airways; by contrast, research at the level of *cells* might explain lung cancer as the transformation of normal lung cells into cancerous ones.

☐ What kind of explanation do you think might arise from research at the *molecular* level?

■ Lung cancer might be explained as the consequence of faulty DNA, perhaps damaged by toxic molecules in tobacco tar.

Each of these is an example of a **'within level' explanation**.

It is also possible to construct '*between level*' explanations, which fall into two types depending on their starting point: **'top-down'** or **'bottom-up' explanations** (already described in Chapter 2). In biological research, the power of reductionism as a guiding principle is such that bottom-up explanations predominate. Thus, in the lung cancer example, biologists investigating the smallest units contributing to the condition (i.e. the genes and tar molecules) would consider that they were researching at the heart of the problem. In a bottom-up explanation of lung cancer the cellular level would be seen as a *consequence* of the genetic abnormality, and in turn the organ and tissue level (problems with lung function) is a consequence of the abnormality in the cells 'below' it in the hierarchy.

Top-down explanations in biomedical research are relatively uncommon. The reason is fairly obvious: it is simpler to relate to complex phenomena as though they can be divided into their component parts and to study each in some degree of isolation from the rest. A top-down explanation of lung cancer would have to be 'holistic' (i.e. take account of all contributing factors), so it would encompass not only human biology but also human behaviour, social, cultural and political factors, the economics of tobacco growing, and so forth, in locating the primary cause of the disease in complex interactions at the topmost level of a hierarchy that most biologists have neither the competence nor the 'tools' to explore.

Two other important types of explanation exist in biomedical research which relate not to an organisational hierarchy but to time.

Developmental explanations focus on the lifespan of individual organisms, from the moment that a new organism begins to take shape to the moment of death. In humans, the developmental trajectory from conception to old age follows a common sequence which, in some respects, appears to be timed by a biological 'clock'. At certain times in the lifespan, significant biological events occur: for example, birth, puberty, the menopause and the degeneration of tissues that accompanies old age.[17] To return to the question we posed earlier about lung cancer, a developmental explanation would view cancer cells as reversions to embryonic cells, which regain the ability to multiply rapidly and move around the body just as they did when the embryo was forming. In the next chapter you will read about another developmental explanation: the 'programming hypothesis' which explains certain adult diseases in terms of experiences in the womb and in infancy. The practical problems of studying developmental biology in long-lived species such as ourselves is one reason why biomedical research has frequently turned to fast-breeding animals as models for humans.

Evolutionary explanations by contrast, encompass the whole of the time in which present-day species have evolved. Human beings and our diseases have a long history in which we have evolved certain biological mechanisms for fending off disease (for example, the immune system, and mechanisms to detect and correct 'mistakes' in our DNA), and in turn the organisms that make their living by infecting us have evolved ways of evading our defences. As our body structure has evolved and adapted to the upright posture characteristic of humans, so we have also developed a tendency to bone disorders such as arthritis, and difficulties in giving birth.[18]

As we mentioned earlier, these different kinds of explanations are not mutually exclusive: a biologist will select the form of explanation that best suits the subject of a specific investigation.

Finally, we end on a note of caution about the use of **metaphors**, which frequently occur in biological explanations of all types. A metaphor is a 'figure of speech' in which a complex phenomenon is described as being *like* something familiar. For example, the human brain is often likened to a computer; earlier we used the metaphor of a coded written message when explaining the function of a gene. Metaphors are often immensely helpful as teaching devices, giving the student of biology a mental 'handle' with which to grasp difficult concepts. But they can also be used to conceal ignorance of what is really going on inside the organism and they can lead to misconceptions.[19] The brain actually has rather a limited resemblance to a computer (see Rose, 1993, in the Further Reading list at the end of this book), and DNA is not actually 'writing a message to the cell'. An over-reliance on the metaphor may mislead us into believing it is more generally true. Like reductionism, metaphors should be used only in a provisional frame of mind.

---

[17]The interaction of sociological and biological inputs to this sequence is discussed in *Birth to Old Age: Health in Transition* (Open University Press, 1985; revised edition 1995).

[18]Evolutionary explanations for biological phenomena are the central theme of *Human Biology and Health: An Evolutionary Approach.*

[19]See the extract from *Illness as Metaphor*, by Susan Sontag in *Health and Disease: A Reader* (revised edition, 1994) which is set reading for *Medical Knowledge: Doubt and Certainty* (revised edition, 1994).

OBJECTIVES FOR CHAPTER 9

When you have studied this chapter, you should be able to:

9.1 Describe the hierarchical organisation of biological systems, from interactions between different organisms to interactions between molecules and atoms, giving examples of biological methods of investigation at each level of organisation.

9.2 Comment on the usefulness and the limitations of the following in biomedical research: diagnostic studies and controlled biomedical experiments; animal models for human disease; reductionism; metaphors.

9.3 Distinguish between different forms of biological explanation for the causes of disease: within-level, top-down, bottom-up, developmental and evolutionary explanations, using examples to illustrate their unique characteristics.

QUESTIONS FOR CHAPTER 9

Question 1 (*Objectives 9.1 and 9.2*)

Briefly describe a diagnostic study you might carry out on a person with diabetes, focusing on the level of biological molecules.

Question 2 (*Objective 9.2*)

Summarise the principal reasons why a controlled biomedical experiment might be carried out on laboratory animals as models (substitutes) for human subjects. What are the main limitations of using animal models in biomedical research?

Question 3 (*Objective 9.3*)

Give a bottom-up (reductionist) and a top-down (holistic) explanation for the cause of tuberculosis, using information from *Medical Knowledge: Doubt and Certainty*.

10 The web of explanations

This chapter rounds off the book with a brief case study. An audio-tape sequence entitled 'Data interpretation: the programming hypothesis' is associated with this chapter. This tape examines the development of a detailed research programme, and gives you practice in interpreting some of the data it produced. More details can be found in the Audiocassette Notes, which also contain graphs and tables that you will need to refer to while listening to the tape.

The 'programming hypothesis'

By this stage in the book, you have been taken through an enormously varied set of methods of discovering and generating knowledge, which led to diverse kinds of explanations and descriptions. In this final chapter, the aim is to review the range of approaches to studying health and disease that have been covered in the book, by showing how they can all come together in providing explanations for how a disease arises.

Although the range of methodologies described in this book is wide, nevertheless some areas of research in health and disease involve aspects of all of them. One important example is the hypothesis, developed since the 1980s by a group of researchers led by the epidemiologist David Barker, that certain adult diseases such as coronary heart disease (CHD),[1] stroke and bronchitis are caused, or at any rate made more likely, by impaired development at specific stages in the womb or in infancy. This impairment is often, in its turn, caused by poverty and deprivation of various kinds. This hypothesis is sometimes called the 'programming hypothesis', on the basis that it claims certain people are 'programmed' to suffer from heart disease or stroke by their experience

in infancy. This hypothesis is in detail much more complicated than can be described in the space available here, and it is controversial; nevertheless it provides an excellent example of a hypothesis resulting from, and related to, many different methodologies.

The programming hypothesis originally arose from the observations that there were very large differences from one part of Britain to another in terms of mortality and morbidity from many diseases; and, furthermore, that these differences could not be explained simply in terms of differences in such things as social class or cigarette smoking between the areas. The researchers then went on to investigate the relationship between the mortality and morbidity from certain diseases in recent years and various measures of mortality and morbidity around the time that the people who are dying in recent years were born. One study (Barker and Osmond, 1986; Clive Osmond is a statistician), for instance, compared the mortality rates from CHD in 212 local authority areas in England and Wales in 1968–78 with infant mortality rates (deaths of infants aged under 1 year per 1 000 live births) for the same areas in 1921–5. They found a strong positive relationship between these two quantities. In other words, areas with a high infant mortality rate in 1921–5 tended to have a high coronary heart disease mortality rate in 1968–78. Barker and Osmond interpreted this result as providing support for the programming hypothesis. (There are many other possible explanations of these data. Barker and Osmond, naturally, discuss some of them in their paper.) Similar studies found similar results in relation to stroke, chronic bronchitis and a few other diseases and, as the hypothesis developed, other kinds of study were used.

□ How would you conduct a case–control study of the hypothesis that CHD is caused by conditions in early childhood?

■ You would find a group of people suffering from CHD, and a comparable control group who did not have CHD. You would ask all of them about (or find records describing) the conditions in which they were brought up.

---

[1] Coronary heart disease is discussed further in *Dilemmas in Health Care*, Chapter 10.

Figure 10.1 *City General Hospital, Stoke-on-Trent (now part of North Staffordshire Hospital), where the cases in a case–control study of the programming hypothesis in relation to CHD (Coggon et al. 1990) were treated. (Photograph: North Staffordshire Hospital)*

In fact, such a study was done in Stoke-on-Trent (Figure 10.1) and Southampton (Coggon *et al.* 1990), and it found that people who were in lower social classes at birth, and people who reported that one or more of their siblings had died in the first year of life, had a higher risk of CHD, even after allowing for age, sex, smoking and current social class. However, the study was inconclusive because the results were not statistically significant.

☐ What does that mean?

■ There was insufficient evidence to rule out the possibility that the observed differences between cases and controls were merely due to the effects of chance.

☐ Suppose the results *had* been statistically significant. Would they then have established the truth of the programming hypothesis in relation to CHD?

■ No; though they would have given it some support. The main snag is that there are other possible explanations for the differences between cases and controls. In particular, all were being asked to answer questions about events a very long time before, and (though the authors of the study claim this was not in fact a problem) some doubt must remain as to whether this long recall period introduced any important biases.

One way of avoiding some of the biases possible in a case–control study is to perform a cohort study. A prospective cohort study would be a very long-term research project, as it would have to follow up people from birth (or before) to death. Instead, Barker's team carried out several retrospective cohort studies; these involved finding detailed past records of births and of such things as weight in infancy for groups of individuals, and then finding the same individuals today and using biomedical analyses to record their state of health. Such studies are far from straightforward, because they require detailed records to exist on the early childhood of people who are now old enough to be developing CHD and other diseases of middle and old age. For this part of their work, Barker's team involved an archivist who used some of the methods of searching for evidence in old documents that you have read about in Chapter 4. One major source of records came from some areas of Hertfordshire, England (Figure 10.2), where sufficiently detailed records had been kept by midwives and health visitors from 1911 onwards, and where the records had survived. Naturally there were difficulties in finding some of the people whose births were recorded, but these Hertfordshire studies (Barker *et al.*, 1989; Barker *et al.*, 1991) and other studies in other areas such as Lancashire provided further evidence for the programming hypothesis.

As previously mentioned, the programming hypothesis remains controversial. One reason for the controversy is that the evidence in favour of the hypothesis comes very largely from observational epidemiological studies.

Figure 10.2 *Were some of these children 'programmed', by their experience in the womb, to have heart disease as adults? Children at Handside School, Welwyn Garden City, Hertfordshire, in 1930. (Photograph: Hertfordshire County Council, Local Studies Library)*

☐ Why is this a problem?

■ Because in studies of this sort it is more difficult to rule out explanations involving confounding factors than with, say, an experiment.

☐ An experiment in humans to investigate the programming hypothesis would be regarded as unethical. (It would also be impractical because it would involve following up the people involved from birth to death.) Are there any alternatives?

■ It might well be considered ethical to carry out an experiment in animals, and if the animal model used was one with a reasonably short lifespan, the experiment would be practicable too.

The research reports from Barker's group do in fact refer to experimental studies on various animal models (including rats and baboons) which demonstrated that even brief periods of malnutrition in infancy had long-lasting effects on the way in which the animals' bodies functioned in later life; in other words 'programming' seems to operate in these animals. Again, this evidence

does not *prove* that 'programming' occurs in humans, because rats and baboons are not humans, but it provides some more evidence in favour of the programming hypothesis in humans.

As is the case with very many hypotheses in health and disease, this is not a situation where it is possible to perform a single, critical, experiment that will be capable of falsifying it. In *principle*, such an experiment could be done, but, as noted above, in practice it cannot. The situation is therefore much less clear-cut. A considerable amount of evidence in favour of the programming hypothesis exists, but holes can be picked in most of it, generally because it is based on observational epidemiological studies. Some evidence *against* the hypothesis exists, but holes can be picked in that too. In the future, there will be more research, but no one piece of evidence is likely to be clear-cut either way. Probably what will happen is that, eventually, enough evidence will build up so that either the great majority of people working in health and disease will believe the programming hypothesis (a *paradigm shift* will have occurred, as described in Chapter 2), or the great majority will not believe it and it will be discarded; we can hope for more clarity than that, but we shall not get it.

Let us suppose that the programming hypothesis becomes more firmly established, and that it is accepted that deprivation in early life does cause CHD and other diseases in later life. This raises the question of how this knowledge might be *used* to decrease the incidence of CHD. According to the hypothesis, the 'programming' works in a biological manner, so that if a person has the 'wrong' experience in the womb or in infancy, their body works in a way that is likely to lead to CHD in middle age or later. It is this biological phenomenon that is the *immediate* or **proximal cause** of the person's CHD (i.e. the 'last link in the chain' of causality). On this basis, one way of intervening to reduce the impact of CHD would be to interfere with the individual's biology in some way, during their life, to remove the increased CHD risk. However, there are less immediate causes of the CHD, under this hypothesis. How did the person come to suffer deprivation in early life? Quite probably, because his or her parents were poor. In that case, the parents' poverty could also be considered a cause of the person's CHD; such a cause which acts less directly is sometimes called a **distal** ('more distant') **cause**. An intervention to reduce poverty would, if this more extended hypothesis is true, also reduce CHD.[2] In order to make a successful intervention of this nature, it is clearly necessary to understand how poverty arises and is maintained in our society; and this understanding requires (amongst others) the explanations and methodologies of social science.

In summary, then, the evidence for the programming hypothesis has come from the use of methods from epidemiology principally, but also from history and biology. Some of the epidemiological studies used methodology (for example, surveys) from social science, and an understanding of social scientific explanations would be necessary for an effective intervention based on the programming hypothesis. All these methodologies play important roles in relation to this area of research.[3]

---

[2]Explanations and interventions of this general nature are discussed again in two other books in this series, *World Health and Disease*, Chapter 10 and *Dilemmas in Health Care*, Chapter 11.

[3]At this point, Open University students should listen to the audiotape 'Data interpretation: the programming hypothesis'. This tape discusses the programming hypothesis, and the work of Barker's team, in more depth. It also discusses the interpretation of some of the data arising from Barker's research programme. You should read the Audiocassette Notes before listening to the tape. They contain graphs and tables of data which you will need to refer to while listening.

A look outward

Having made the case that a wide range of methodologies are crucial to a full understanding of health and disease, this book now ends with a very brief look outward to how the various methodologies figure in the rest of this series. The first book in the series, *Medical Knowledge: Doubt and Certainty,*[4] is concerned with sociology, social anthropology and history, though it also introduces some of the methods used in clinical medicine. The next book after this one, *World Health and Disease,*[5] largely uses data gathered using the methods of epidemiology and demography. *Human Biology and Health: An Evolutionary Approach,*[6] as its title suggests, is largely concerned with biological knowledge and explanations, but also involves social anthropology and history. The other books in the series each use a wider range of explanations and methodologies. *Birth to Old Age: Health in Transition*[7] looks at all parts of the human life cycle, drawing together explanations from biomedicine and epidemiology as well as social science. *Caring for Health: History and Diversity*[8] and *Dilemmas in Health Care*[9] deal with the provision of health services. *Caring for Health: History and Diversity* involves a major discussion of the history of health services; both books use social science to explore and explain the ways that health services operate in various societies; *Dilemmas in Health Care* includes discussion of the role of epidemiological evidence (such as that from clinical trials) in the development of health-service provision, and also a study of how biological, epidemiological and other evidence about the causation of CHD has influenced health-service provision. *Experiencing and Explaining Disease*[10] takes as its subject the way that social scientific, historical, biological and epidemiological explanations of particular diseases interact and contrast. All these books draw on the methodologies introduced in *Studying Health and Disease*. In studying them you will be developing further your understanding of the methods you first met here.

---

[4]*Medical Knowledge: Doubt and Certainty* (Open University Press, revised edition, 1994).

[5]*World Health and Disease* (Open University Press, 1993).

[6]*Human Biology and Health: An Evolutionary Approach* (Open University Press, 1994).

[7]*Birth to Old Age: Health in Transition* (Open University Press, revised edition, 1995).

[8]*Caring for Health: History and Diversity* (Open University Press, revised edition, 1993).

[9]*Dilemmas in Health Care* (Open University Press, 1993).

[10]*Experiencing and Explaining Disease* (Open University Press, revised edition, 1995).

OBJECTIVE FOR CHAPTER 10

When you have studied this chapter, you should be able to:

10.1 Explain and give examples of the role of sociological, historical, epidemiological and bio-medical research methods in studying health and disease.

Appendix

Table of abbreviations used in this book

Abbreviation	What it stands for
AFP	alpha-fetoprotein
AIDS	acquired immunodeficiency syndrome
CHD	coronary heart disease
CT	computed tomography
DNA	deoxyribonucleic acid
GHS	General Household Survey
GP	General Practitioner
HIPE	Hospital In-Patient Enquiry
HIV	human immunodeficiency virus
HMSO	Her Majesty's Stationery Office
ICD	International Classification of Diseases (Injuries and Causes of Death)
MRC	Medical Research Council
MRI	magnetic resonance imaging
NHS	National Health Service
NTD	neural-tube defect
OPCS	Office of Population Censuses and Surveys
PNMR	perinatal mortality rate
RCT	randomised controlled trial
RNA	ribonucleic acid
SMR	standardised mortality ratio
TB	tuberculosis

References and further reading

References

Allen, R. E. (ed.) (1990) *The Concise Dictionary of Current English*, 8th edn, Clarendon Press, Oxford.

Atkinson, P. (1977) Personal communication, quoted in Hammersley, M. (1979) *Data Collection Procedures*, Book 4 in DE304 Research Methods in Education and the Social Sciences, Open University, Milton Keynes.

Barker, D. J. P. (ed.) (1992) *Fetal and Infant Origins of Adult Disease*, British Medical Journal, London.

Barker, D. J. P., Godfrey, K. M., Fall, C., Osmond, C., Winter, P. D. and Shaheen, S.O. (1991) Relation of birth weight and childhood respiratory infection to adult lung function and death from chronic obstructive airways disease, *British Medical Journal*, **303**, pp. 671–5. Reprinted as Chapter 14 in Barker (1992).

Barker, D. J. P. and Osmond, C. (1986) Infant mortality, childhood nutrition, and ischaemic heart disease in England and Wales, *Lancet*, **i**, pp. 1077–81. Reprinted as Chapter 1 in Barker (1992).

Barker, D. J. P., Winter, P. D., Osmond, C., Margetts, B. and Simmonds, S. J. (1989) Weight in infancy and death from ischaemic heart disease, *Lancet*, **ii**, pp. 577–80. Reprinted as Chapter 13 in Barker (1992).

Becker, H. S. (1964) Problems in the publication of field studies, in Vidich, A. J., Bensman, J. and Stein, M. R. (eds) *Reflections on Community Studies*, John Wiley & Sons, New York. Reprinted in Bynner, J. and Stribley, K. M. (eds) (1979) *Social Research: Principles and Procedures*, Open University Press, Milton Keynes.

Becker, H. S. (1970) *Sociological Work: Method and Substance*, Aldine, Chicago.

Becker, H. S. and Geer, B. (1957) Participant observation and interviewing: a comparison, *Human Organization*, **XVI**, pp. 28–32.

Beischer, N. A., Evans, J. H. and Townsend, L. (1979) Studies of prolonged pregnancy: I The incidence of prolonged pregnancy, *American Journal of Obstetrics and Gynecology*, **103**, pp. 476–82.

Blaxter, M. (1990) *Health and Lifestyles*, Tavistock/Routledge, London.

Booth, C. (1886–1902) *The Life and Labour of the People of London* (17 volumes), Macmillan, London.

Bowley, A. L. and Burnett-Hurst, A. R. (1915) *Livelihood and Poverty: a Study of the Economic Conditions of Working Class Households in Northampton, Warrington, Stanley and Reading*, Bell, London.

Brown, G. and Harris, T. (1987) *Social Origins of Depression: a Study of Psychiatric Disorder in Women*, Tavistock, London.

Carr, E. H. (1971) *What is History?* Penguin Books, Harmondsworth, Middlesex.

Cartwright, A. and Seale, C. (1990) *The Natural History of a Survey*, King's Fund, London.

Coggon, D., Margetts, B., Barker, D. J. P., Carson, P. H. M., Mann, J. S., Oldroyd, K. G. and Wickham, C. (1990) Childhood risk factors for ischaemic heart disease and stroke, *Paediatric and Perinatal Epidemiology*, **4**, pp. 464–9. Reprinted as Chapter 12 in Barker (1992).

Daintith, J. and Isaacs, A. (1989) *Medical Quotations,* Collins, London and Glasgow.

Department of Employment (1992) *New Earnings Survey 1992, Part A*, HMSO, London.

Doll, R. and Hill, A. B. (1956) Lung cancer and other causes of death in relation to smoking: a second report on the mortality of British doctors, *British Medical Journal,* **ii**, pp. 1 071–81.

Doll, R. and Peto, R. (1976) Mortality in relation to smoking: 20 years observation on male British doctors, *British Medical Journal*, **2**, pp. 1 525–36.

Evans, L. (1993) The Human Genome Project, *Biological Sciences Review*, **5** (5), pp. 2–5.

Finch, J. (1984) 'It's great to have someone to talk to': ethics and politics of interviewing women, in Bell, C. and Roberts, H. (eds) *Social Researching: Politics, Problems, Practice,* Routledge, London. Reprinted in Hammersley, M. (ed.) (1993) *Social Research: Philosophy, Politics and Practice,* Sage, London, pp.166–80.

Gallup (1986) *Alternative Medicine,* 12–18 August, Gallup.

Glaser, B. G. and Strauss, A. L. (1966) *Awareness of Dying,* Weidenfeld and Nicolson, London.

Glaser, B. G. and Strauss, A. L. (1967) *The Discovery of Grounded Theory,* Aldine, Chicago.

Goldstein, J. (1987) *Console and Classify: The French Psychiatric Profession in the Nineteenth Century,* Cambridge University Press, Cambridge.

Goncourt, E. and J. (1956) *Journal des Goncourts, Mémoires de la vie littéraire,* 4 vols, Fasquelle & Flammarion, Paris. (1st edition 1879–1890.)

Guillain, G. C. (1959) *J.-M. Charcot 1825–1893, His Life His Work,* trans. P. Bailey, Pitman Medical Publishing Co., London.

Hall, M. B. (1965) *Robert Boyle on Natural Philosophy: An Essay with Selections from his Writings,* Indiana University Press.

Hammersley, M. and Atkinson, P. (1983) *Ethnography: Principles in Practice,* Routledge, London.

Hollingsworth, T. H. (1969) *Historical Demography,* The Camelot Press Ltd., London and Southampton.

Horgan, J. (1992) Profile: Karl R. Popper, the intellectual warrior, *Scientific American,* November, pp. 20–1.

James, M. (1994) Hysteria and demonic possession, in *Health and Disease: a Reader*, Davey, B., Gray, A. and Seale, C. (eds) (2nd edn), Open University Press, Buckingham.

James, N., Laurence, K. M. and Miller, M. (1980) Diet as a factor in the aetiology of neural tube malformations, *Zeitschrift für Kinderchirurgie*, **31**, pp. 302–7.

Jones, E. (1977) *The Life and Work of Sigmund Freud*, ed. and abridged by L. Trilling and S. Marcus, Penguin Books, Harmondsworth, Middlesex. (1st edition, 3 vols., 1953–7, *Sigmund Freud: Life and Work*, Hogarth Press, London.)

Kinsey, A. *et al.* (1948) *Sexual Behaviour in the Human Male*, W. B. Saunders, Philadelphia.

Kinsey, A. *et al.* (1953) *Sexual Behaviour in the Human Female*, W. B. Saunders, Philadelphia.

Kuhn, T. (1962) *The Structure of Scientific Revolutions*, University of Chicago Press, Chicago.

Laurence, K. M. (1989) A declining incidence of neural tube defects in the U.K., *Zeitschrift für Kinderchirurgie*, **44**, p. 51.

Laurence, K. M., Campbell, H. and James, N. (1983) The role of improvement in the maternal diet and preconceptional folic acid supplementation in the prevention of neural tube defects, in Dobbing, J. (ed.) (1983) *Prevention of Spina Bifida and Other Neural Tube Defects*, Academic Press, London.

Laurence, K. M., James, N., Miller, M. and Campbell, H. (1980) Increased risk of recurrence of pregnancies complicated by foetal neural tube defects in mothers receiving poor diets, and possible benefits of dietary counselling, *British Medical Journal*, **281**, pp. 1592–4.

Laurence, K. M., James, N., Miller, M., Tennant, G. B. and Campbell, H. (1981) Double-blind randomised controlled trial of folate treatment before conception to prevent recurrence of neural-tube defects, *British Medical Journal*, **282**, pp. 1509–11.

Lofland, J. (1971) *Analyzing Social Settings*, Wadsworth, Belmont, California.

Marsh, C. (1982) *The Survey Method: the Contribution of Surveys to Sociological Explanation*, Allen and Unwin, London.

Medawar, P. (1991) Is the scientific paper a fraud?, in *The Threat and the Glory*, (paperback edition), Oxford University Press, Oxford.

Micale, M. (1989) Hysteria and historiography: a review of past and present writing, *History of Science*, Part 1, December 1989; Part 2, March 1990.

MORI (1989) *Alternative medicine*. 21–25 September, MORI.

Moser, C. and Kalton, G. (1971) *Survey Methods in Social Investigation*, 2nd edn, Heinemann Educational Books, London.

MRC Vitamin Study Research Group (1991) Prevention of neural tube defects: Results of the Medical Research Council Vitamin Study, *Lancet*, **338**, pp. 131–7.

Murphy, M. G. (1973) *Our Knowledge of the Historical Past*, The Bobbs-Merrill Co. Inc., Indianapolis & New York.

OPCS (1986) *Occupational Mortality: The Registrar-General's Decennial Supplement for Great Britain, 1979–80, 1982–83*, Series DS, no. 6, part 1, HMSO, London.

OPCS (1991) *Key Population and Vital Statistics, Local and Health Authority Areas 1990*, Series VS no. 17, PP1 no.13, HMSO, London.

OPCS (1992a) *Birth Statistics: England and Wales 1990*, Series FM1, no. 19, HMSO, London.

OPCS (1992b) *Mortality Statistics, Perinatal and Infant, Social and Biological Factors: England and Wales 1990*, Series DH3, no. 24, HMSO, London.

OPCS (1992c) *1991 Census, County Report for Buckinghamshire*, Part 1, HMSO, London.

OPCS (1992d) *Mortality Statistics, Area: England and Wales 1990*, Series DH5 no. 17, HMSO, London.

Open University (1979) *Classification and Measurement*, DE304, Block 5, The Open University, Milton Keynes.

Open University (1983) MDST 242 *Statistics in Society*, Unit C3 *Is My Child Normal?*, The Open University, Milton Keynes.

Oyama, S. (1989) Ontogeny and the central dogma: Do we need the concept of genetic programming in order to have an evolutionary perspective?, pp. 1–34 in Gunnar, M. R. and Thelen, E. (eds) Systems and development, *The Minnesota Symposia on Child Psychology*, **22**, Lawrence Erlbaum Associates, Hillsdale, New Jersey.

Porter, R. (1986) *English Society in the Eighteenth Century*, Penguin Books, Harmondsworth, Middlesex. (1st edition 1982, Penguin Books, Harmondsworth, Middlesex.)

Porter, R. and Wear, A. (eds) (1987) *Problems and Methods in the History of Medicine*, Croom Helm, London.

Registrar-General for Scotland (1991), *Annual Report 1990*, no. 136, General Register Office, Edinburgh.

Rose, S. (1988) Reflections on reductionism, *Trends in Biological Science*, May, pp. 161–2.

Rose, S. (1993) *The Making of Memory*, Bantam Press, Uxbridge.

Rose, S., Lewontin, R. C. and Kamin, L. J. (1984) *Not in Our Genes*, Pelican Books, London.

Roth, J. (1957) Ritual and magic in the control of contagion, *American Sociological Review*, **22**, pp. 310–14.

Rowntree, S. (1902, new edn 1922) *Poverty: a Study of Town Life*, Longman, London.

Schweitzer, P. (ed.) (1985) *Can We Afford the Doctor?*, Age Exchange, London.

Selvin, S. (1991) *Statistical Analysis of Epidemiological Data*, Oxford University Press, New York.

Sharma, U. (1990) Using alternative therapies: marginal medicine and central concerns, in Abbott, P. and Payne, G. (eds) *New Directions in the Sociology of Health*, Falmer Press, London, pp. 140–52.

Showalter, E. (1987, new edn 1991) *The Female Malady: Women, Madness and English Culture, 1830–1980*, Virago Press, London. (First published 1985, Pantheon Books, New York.)

Silverman, D. (1985) *Qualitative Methodology and Sociology*, Gower, Aldershot.

Smith-Rosenberg, Carroll (1972) The Hysterical Woman: sex roles and role conflict in nineteenth-century America, *Social Research*, **39**, pp. 652–78.

Smithells, R. W., Sheppard, S., Schorah, C. J., Seller, M. J., Nevin, N. C., Harris, R., Read, A. P. and Fielding, D. W. (1980) Possible prevention of neural-tube defects by periconceptional vitamin supplementation, *Lancet*, **i**, pp. 339–40.

Statistical Society of London (1848) Report of an investigation into the state of the poorer classes in St George's-in-the-East, *Quarterly Journal of the Statistical Society of London*, **II**, pp. 193–250.

Strong, P. M. (1979) *The Ceremonial Order of the Clinic*, Routledge and Kegan Paul, London.

United Nations (1991) *1989 Demographic Yearbook*, United Nations, New York.

United Nations (1992) *1990 Demographic Yearbook*, United Nations, New York.

Veith, I. (1965) *Hysteria: The History of a Disease*, Phoenix Books, The University of Chicago Press, Chicago.

Wells, A. F. (1935) *The Local Social Survey in Britain*, Allen and Unwin, London.

Whyte, W. F. (1943) (3rd edn, 1981) *Street Corner Society: The Social Structure of an Italian Slum*, University of Chicago Press, Chicago.

Wolpert, L. (1992) *The Unnatural Nature of Science*, Faber and Faber, London and Boston.

Wrigley, E. A. (ed.) (1966) *An Introduction to English Historical Demography from the Sixteenth to the Nineteenth Century*, Weidenfeld and Nicolson, London.

Wrigley, E. A. and Schofield, R. S. (1981) *Population History of England 1541–1871*, Edward Arnold, London (paperback edn, 1989, Cambridge University Press, Cambridge).

Further reading

If you are interested in pursuing some of the general methodological and philosophical ideas you met in Chapter 2 of this book, you might wish to read the following books.

Positive Philosophy by L. Kolakowski (1972, Penguin Books, Harmondsworth). See particularly Chapter 1, 'An overall view of positivism'.

The Dilemma of Qualitative Method, by Martyn Hammersley (1989, Routledge, London and New York; republished as a paperback in 1990). See particularly Chapter 1, 'Philosophy and the human sciences in the nineteenth century' for a lucid account of positivism and the emergence of the social sciences at the turn of the last century.

The last-mentioned book, as its title indicates, deals with (among other things) aspects of qualitative social science. Other sources of further information about qualitative methodology include the following.

'On feminist methodology', by Martyn Hammersley, an article published in 1992 in the journal *Sociology* (**26**, 2, pp. 187–206). A discussion of the problems raised in feminist methodology, with replies from two feminist researchers.

Ethnography: Principles in Practice by Martyn Hammersley and Paul Atkinson (1983, Routledge, London) is an excellent outline of the main principles and problems of the method, including interviewing, with extensive use of quotations from ethnographic studies.

Qualitative Methodology and Sociology by David Silverman (1985, Gower, Basingstoke) is a more advanced text which describes the philosophical underpinnings of qualitative methods, and gives more detail on methods not covered in this book, such as ethnomethodology and discourse analysis.

If you wish to read more about how historical research is done, the following are useful.

Population History of England 1541–1871, by E. A. Wrigley and R. S. Schofield (1989, Cambridge University Press, Cambridge; originally published in 1981 by Edward Arnold, London) is a lengthy, in-depth demographical study, providing a comprehensive, if somewhat complex, account of how the quantitative approach to history can be put into practice.

The Historian's Craft by Marc Bloch (1992, Manchester University Press, Manchester; translated from the French by Peter Putnam, with a preface by Peter Burke). The author, a French Jewish Professor of History at the Sorbonne, was shot by the Nazis in 1944 before this work was completed. Nevertheless, this essay offers a clear and incisive account of his personal approach to the study of history and is a valuable introduction to the subject.

What is History? by E. H. Carr (1971, Penguin Books, Harmondsworth, Middlesex) is a short and easily accessible text, which addresses such issues as the selection process at work in the production of historical 'facts' and how historians are themselves influenced by the standards of their own time and place.

The following books cover various aspects of quantitative research in the social sciences.

The Social Survey in Historical Perspective 1880–1940, edited by M. Bulmer, K. Bales and K. K. Sklar (1991, Cambridge University Press, Cambridge) is an illuminating collection of articles describing the ways in which modern social survey methods developed. It contains many interesting examples of how things used to be done.

Surveys in Social Research by D. A. de Vaus (3rd edition, 1991, UCL Press/Allen and Unwin, London; first edition published by Allen and Unwin in 1986) is a comprehensive and practical guide to all aspects of the modern social survey.

The Survey Method: the Contribution of Surveys to Sociological Explanation by C. Marsh (1982, Allen and Unwin, London) is a defence of the social survey against its critics. It is particularly good on sensitive ways of measuring meaning.

Many books on statistics and epidemiology cover technical material which goes far beyond this book. The following are our favourites out of an enormous range of available books.

Practical Statistics for Medical Research by D. G. Altman (1991, Chapman and Hall, London) is a particularly clear and interesting book on medical statistics; however, it goes far beyond what is required for this series of books.

Statistics for Health Management and Research by M. Woodward and L. M. A. Francis (1988, Edward Arnold, London) is a clear and reasonably comprehensible book on statistics, aimed particularly at health-service managers. This book has the virtue that it discusses techniques appropriate to, and uses examples from health and disease, without assuming the technical knowledge of medicine, nursing or another health-care profession.

The British Population by D. Coleman and J. Salt (1992, Oxford University Press, Oxford) is a very comprehensive handbook on all aspects of the demography (and many aspects of the epidemiology) of Britain. It is absolutely fascinating, if you like that sort of thing. The style of the book is readable and not too technical; if you managed Chapters 6 to 8 of this book without too much trouble, you should cope with Coleman and Salt.

Causal Relationships in Medicine: a Practical System for Critical Appraisal by J. M. Elwood (1988, Oxford University Press, Oxford) is a particularly clear explanation of detailed aspects of epidemiological studies, including clinical trials and statistical analysis. The book is aimed at doctors and other health workers.

Making Sense of Data by J. H. Abramson (1988, Oxford University Press, New York) is a reasonably short and clearly-written book which aims to teach epidemiology through a series of short chapters with large numbers of self-assessment questions.

Prevention of Spina Bifida and Other Neural Tube Defects, edited by J. Dobbing (1983, Academic Press, London) is the record of a conference at which most of the key researchers in the area made their positions clear, around the time of the main controversy about the setting-up of the MRC trial discussed in Chapter 8. To understand the book fully requires some biomedical knowledge.

Methodological Errors in Medical Research: an Incomplete Catalogue by B. Andersen (1990, Blackwell Scientific Publications, Oxford) is an excellent guide on how not to do it! Plenty of proof that professional medical researchers can make mistakes as bad as yours. The book does assume knowledge about statistical methods and about medicine that is beyond the scope of this series of books.

Clinical Epidemiology: a Basic Science for Clinical Medicine by D. L. Sackett, R. B. Haynes, G. H. Guyatt and P. Tugwell (2nd edition, 1991, Little, Brown and Company, Boston) is a first-rate book on how to apply the methods and principles of epidemiology in clinical medicine. It is aimed at clinicians; if you are not one, some of it may make little sense to you.

Fetal and Infant Origins of Adult Disease, edited by D. J. P. Barker (1992, published as a book by the British Medical Journal, London) is a collection of 31 papers by David Barker and his colleagues on the 'programming hypothesis' discussed in Chapter 10. It provides a very interesting example of how epidemiological evidence from many sources has been brought together to build up a hypothesis. Naturally, however, the arguments *against* the hypothesis are not well represented.

Finally, the following publications relate to biomedical research.

'Using animals in medical research' (an article published in 1993 in the *British Medical Journal,* **306**, pp.1 019–23). This review in the News section of the BMJ gives a summary of the conditions under which animal experiments are carried out in Britain, the USA, Scandinavia, Canada, Japan, France and Germany, together with a discussion of current debates about the ethics of animal research in those countries.

The Making of Memory by Steven Rose (1993, Bantam Press, Uxbridge) is a readable and personal account of the history of brain science which reveals the insider's view of what scientists do and why. It explores the strengths and pitfalls of the scientific method in a biological context and tackles difficult ethical questions, for example about the use of animals in research. Winner of the Science Book of the Year Prize in 1993.

Answers to self-assessment questions

Chapter 1

1   No. Even if, for example, there exists a simple biological explanation, say in terms of infection by a particular micro-organism or of exposure to a particular toxic chemical, the question arises as to why some people are infected or exposed and others are not. Generally these questions do not have biological explanations (or at any rate, not simple ones).

2   (a)   This is a question for a historian, though a social scientist or a biologist may be able to contribute to the study of the meaning of the definitions used.

(b)   This is clearly a biological question.

(c)   This is the kind of question studied by epidemiologists, though since it looks at the past, historical research methods would be very relevant too. Also, the question of defining the social status of different areas arises, and social science is relevant to answering it.

(d)   This question would be of interest to a social scientist.

Chapter 2

1   (a)   Not surprisingly, you probably came up with the same hypothesis as Fleming—that a chemical produced by the mould was killing the bacteria. This is a scientific hypothesis in Popper's sense of the term because it leads to a testable prediction: namely, if the chemical produced by the mould is collected, it should be able to kill bacteria. Today we know the mould chemical as *penicillin*.

(b)   Since you began with an observation of an event that was detected objectively with the senses (visible clear patches with mould growing in them), and then used this as the basis for a plausible explanation (moulds produce anti-bacterial chemicals) that contained more information than the actual observations, you were using *induction*. Deduction involves reasoning alone, not based on observations of the real world. This is the process you used when you 'reasoned out' a testable prediction from your hypothesis.

(c)   You need to ensure that the experiment is controlled in two senses: first, that as many as possible of the materials, techniques and conditions under which the experiment is carried out are known and kept 'under control' so that extraneous interventions do not creep in and affect the results. Second, you would evaluate the ability of the mould chemical to kill bacteria by adding it to 'test' dishes of bacteria, and ensuring that no trace of it (or of the mould itself) was present in 'control' dishes of bacteria that were identical to the test dishes in all other respects. The comparison of tests and controls is an essential safeguard in experimental science because it helps to exclude the possibility that results are due to chance, or to something in the experimental design other than the substance or situation under test.

2   In the popular version, Fleming made his greatest discovery in the ideal scientific frame of mind—objective neutrality. He simply observed a novel phenomenon as a result of his close attention to the details he could see with his own eyes. He was not acting from a preconception that moulds produce chemicals that damage bacteria. In 'ideal' science the scientist discovers 'facts' about the material universe, which are revealed by systematic observation and measurement.

3   It is an example of biological determinism: the speaker asserts that women are determined by their biological nature (i.e. their genes) to be better fitted than men for the task of looking after children. This view is a consequence of taking the scientific tradition of reductionism to the extreme position of reducing all human behaviour to the dictates of human genes.

4   The traditional written sequence of published scientific research (introduction, previous work, methods, results, discussion) follows the idealised sequence of scientific methods of investigation and serves to conceal the fact that the researcher virtually always begins with hypotheses ('adventures of the mind') which leads him or her to devise the experiments which put those imaginative, inspirational hunches to the test. The neutral self-effacing language of the scientific paper elevates the status of 'observation' to 'fact' and disguises the *provisional* status of hypotheses, which are simply logical representations of *current conjecture* about the world and in time may be discarded.

Chapter 3

1 The doctor explains to the researcher (his 'audience') that he has presented a false impression to the mother, and explains his reasons for this. But the doctor may be exaggerating his concern over the reaction to the rattle, in order to impress the researcher with the precision and rigour with which he carries out his work.

2 They are not always to be believed, even if they consist of statements by doctors and magistrates. The people filling them in may wish to create a certain impression for others who read them, and therefore omit or cover up certain facts.

3 We cannot generalise from a case of one. We don't even know if this instance of his behaviour is typical of this paediatrician on other occasions. Observation of a large, representative sample of paediatricians would be necessary to establish typical behaviour. This is rarely possible in ethnographic work.

4 He would need to show that he had observed many instances of racial stereotyping over a period of time, and that he had searched both in collecting data and in analysis of his field notes for instances which contradicted this view. For example, if he collected examples of paediatricians saying that racial stereotypes were *not* involved in their assessments, he would need to show that he had observed these same doctors at work and found that their actions contradicted their words.

Chapter 4

1 Showalter's sources for this extract are letters by Virginia Woolf and the diary of Alice James. These provide personal insights into neurasthenia and the rest cure from the patients' point of view. The historian might enquire whether the authors intended these works for publication as they may be less than entirely candid if the general public was the audience anticipated. Letters and diaries are typical sources for narrative history.

2 Showalter's methodology is qualitative. The relationship between women, madness and English culture which Showalter investigates is concerned with subtle and complex cultural meanings, and personal and subjective experiences. These cannot be stated in numerical terms.

3 The extract is an example of a feminist social history. It is specifically feminist in its concern with women's experience of the attitudes of the male medical profession. The analysis of the doctor–patient relationship in terms of gender and power differentials is related to the broader social context in which women held a subordinate position.

Chapter 5

1 (a) The units of analysis would be the old people themselves. The variables would be the things on which the old people varied, i.e. the answers they gave to the questions asked.

(b) Qualitative interviewing does not involve asking all respondents the same questions so it is difficult to construct a data matrix. The method can lead to data that is quantified if researchers analyse the content of each interview and apply ratings or category systems to aspects of what people say. The same is true for qualitative material gained from open-ended questions in structured interviews. It would have the advantage of allowing the elderly people to express their needs in their own terms, rather than choosing from a pre-specified list. But such research is time-consuming if done on a large scale.

Structured interviews would be less time-consuming, could involve some opportunities for open-ended comment, and could ensure that things that were within the power of the social services department to provide were asked about. Presenting a list could be a way of bringing needs to peoples' attention. However, the questions asked might constrain respondents to answering on topics and with terms that they would not normally use or think important.

2 Independence, like health, is a concept for which there are multiple indicators. The researchers could include things such as being able to dress, cook and eat without help. They could also attempt to measure mobility, but asking about this could prove tricky. If the researchers ask the old people how easily they can get about, for instance, their answers may appear similar but mean very different things. More knowable or 'objective' measures, such as being able to get to the shops, to climb the stairs, or just to walk unaided, would allow the questions and answers to be more precise, but do not tap the individual's subjective feelings about how independent they are.

The researchers would need to ensure that whatever questions were asked got the same answers without being biased by who was doing the interviewing, so different researchers might have to interview the same person twice to check on this aspect of reliability. They might also want to test the *criterion validity* of their measure by comparing the results with some other measure, perhaps ratings made by home helps who visit the old people.

3 These questions are unsatisfactory on several grounds. Question A is ambiguous. Is someone who smokes a cigar once a year 'a smoker'? Some people may classify themselves as 'a smoker' if they smoke rarely; others may not. Question B is too vague. The respondent could answer according to the amount smoked, the type of tobacco smoked (cigarette, pipe, cigar), whether he or she inhales, and so on. In addition, it is not clear what a non-smoker is supposed to do with this question. Question C is leading in that it emphasises the 'evil' of smoking. It also constrains the respondent to give exactly one of only four answers. A respondent may feel that none of these is appropriate or that several of them are.

4 Americans are not necessarily representative of all humans. The sample was self-selected: volunteers for the study might have been different in their sexual behaviour from non-volunteers.

Chapter 6

1 (a) The row percentages for Table 6.7 are as follows:

Table 6.7 Percentages of people in each age group in two Buckinghamshire districts in 1991

| District | Age group/years | | | | |
	0–19	20–39	40–64	65 and over	Total (= 100%)
Milton Keynes	30.6	34.0	25.4	10.0	176 330
Aylesbury Vale	27.0	31.1	29.6	12.3	145 931

(b) Compared with Aylesbury Vale, Milton Keynes has a younger population. In particular, Milton Keynes has proportionately more children and younger adults (0–19 and 20–39 years) and proportionately fewer older people (40–64 and 65 years and over) than Aylesbury Vale.

2 (a) The perinatal mortality rate per thousand births is

$$\frac{607}{63\,995} \times 1\,000 = 9.5$$

(b) Generally speaking, the PNMR increases as we go from social class I to social class V. Perinatal mortality is far more of a problem in the families of unskilled manual workers than in the families of well-paid men in non-manual occupations.

3 (a) The relationship is positive, because the points on the scatter diagram slope upwards from left to right.

(b) The higher the lung cancer SMR for men in an occupational group, the higher is the SMR for married women whose husbands are in the same occupational group. So, in terms of the meanings given to these quantities in the question, the higher the mortality from lung cancer is for men in a particular group of occupations, the higher will be the lung cancer mortality for women married to men in that group of occupations.

(c) No. There is nothing in these data to show that the relationship is causal. The diagram itself provides no *explanation* of why the quantities are related. (In fact it is extremely unlikely that the relationship *is* a direct causal one in this sense.)

(d) The data are cross-sectional. They were collected by studying a whole population over a reasonably short period of time (four years, which were combined to provide the data), rather than by following up individuals over a long time and examining changes over time. One important reason for being cautious in interpreting cross-sectional data like these is that they tell us nothing about whether the positive relationship was present in other periods.

4 The mean is
$$\frac{total}{size} = \frac{593}{7} = 84.7$$
In order, the seven numbers are 75, 80, 82, 83, 88, 90, 95. The median is the middle value, 83.

Chapter 7

1 An epidemiologist would be interested in all of these except, possibly, (iii). That is, because epidemiology is the study of health and disease in populations, (i), (ii) and (iv) are of direct interest. But Mr Lawson's case *in itself* would not be studied in epidemiology. However, an epidemiologist might well be interested in a systematic comparison of a group of people that included Mr Lawson with some other group, and Mr Lawson's diagnosis could be relevant to this comparison.

2 (a) The crude birth rate per thousand (total population)

$$= \frac{number\ of\ births}{total\ population} \times 1\,000$$
$$= \frac{65\,973}{5\,102\,400} \times 1\,000$$
$$= 12.9$$

(b) The crude death rate per thousand (total population)

$$= \frac{\text{number of deaths}}{\text{total population}} \times 1\,000$$

$$= \frac{61\,527}{5\,102\,400} \times 1\,000$$

$$= 12.1$$

(c) The general fertility rate per thousand women of childbearing age

$$= \frac{\text{number of births}}{\text{number of women aged 15–44}} \times 1\,000$$

$$= \frac{65\,973}{1\,121\,469} \times 1\,000$$

$$= 58.8$$

3 The doctor certifying the death will enter stomach cancer as the cause on Mrs Wells' certificate of cause of death. This will go to the local registrar, and eventually to OPCS in London. Coders there will convert the information to an ICD number. Mrs Wells' death will then be added to the total of stomach cancer deaths for women of her age and last occupation (or her husband's occupation if she was married or a widow), who lived in Lancashire. This total will be among the figures eventually published by OPCS.

4 (a) The SMR was used because the age structure differs from one occupational group to another. If crude death rates were used, one group might appear to have a high death rate merely because it contained more older people. Standardisation for age, for example by calculating the SMR, avoids this problem.

(b) Taking the welders first, there were 46 per cent more deaths from lung cancer in this group than would have occurred had national male age-specific death rates applied to this group. For office managers, 45 per cent fewer deaths occurred than would be the case if national rates had applied. Thus, allowing for age, lung cancer affects male welders to a much greater degree than male office managers.

5 First, the expectation of life at birth *in 1987* would be less than 35 + 44.3 years, because it is the mean lifetime of the whole of a birth cohort, whereas the 44.3 figure excludes those who died before age 35. (In fact, the expectation of life at birth for females in 1987 was 78.1.) Second, the expectation of life at birth *in 1952* is less still, because death rates generally fell between 1952 and 1987. You read in this chapter that the expectation of life at birth for females was 77.9 years in 1989, over six years longer than the 1952 figure. (Remember that life expectancy is the average length of life of a *hypothetical* cohort.)

6 (a) The incidence rate for 1982

$$= \frac{5}{56\,300} \times 100\,000$$

$$= 8.9 \text{ per } 100\,000$$

(b) The prevalence rate at 30 June 1982

$$= \frac{119}{56\,300} \times 100\,000$$

$$= 211.4 \text{ per } 100\,000$$

Chapter 8

1 (a) This was a retrospective case–control study, because it compared a group of cases with a group of controls, and looked back at their past history.

(b) No. With a case–control study, one finds a group of cases and a group of controls. It could then be worked out what proportion of people with lung cancer were heavy smokers, for example. But this is not the same thing as the proportion of heavy smokers who die from lung cancer. This can only be calculated by finding a group of smokers and *then* counting how many die of lung cancer, that is by doing a cohort study. (In fact, it *is* often possible to estimate a *relative* risk from a case–control study, but this involves the use of statistical techniques beyond the scope of this book.)

(c) The relative risk is 166/7, or about 24. On the basis of the Doll and Hill data, heavy smokers are 24 times as likely to die from lung cancer than are non-smokers.

2 (a) Because there is no established cure, the other group may receive no active treatment. However, this control group should be given a placebo.

(b) At random, to make it unlikely that the two groups differ systematically in any way (except, of course, that only one group receives the new drug).

(c) No, the doctor should not know, as this may bias the assessment in some way.

(d) 'The average rating of patients receiving the drug is the same as the average rating of those receiving the placebo.' (Note that the null hypothesis refers to the *average* ratings.)

(e) '$P = 0.25$' means that, if the null hypothesis is true, the probability of a result as extreme as that actually observed would be 0.25 (i.e. one chance in 4, because $1/4 = 0.25$). This is not small enough to reject the null hypothesis. In other words, the difference is 'not statistically significant'. However, this does not *definitely* mean that the drug has no effect. It *may* have no effect; or it may be that the drug *does* have an effect, but the trial did not provide enough evidence to establish it.

Chapter 9

1 The most important biological molecules in diabetes are the hormone insulin and the simple sugar glucose. A diagnostic test on a person with diabetes might be to measure the amounts of these molecules circulating in the plasma (the fluid fraction of blood), when the person had been fasting and again after consuming a known quantity of glucose. In a diabetic person, both the fasting level and the level after a glucose 'meal' would be abnormally high for glucose and low for insulin.

2 Animal models might be chosen because the experiment:

(a) was considered to be unacceptably risky or distressing or unethical to conduct on human subjects;

(b) would take too long to conduct on humans because it investigates biological development or degeneration, which take decades to complete, or involves reproductive processes which occur infrequently in humans;

(c) requires large numbers of similar subjects to ensure that the results are statistically valid and can be verified by repeating the experiment.

The main limitations of animal models are:

(i) no matter how closely related the chosen species is to humans in terms of its anatomy, physiology and biochemistry, it is not human and must differ in a variety of biological respects which may affect the outcome of the experiment;

(ii) many important diseases affecting humans have no equivalents in other animals;

(iii) important ethical objections have been raised against the use of animals in experiments.

3 A bottom-up explanation would locate the primary cause of TB in a particular type of bacterium that grows in and damages body tissues, often in the lungs. A top-down explanation would start with the social conditions that render people vulnerable to these bacteria as a consequence of inadequate nutrition and overcrowded and insanitary housing.

Acknowledgements

Grateful acknowledgement is made to the following sources for permission to reproduce material in this book:

Figures

Figure 4.1 Bucks County Record Office; *Figure 4.2* Royal Society of Medicine Photographic & Film Unit; *Figure 4.3* British Library; *Figure 5.3* Cartwright, A. and Seale, C. (1990) *The Natural History of a Survey*, King's Fund © Institute for Social Studies in Medical Care; *Figure 7.6* The design of the medical certificate of cause of death is Crown Copyright and is reproduced with the permission of the Controller of Her Majesty's Stationery Office; *Figure 7.7* Office of Population, Censuses and Surveys (1991) *Key Population and Vital Statistics: Local and Health Authority Areas*, Series VS no. 17, PP1 no. 13, reproduced with the permission of the Controller of Her Majesty's Stationery Office; *Figure 9.1a* Wellcome Museum of Medical Science and Wellcome Medical Foundation; *Figures 9.1b, 9.1c, 9.2* Mike Levers/Open University; *Figure 9.1e* Mike Stewart; *Figure 9.1g* antibody, courtesy of R. Dourmashkin and Gower Medical Publications; DNA courtesy of J. Griffith, from Griffith, J., Huberman, J.A. and Kornberg, A. (1971) Electron microscopy of DNA-polymerase bound to DNA, *Journal of Molecular Biology*, **55**, 209–214, Plate 1b; *Figures 9.3a,d* Milton Keynes General Hospital; *Figure 9.3b* Dr Marjorie England; *Figure 9.3c* Siemens plc; *Figure 9.4* National Medical Slide Bank; *Figure 10.1* North Staffordshire Hospital; *Figure 10.2* Hertfordshire County Council, Local Studies Library.

Text/Boxes

Box 3.1 Glaser, B. G. and Strauss, A. L. (1967) *The Discovery of Grounded Theory*, Weidenfeld and Nicolson, London © Barney G. Glaser and Anselm L. Strauss.

Tables

Table 5.1 Blaxter, M. (1990) *Health and Lifestyles*, Tavistock/Routledge, London © 1990 Mildred Blaxter; *Table 5.3* Cartwright, A. and Seale, C. (1990) *The Natural History of a Survey*, King's Fund © Institute for Social Studies in Medical Care; *Tables 8.1, 8.3* Laurence, K. M., Campbell, H. and James, N. (1983) The role of improvement in the maternal diet and preconceptual folic acid supplementation in the prevention of neural tube defects, in Dobbing, J. (ed.) *Prevention of Spina Bifida and Other Neural Tube Defects*, Academic Press, London.

Un-numbered photographs/illustrations

p. 4 By permission of the librarian, Glasgow University Library; *p. 10, p. 14 (right), p. 24, p. 27, p. 104* Mike Levers/Open University; *p. 14 (left)* Marion Hall; *p. 15* Karl Popper.

Index

Entries and page numbers in **bold type** refer to key words which are printed in **bold** in the text. Indexed information on pages indicated by *italics* is carried mainly or wholly in a figure or a table.